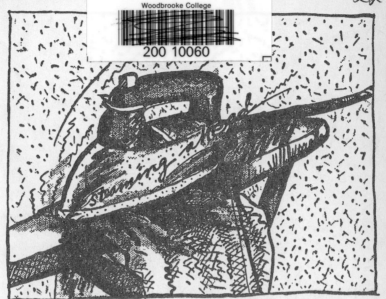

Jewish Women in London Group

Generations of Memories
Voices of Jewish Women

The Women's Press

First published by The Women's Press Limited 1989
A member of the Namara Group
34 Great Sutton Street, London EC1V 0DX

British Library Cataloguing in Publication Data

Generations of memories: voices of Jewish women.
  1. Great Britain. Jewish women. Social life,
  history
  I. Jewish women in London Group
  941'. 004924

  ISBN 0–7043–4205 7

Phototypeset by Input Typesetting Ltd, London

Reproduced, printed and bound in Great Britain by
BPCC Hazell Books Ltd
Member of BPCC Ltd
Aylesbury, Bucks, England

To our grandmothers, our mothers
and to our daughters

Acknowledgments

We would like to thank all the women whose life histories we recorded for the Jewish Women in London Archive for telling their stories to us.

As the editors of this book we would like to thank all the women who have been or are still members of the Jewish Women in London Group, especially Debi Alper, Ruth Cohen and Brenda Factor. We would especially like to thank Sue Libovich for concentrated, detailed comments on earlier drafts, and for helping us all to get this book finished.

Thanks also to Heather Lyons for detailed and helpful comments on successive drafts of large sections of the book.

Esther Held and Barry Davis gave advice on Yiddish transliteration, but the responsibility for the final form rests with us.

Photographs were copied for the archive and reproduced for the book by Latent Image, Reading. Recent portraits were by the Out Take Collective, London. The portrait of Rose Kerrigan is reproduced courtesy of the photographer, Philip Wolmuth.

Jeanette Copperman thanks family and friends, in particular colleagues at the Waterloo Action Centre, for their support.

Hannah Kanter thanks family and friends for forbearance, help with childcare and comments on the manuscript, and Frances Carter for all the work done together on a previous project, some of which now appears in this book. Thanks especially to David Mazower for all his help, and to him and our daughters Nina and Clara for putting up with all the meetings.

Jeanette Copperman
Hannah Kanter
Judy Keiner
Ruth Swirsky

Our memories are very long;
sometimes I think I inherited
generations of memories of memories
before anyone told me anything.

Sheila Shulman, *Pome for Jackie*

CONTENTS

The names of some of the women interviewed have been changed
at their request, as have most of the names that appear in their life
stories.

About the Project

This book of life stories is part of a wider project undertaken by the Jewish Women in London Group from 1984 to 1988. The project was funded for two and a half years, first by the Women's Committee of the GLC and later by the London Boroughs Association. This enabled a number of women in the group to be paid for some of the work they did for the project.

The project was set up with the primary aim of recording the life stories of Jewish women through oral testimonies. The thematic focus of the project was migration – all the women interviewed were first- or second-generation immigrants.

An archive of interviews with 44 women and of photographs has been set up. The interviews have been either summarised or fully transcribed, or both. The women we interviewed were born in many countries – England, Scotland, Ireland, Russia, Poland, Rumania, Hungary, Czechoslovakia, Germany, Austria, Israel, Italy, Morocco, Persia, India, the United States, South Africa. Some of them were both daughters of immigrants and then immigrants themselves. The largest single group comprised women born in England, Scotland or Ireland, daughters of immigrants from Eastern Europe. Almost as large was the group comprising refugees from Nazi persecution in the late thirties and those who survived the Holocaust in concentration camps or in hiding. The third-largest group comprised Sephardi women from Asia and Africa, with different religious and cultural traditions from European Jews.

The women we interviewed differed from one another not only in their country of origin but also in their religious observance (or lack of it), their class, their race and their politics; in whether they were married or single, lesbian or heterosexual, mothers or childless. Most were in their sixties and seventies when they were interviewed, though the age range was 43 to 98. We wanted to be positive about and highlight women who had not led conventionally Jewish lives as well as women who had lived according to Jewish tradition and custom.

The book is only one aspect of the ways in which we have developed the material collected. Using the interviews and photographs in the archive, we have produced a tape/slide show and video, *Three Jewish Women*, which draws on the lives of a woman from the East End of London, an Austrian refugee from Nazism and a woman from the Bene Israel community in Bombay. An exhibition entitled *Daughters of the Pale* is based on the experiences of those women who were daughters of immigrants to Britain from Eastern Europe around the turn of the century. A second exhibition focusing on those women who were refugees from Nazism in the thirties is being produced.

Both *Three Jewish Women* and *Daughters of the Pale* have been taken out into the community and seen by thousands of people. The tape/slide show and video have been seen by many groups, both Jewish and gentile, from young children to older people. The exhibition has been set up in schools, colleges and universities, in libraries, community centres, festivals, synagogues and other venues.

Jewish Women in London also made a major contribution to *The Jewish East End Education Pack*, both through providing extensive material from our archives, and in the production of the pack.

Many women have participated in the Jewish Women in London group over the last five years. All but one of us are Ashkenazi Jews and all are European in origin. Most of us are heterosexual; some of us are lesbians. Many of us are also immigrants or daughters of refugees. The ways in which our own experiences differ from one another's and in which we are different from gentile feminists in the Women's Liberation Movement are many and complex. This has been paralleled by what we have learned from the older Jewish women we have interviewed. They too have had vastly different experiences – from one another and from gentile women of their generation.

The eight life stories contained in the book are part of the wider project; the introduction draws on the experiences of all 44 women interviewed and on what we learned from them and about them, as well as what we learned about the process of narrating and recording life stories during the three years of interviewing.

Introduction

STARTING POINTS

Jewish Women in London was originally formed in 1984. It was part of a British Jewish Feminist Movement which had grown from small beginnings to hold a first National Jewish Feminist Conference in 1982. Most of us who founded the group had begun to rethink our identity as Jewish women in the many local Jewish Feminist Groups that were subsequently set up. We were becoming aware of how many of us felt excluded or had excluded ourselves from our Jewishness, or kept our Jewishness separate from our feminism. Now we were redefining our identity as Jewish feminists, bringing together a positive sense of ourselves as Jews and as women. In coming to terms with our identities, we had also to reconsider the lives of our own mothers, and this led us, as Jewish women, towards exploring our own history, a history which has only begun to be written. Our interests were diverse, but we were certainly impelled by a common concern; most of us had no sense of historical continuity in our families' lives. For all of our families, within the last few generations, had migrated – across Europe or across continents.

We might know the bare facts behind these upheavals: response to poverty, repression and pogrom; the need to flee Nazism. Some of us had felt a protectiveness towards our parents and grand-parents when we knew they had had such traumatic experiences. As children and even later, these feelings inhibited our sense of what questions we were allowed to ask or even to frame for ourselves. Some parents refused to talk about the past. Others wanted to shelter us as children from the pain they had lived through, and tried to stress the links between their present sense of security and the more comfortable parts of their personal histories. But whether our parents were silent or whether they constantly repeated certain family stories, we all shared a growing sense that we wanted to know more.

Over the first three years of the project we set out to interview women who were either immigrants or the daughters of immigrants to Britain. We were very conscious that there was a stereotype of the Jewish woman as wife and mother, with her horizons stretching no further than the household and the vision of a better life for her children. We did not set out to shatter that stereotype but to enable women who had lived lives within the mainstream Jewish community to reveal, through their own stories, just how much more tenuous and hard-fought than the rosy myths suggest, the position of Jewish people in Britain has been. And we set out to go beyond the stereotype. We wanted to include both single women and women who were living without men, some by choice as lesbians or divorcees, some as widows. We wanted to include women who had been politically active and women who had worked or lived unconventionally.

When we first formed the group, it was as feminists who had only slowly come to recognise that we had for many years seen other people's histories and political struggles as our own. Most of us had at some time seen ourselves as members of a sisterhood of women whose history took in the suffragettes, the factory girls and the great women campaigners for sexual emancipation, but not our history as Jewish women. There was no link between history as we knew it from home and our place in modern Britain, between childhood stories and our adult experience. Our parents' stories belonged to a different history; they lived on the margins of the textbooks we met at school.

For those of us who grew up in Britain, the school history we learned was the one in which English kings and one or two queens led a triumphant march from the Stone Age to the present day. It was followed by a history of the Greeks and Romans which didn't mention their occupation of the Jews' land and the consequent oppression of the Jews, or the contribution the Jews made to resistance against their empires. The rest of school history was a cosy anglocentric celebration of a past in which the other peoples of the world were by and large either subject peoples or enemies. Usually, that history stopped at the First World War. And the ordinary people of Britain were presented as a monolithically white, English-speaking mass who either lined the streets to cheer the great or erupted dangerously as mobs.

Some of us encountered Jewish history at school in the shape of scripture lessons; some of us went to *cheder* as well, where we also learned to read Hebrew. This history was largely based on Bible stories of the tribes of Ancient Israel. Where women played any part at all, they were just as likely to have been temptresses and schemers, like Jezebel and Delilah, as heroines, like Esther and Deborah.

Our mothers' stories were very different. For most of us, 'our' history was one which included flight from persecution and sometimes the threat of death, and subsequent migration from country to country. There are few of us who have grown up in the same countries as our mothers, and some of them in turn had come to live in different countries from their mothers or their grandmothers. The stories they had to tell us were often of the ways of their own families as part of the Jewish communities of Middle and Eastern Europe; of lives sometimes lived in poverty and fear, more rarely in an insecure prosperity. There were also stories which told of lives strong in resisting oppression, and others which told of becoming part of a middle-class establishment, which later only too readily turned its back on them.

Through these stories many of us learned that it was the women in our families who had so often been the ones responsible for taking on those movements across continents to safe homes. It was the women who kept the memory of who and what had been in the past. For those of us who came from religious backgrounds, it was often the women who found ways to give us a consciousness of Jewishness as more than a religion, a nationality, a personal identity. For them, it meant a way of life which shaped every aspect of their existence.

CHOOSING AN APPROACH THROUGH ORAL HISTORY

We wanted to know what Jewish women's lives were like. But women are scarcely mentioned in conventional Jewish histories. It is an irony that histories of Jews by Jews, which are scarcely acknowledged in mainstream historical accounts of countries where Jews lived for centuries, echo the marginalisation of women in orthodox academic history. Jewish women's experiences and perceptions have either been obscured or absorbed into descriptions of men's lives. Yet we know that Jewish women's contributions to the family economy in Eastern Europe prior to their arrival in England were vital, often the only ones when men were absent in the army or peddling or studying, or had gone abroad in advance of the rest of the family.

Like other historians of lives which have not to date been considered worthy of documentation, we turned to oral history. We wanted to talk to Jewish women about their personal experiences of living through the great upheavals of Jewish life in this century. We were not aiming to generate vast arrays of statistics or to establish the definitive history of Jewish women's domestic, working and political lives.

The task was far greater than we had ever imagined in 1984, when we first formed as a group, for there is no single Jewish women's history. Instead, there are a number of Jewish women's histories, for Jewish women have lived in countries as diverse as the Yemen, Lithuania, Germany and India and their lives are shaped by the histories of those countries as well as having an internal dynamic of their own. We wanted to represent the range and diversity of Jewish women's experience and set out to explore the ways in which Jewish women's identities are constructed and developed, within and against historical and life events.

The impulse behind the broad focus of the interviewing which was central to our project was not just to 'find out' but to go further and challenge the stereotyped assumptions we have referred to about who Jewish women were and what their lives were like. These assumptions are widely held in the world in general and also within the Jewish community itself.

This broad focus brought its own problems. We came to the project seeing in feminist oral history a range of different possibilities. Oral history seemed to be a method particularly appropriate for use by feminists, since feminism has always respected the individual voice, saying that we have much to learn from each woman's life. However, we soon found that in interviewing we were not simply 'giving women a voice'; the interview process was not a simple channel through which the woman's experience flowed. Who we as interviewers were, and the questions we asked, however 'neutral' we tried to make them, were two of the many factors influencing what women chose to talk to us about.

LIFE HISTORIES AND LIFE EXPERIENCES

The life history approach focuses on the way in which historical time and place and personal experience are lived out by individual women. At birth women are dealt a hand in terms of time, place and family circumstances. In reading these life histories there is a strong sense of the power of chance, of both the randomness of the hand dealt and the chance of later events. As Jews we may be particularly conscious that by a fluke of time and place we exist or are still alive, as against the millions that perished.

In narrating their life histories, the women incorporated both personal and historical events. However, there is a distinction between the individual women's subjective descriptions of incidents and responses and any claims to making a general analysis of an historical event or process itself. For example, no mainstream history of the Holocaust can adequately tell us about the subjective meanings of that experience for those who were its victims and its survivors. At the same time, no series of individual narratives can provide an analysis of the Holocaust. In recording these life stories, we have not set out to produce conventional history. Our approach to oral history stresses the story-making dimension of life histories.

The eight life stories which we have selected are not and could not be representative of Jewish women's experiences, just as no single book could represent the full range of British women's experiences. Each woman's life story is valuable for what it reveals of the ways in which women's lives are lived out and identities are constructed within the framework of gender, ethnicity and class. Some women shared their insights into those processes, and the life stories included in this collection are characterised by such insight. Many of the events that have affected Jewish people's lives in the twentieth century have been traumatic: family separations because of the pressures of anti-Semitism, and behind some of those separations, a history of massacre. Some of these accounts are harrowing, but all are characterised by strength and optimism. Whatever the sadnesses and pain of their lives, none of these women sees herself as a victim. All are strong and positive women.

The experiences of all the women interviewed are diverse. What they share, which is central to Jewish experience, is a history of migration, as immigrants and refugees or as the daughters of immigrants and refugees. This common thread of migration, with its separations, dislocations and attempts to reconstruct lives in new contexts, runs through these life stories. As with ourselves, it is a common Jewish experience that mothers and daughters are not born and brought up in the same place. The generation into which a woman is born has a critical effect on the way in which her identity is constructed. For these Jewish women there is not only the difference of generation that separates them from the experiences of their mothers but also the dislocation of migration, their mothers' or their own.

One of the impulses to undertake this project derived from the significance of our own mothers' stories of their lives and of their family histories in the development of our own personal and social identities. As we have explored the nature of both memory and the presentation of a life's events, it has become increasingly clear to us that it is just as important to understand the nature of the women's perceptions as to learn about the events that they have described.

The narration of a life story is woven out of the stories we tell ourselves before we tell them to others. We return to our memories again and again and in retelling these stories to ourselves, we reshape our past – but we reshape it from within a specific present. The contours of those memories change as our relationship to the present changes. Oral history has to contend with issues of authenticity and truth and of silence and omission. In treating life histories as storytelling, as a mythologising of dreams and aspirations and memories, the silences and distortions become part of that reshaping. In a sense, the point of the story lies not in what happened in the past, but in the interpretation from the present.

It is rare that a woman is given the opportunity to talk about her life in its entirety, to be encouraged to reveal as a whole a story which exists in her memory as unarticulated fragments, and then to comment on the edited version of the story in an afterword. Some women would welcome that opportunity, but for others the process can be painful if not devastating. In telling their story women are giving a solidity to memories which can be profoundly disturbing, particularly where the events lived through were extremely traumatic ones.

It is a common experience, for example, of Holocaust survivors and refugees that during the decades since the Holocaust they have coped by submerging their memories. It is only now, over 40 years later, that they are beginning to talk about those experiences and that the effects of the trauma are making themselves fully felt. One of the refugees from Germany we interviewed became fearful that in revealing her life story, which included membership of the Communist Party, she might lose her passport and be deported. The knowledge that interviews can have this sort of effect emphasises the need for responsibility on the part of oral historians. If they are to draw out new responses from women as they relive past events and experiences, these women cannot then be left to deal with those feelings alone.

However, the opportunity to recall and narrate their life stories has been a positive experience for many of the women. For one, the interviews played an important role in the process of profoundly redefining her identity, her relationships and the direction of her life, a process which is ongoing. The warmth that was shared in that process of narrating and recording a life story can be heard on the tapes but is partly lost through the process of transcribing, and is inevitably edited out in the transformation of a transcript into a published life story. But that warmth between older and younger women, and between the women themselves, has not been lost; contact has been maintained and friendships have developed.

11

The life stories published here are those of women who have lived full lives. But they are unlikely to be recognised as such according to the conventional expectations contemporary Jewish culture has of women. On the other hand, simply trying to interpret these lives using existing feminist interpretations of how gender organises identity is not an adequate substitute. Much work done by white gentile feminists, while presented as if universal, is culturally ethnocentric and offers little insight into our relationship as Jewish women to the world. The lives of those women born and brought up in Britain (let alone those born and brought up in Europe) in some respects resemble those of gentile women of the same generation, but they differ significantly in others. The terrain in which those lives have been mapped out is different; the Jewish East End was different from the white gentile East End. The view from a little terraced house may be the same, but the interior view is different.

THE EXPERIENCE OF THE OUTSIDER

There is a real sense in which many of the women here are outsiders who, because of their experiences, no longer fit in the world into which they were born. Some have been torn from it by force of circumstance, or by events which have for ever alienated them from it. Maya Nagy's sense of being an outsider stems from being a Jewish child of a divorced parent growing up in an anti-Semitic small town in Hungary and somehow not fitting into the Jewish or the gentile community as a result. Rita Altman is an outsider in so many ways: as an *Ostjudin*, an Eastern European Jew, in a more assimilated Jewish community in Germany, and then as a refugee in this country, and lastly as an abused child, something she only included in her chapter once the interviews were over and the editing was in progress. Elli Adler, a child of a gentile mother, brought up without any religious background though with a sense of her Jewishness through her father's side, suddenly at the mercy of racial anti-Semitism, at risk from Nazism, came to this country at the age of 13. Yet here, as soon as she reached 16, she became on the one hand an enemy alien and on the other, in the eyes of some of her colleagues at work, 'a dirty Jew'.

Others, like Ena Abrahams, see themselves as having lived a life between two worlds, as the daughters of East European Jewish immigrants to this country. Her story exemplifies the price that had to be paid for the education that many Jewish parents sought for their children. Her Jewish identity was denied or minimised, and she was actively discouraged from speaking her mother tongue. It was the particular aspects of her life as the child of poor working-class parents that made her assume adult responsibilities when still a young child.

There are many parallels with Ena's experiences in Ruth Adler's account of her life. Her early politicisation led to fulfilment and a sense of positive purpose; her later disillusion with the Communist Party (CP) left her outside both the world of her youth and the political party to which she had committed herself. For Rose Kerrigan, the only interviewee included who has retained a life-long allegiance to the CP, political commitment meant the rejection of religious belief, but not of Jewish values.

Asphodel was orphaned as a child and struck out on her own when she left school, living an unconventional life and only later reasserting her Jewish identity within the context of her involvement in women's spirituality, which is rooted in her own childhood experiences.

Miriam Metz, as the daughter of Yiddish-speaking refugees in the East End of the forties and fifties, grew up with a sense of being dislocated in time, because so many of the children she grew up with had English-born parents and the immigrant generation was thought of as an elderly one. Lesbianism and feminism subsequently separated her socially if not emotionally from the East Enders she knew in her childhood. That sense of separation has been underlined by the physical demolition of much of the Jewish East End in recent years.

We did not wish to impose our own political agendas on the women we interviewed. In deciding how to explore the politics which women held in their earlier lives, or hold now, we made the decision that we would not specifically question women on their stances on particular political positions such as socialism, communism, Zionism and Thatcherism. However, some women did see their political commitments as key elements in their life stories. It is perhaps no accident that the CP played a central role in three of the published life stories of women who were brought up in Britain. In the first place, London was a centre for political exiles, Jewish and gentile, in the late nineteenth century. Secondly, some Jewish immigrants had been politicised by their experiences in Eastern Europe, even if they were not members of a political group. Rose Kerrigan's politics developed through contact with her own father's political ideals and the political education he gave her; Ruth Adler became politicised as a young woman through contact with two young immigrants (one of whom she was later to marry) who frequently visited her home. Then, too, the perceptions and consciousness of being an outsider in British society shaped the aspirations and yearnings of a young woman. Fascism in the thirties was a direct threat for Jews, and the CP attracted many young Jews through its anti-fascist work. For those women, of whom Asphodel was also one, the CP offered the possibility of transforming those dreams and aspirations, perhaps in the way that the feminist movement does for us today. All three women now look back on those experiences from very different perspectives.

For a fourth woman among our interviewees, Maya Nagy, the CP has had a very different meaning and impact on her life. While she was not herself politically active, her story hints grimly at the nature of the experience of being under Stalinist domination in post-war Hungary.

Some women were drawn to Zionism too as an explanation of and a potential solution to the experience of the Jews. In this collection of life stories, it does not appear to have played a particularly significant part. All the women accept the justification for the establishment of the State of Israel. Some have developed a critical attitude to the actions of the Israeli state, recognising its significance for Jews but demonstrating a keen awareness of the rights of the Palestinians.

14

REFLECTING ON THE PAST

Each chapter represents an individual response at a particular moment. Each began as a 'fragment of a fragment' – that is, of that woman's history caught on a tape recorder on, say, a wet Tuesday in February.

For most of the women, being presented some time later with, as one of us put it, an 'autobiography that they had not written' was a disturbing experience and added another dimension to the vexed question of 'giving a voice'. Those interviews, a record of a series of moments in which what was said, or what was left out, was influenced by complex factors, were then transcribed and edited. Our policy in editing for publication was to offer editorial control to the women interviewed. Afterwards, each woman was also invited to contribute a written afterword.

The women who were interviewed had the experience of reading a typed, unedited transcript which presented them with how they felt and what they said on a particular occasion. Some found the very fact of seeing it in print quite painful. At a later stage, those women whose life stories are included in this collection read edited transcripts of their interviews, and many of them felt dissatisfied. This raises questions about the differences between an oral narrative and an autobiography. Oral testimonies are able to capture the richness of people's speech and these life stories have a vividness which written pieces often lack. Yet the point for these women was that they felt they didn't have direct control over their words. The strong reactions to seeing something which had been experienced as ephemeral suddenly enshrined as a 'life story' meant that some women chose to withdraw their material from the book.

When we set out to select women for the project, as part of our commitment to going beyond stereotypes, we made it one of our first priorities to include Sephardi women, particularly those from the Mizrachi communities, and women who were lesbians. Yet we found that women from these two groups were among the most reluctant to see their stories in print, even though we did succeed in interviewing a number of them, and their stories have contributed both to our archive and to our tape/slide show, *Three Jewish Women*. Often it was only after a long period of work and shared discussion around draft chapters that the women concerned finally decided that they did not want their stories published in this book.

From this disappointment, we have learned – the hard way – much about the strength of Sephardi/Mizrachi Jewish women's solidarity in not entrusting their experiences to an unknown audience. Some women were very reluctant to say anything about personal experiences. Others shared with us some moving evocations of their home communities as well as bitter insights into the lived reality of racism and anti-Semitism in Britain. But these were a minority. We began to wonder whether we had struck some particularly unique characteristic of Sephardi Jewish women, or whether we ourselves lacked skills as interviewers, so frequently did we encounter either reluctance to talk or withdrawal once an interview had taken place.

In fact, women from a range of backgrounds were reluctant to give interviews or to contemplate publication, and we do not think that reluctance to speak in a public form is uniquely a characteristic of women from Middle Eastern and Third World cultures. We do recognise, though, that there are particularly strong traditions among many of these communities, which place great importance on strength and shared trust within known circles, and strong reservations about extending that trust outside it.

In the case of the lesbians we interviewed, it was very clear that the recent onslaught of media and right-wing anti-homosexual campaigns and legislation in Britain has had a very real impact. Otherwise active and courageous women feel they cannot safely make their histories public. Several lesbians also felt under pressure to respond to overt or anticipated family hostility to their identification.

In retrospect, we have begun to question whether oral history, which is usually seen by Western feminists, socialists and other radicals as offering a voice to those who are not usually heard, needs to be seen as a much more limited and culturally specific form of investigation. We have become aware that few academic oral historians give interviewees the opportunity to review their interviews once given and that these are edited and published without further reference back to the interviewees. Oral history, which often bases its credentials on being a people's history, can become a vehicle for individual achievement and primarily a resource for groups of academic and political onlookers rather than one for the speakers themselves. In giving interviewees the opportunity to review and comment on their chapters, and the right to veto where preferred, we have tried to give the women as much control as possible over their stories.

These are life stories, told rather than written, which have their own shape dictated by a particular interaction and the constraints of time. They become something different when written down – stories which, although partly shaped by chronological events, are also edited in order to echo and pinpoint certain themes formally. It takes one a long way from the wet Tuesday morning.

On the other hand, it can seem further than it in fact is. Maya Nagy responded to her chapter with praise, saying how happy she was that in editing her interviews something coherent and whole had been made out of a life which seemed to her to be without shape. Yet in fact very little had been done in terms of shaping to change the stories she had told over a long period of time.

What many of the interviews share is a sense of identity as something which is always being modified through time, not as a static label. For many of the women, where home is has been a result of chance: they or their parents have been buffeted by events into flight or the consequences of not being able to flee. The centrality in many of their stories of being defined by others is matched by their awareness of losing a sense of self in relation to place and family. The effect of cumulative loss of one kind or another has made them particularly alert to the way in which questions of identity are constantly being used to challenge and circumscribe Jewish existence, in Britain as well as in other countries. Jews have been told by other, often hostile people who and what they are, and what they should conceal if they want to get on, or even survive – their Jewish names, the Yiddish language. As Rita Altman says, you need to know your own history to understand what is being asked of you.

Exploring the History of
Jewish Settlement in Britain

Most people are unaware that far from being relatively recent, happily absorbed immigrants to the UK, Jews have had a much longer and more tragic history here. There were Jewish communities all over England in the early Middle Ages. They had a flourishing communal life and contributed substantially to the economic life of the country. They were also subjected to anti-Semitic restrictions and taxes, harassment and to the stock anti-Semitic libel that they killed Christian children to use their blood for Pesach matzos. Jews were murdered on the strength of these libels, and, in the most tragic of these events, 200 Jews in York committed suicide under siege in 1190 rather than face forcible conversion or death at the hands of the mob. England expelled all Jews in 1290, having first stripped them of their property, and thus became the first country in the world to carry out a policy of total and permanent expulsion of a minority people from every part of a country (though Jews were expelled from more localised areas in Europe both before and after this date).

Anti-Semitism persisted in England even when no Jewish community had lived there for hundreds of years. Very small numbers of individual Jews did in fact manage to enter and survive in England during the subsequent centuries, usually by keeping their religion secret. But they were officially allowed to settle in England again only in 1656, during the time of Cromwell's republic. The small communities of Jews who settled in the following 100 years or so were from the Sephardi Jewish tradition, descendants of the Spanish and Portuguese Jews expelled from those countries in the fourteenth and fifteenth centuries. The Sephardim who came to this country thus form the oldest Jewish community in Britain today and are the backbone of the Anglo-Jewish establishment. There was no significant settlement of Jews from the Ashkenazi, or German and Eastern European, tradition until the mid-nineteenth century, when significant numbers of German, Dutch and subsequently Eastern European Jews began to come to Britain as a country offering greater opportunities.

There have been three major waves of immigration of Jews to Britain in the last 100 years. The first and largest, from Eastern Europe, took place mainly between the years 1880 and 1905. There is a real sense in which the Jews of Eastern Europe formed an Ashkenazi national group, cutting across existing national and imperial boundaries, with its own social and cultural institutions, its own language and its own internal divisions.

The millions of Jews who were under Russian imperial rule suffered increasing economic restrictions, poverty and persecution. Since the eighteenth century they had been compelled to live in a designated part of the Western Russian Empire, the Jewish Pale of Settlement. Jews in other Eastern European countries also faced similar though less severe restrictions. Economic conditions for Jews also became increasingly difficult as the rise of industrialisation and new patterns of trade cut away their traditional small business and middleman roles. Only a tiny minority benefited from these changes to become members of a prosperous, new middle class. Many Jews saw in America and industrialised Western Europe the prospect of new economic life and political and personal freedom.

During the latter part of the nineteenth century and the early twentieth century millions of Jews from Russia, Poland, Lithuania, Galicia and Rumania – which is to say, the Russian and Austro-Hungarian empires – emigrated. They moved to other parts of Europe, North and South America, Australia, southern Africa and Palestine; in fact, anywhere that offered hope of a better life. During this period hundreds of thousands of Jews entered Britain, though some stayed only temporarily, later migrating further west or south. Entry to Britain was severely curtailed after the Aliens Act of 1905, which was aimed particularly at restricting Jewish immigration to a minimum.

For the Jews of Eastern Europe, the First World War was a catastrophe. Many of the great Eastern European battlefronts of 1914–15, which rarely figure in British or American histories of the war, devastated and burnt down the great centres of traditional Jewish village life in Poland, Russia and Hungary. Hundreds of thousands of Jews then became refugees, often moving to Vienna or Berlin. In these and other great European cities there were well-established, openly anti-Semitic political parties, and they found convenient targets in these mostly impoverished newcomers.

After the First World War, some of the newly independent Eastern European countries such as Poland and Rumania gained their statehood subject to guaranteeing the rights of their very substantial Jewish minority, and of others, to continuing communal autonomy. From the start, these rights were either ignored, steadily watered down or cancelled out by overtly anti-Semitic legislation. Many thousands of Jews died in pogroms instigated by Ukrainian nationalists in 1919–20. The Polish state became embroiled in war with Russia and the anti-Semitism of the Polish army drove many young Jewish men into flight over the borders into Germany and other countries, where they lived a precarious existence of state-lessness.

Small numbers of these Eastern European refugees did manage to enter Britain in the twenties, within the narrow scope offered by the Aliens Act. The traditional Jewish refugee haven of the USA was all but closed by covertly anti-Semitic immigration legislation which had been adopted in the early twenties. It allotted minute quotas of places to those countries from which the most oppressed Jews were seeking to flee, especially Poland and the Ukraine, and much larger quotas to Anglo-Saxon Western European countries. Many of the Eastern and, later, Central European Jewish refugees were able to settle in more hospitable countries like Holland and France, where they were to be among the first from those countries deported and murdered by the Nazis.

When Hitler came to power in 1933, the previous trickle of Jewish immigration swelled into a second wave that was to bring some 75,000 Jews to Britain. It was now extremely difficult for Jews to gain permits for entry into Britain. In addition to the barrier of the Aliens Act, it was accepted unquestioningly that high unemployment in Britain meant that immigration had to be held down to a minimum, although, then as now, some of the largest concentrations of the unemployed were in areas, such as the Clyde, Teesside, South Wales and Northern Ireland, to which very few immigrants sought to go.

Public reactions of sympathy for Jews after the state-organised horrors of Kristallnacht in 1938 enabled nearly 10,000 children from Germany, Austria and Czechoslovakia, most of whom were Jewish, to be admitted to Britain through the Children's Transport programmes. Ironically, it was that great preoccupation of the British upper and middle classes, the 'servant problem', which was to open the door to a large number of Jewish women refugees from Nazi Germany and the countries threatened by Germany – Czechoslovakia and Austria. Permits were potentially available for women (and men) who agreed to enter domestic service, and this opened the way for the majority of Jewish women who had neither wealth nor professional qualifications.

While there were a good number of generous British people who committed themselves to using this way of rescuing Jewish women by offering service vacancies, there were others who were much more exploitative in their attitudes. Even the widespread pre-war knowledge of the atrocities and relentless persecution suffered by Jews under the Nazis, publicised by *Picture Post*, cinema newsreels and other popular media, did not prevent some gentile and Jewish British people from deriding the situation and the experiences of the refugees.

In the light of the increasing reluctance of other countries to offer Jews refuge from the twenties onwards, it was hardly surprising that the initially small, politically committed Zionist movement to settle in Palestine was greatly swelled by refugees who simply wanted a home. The British consistently tried to reduce and finally close Jewish entry into Palestine, partly for their own political purposes and partly in response to the demands of the Palestinian Arabs. The struggles in Palestine began to have repercussions on the security of Jews who lived in other Arab countries.

Jewish settlement in the Mediterranean countries and the Near and Middle East goes back well over 2,000 years, and for most of that time relations between the Jews and their Islamic neighbours were cordial and peaceful. The already substantial numbers were swelled by the expulsion of the Sephardi Jews from Spain and Portugal in the fourteenth and fifteenth centuries. The term Mizrachi is usually used to refer to those Jews from the Sephardi tradition who originate from the Arab and other Middle Eastern countries and India.

The struggles against the British in India and Persia, which was part of the British sphere of influence, also began to open up divisions between the majority of Jews of those countries and their compatriots.

As with other colonial powers, like the French in Morocco, the British often exploited particular ethnic minorities as unequal allies or scapegoats in the course of struggles against mass popular movements for independence. These undercurrents of empire cropped up in some of our interviews with Jewish women from these countries, sometimes as a painfully remembered sense of a point at which a long historical relationship was severed. Others we interviewed identified with the national struggle against a racist colonial rule.

After the Second World War, Britain did little to offer a home to Holocaust survivors, although, as has recently become clear, it offered shelter to some of the Nazis' murderous Eastern European collaborators, seeing them as useful anti-Communist sources. One factor in the general British reluctance to give Jews a home was the continuing anti-Semitism of sectors of the British Civil Servant ruling caste. Comments by officials of the Foreign Office on the margins of departmental records of the period can be found speaking of 'wailing Jews' trying to push their case.

Another factor was British determination to avoid doing anything that would fuel the pressure from Jewish Holocaust survivors to be allowed to enter Palestine. Offering an alternative home in Britain was not seen as a suitable strategy, because it was thought that the Jews might then seek to use Britain as an easier transit point for Palestine. Ironically, there was a desperate shortage of labour in post-war Britain and over half a million gentile European migrant labourers were brought in.

With the coming of the more prosperous post-war period, new political upheavals enabled a third, much smaller wave of Jewish people to come to Britain. The 1956 Hungarian uprising brought Jews fleeing from Hungary; a few months later, the Suez invasion by Britain, France and Israel led to the expulsion or flight of Jews who had British passports from Egypt. Anti-Semitism in Poland after the 1967 Six-Day War in Israel caused many of the few remaining Polish Jews to leave Poland.

The outraged and angry response of the Arab countries to the establishment of Israel in 1948 included punitive laws against the Jews of those countries and led to the flight of a first, massive wave of Jews. There were then subsequent flights of large numbers of those who had remained, following the wars with Israel in 1956 and 1967. Additionally, the ending of British colonial rule and spheres of influence in India, Iraq and Aden further added to the Jewish communities' anxieties about the security of their future in their long-established homes.

Throughout the fifties the steady process of immigration to Britain of Sephardi/Mizrachi Jews continued from countries such as India, Morocco and Aden. There was already a significant Persian Jewish community in London, dating from the 1920s. Most of the 30,000 Israelis who have settled in Britain since the 1960s originated in Arab countries such as the Yemen and Iraq. Many of the Sephardi/Mizrachi women we interviewed had, like some of the refugees from Europe, come to England only after a period of settlement in Israel. A small number of Israelis have come to settle in Britain because of their opposition to Zionism or to the present policies of the Israeli state.

Thousands of Jews from South Africa have settled in Britain since the fifties, mainly in opposition to the rule of apartheid and its consequences, or for more pragmatic and personal reasons in the period following. Their white status, their professional qualifications and their relative wealth allowed them an entry refused to people from black Commonwealth countries.

There are also small numbers of recent Jewish émigrés to Britain from the Soviet Union, although the vast majority who leave settle in the USA and Israel.

After the Second World War, it seemed inconceivable that there would ever again be the prospect of a new wave of Jewish refugees from persecution in Europe. It seemed inconceivable too that after the Second World War fascists and overt racists would be elected to parliaments in Europe. However, there have been repeated successes by the racist and covertly anti-Semitic French National Front Party in successive elections in the 1980s. Early in 1989, a neo-fascist party in Berlin, with an unrepentant ex-SS officer at its head, made substantial electoral gains.

RUTH ADLER
Woman of the Eighties

Ruth Adler was born in London in 1912, months after her parents arrived from Poland. When Ruth was still a baby, her mother took her to Warsaw to visit her family and they were unable to return to Britain for the duration of the First World War. She spent her early childhood with her mother's family, living a traditional, orthodox Jewish life, speaking only Yiddish. She returned to the East End of London when she was seven and, although her family were not observant, she grew up in an almost entirely Jewish environment. In the 1920s, despite steady migration out of the area, there were still between 100,000 and 150,000 Jews living in the East End.

Although Ruth attended a Jewish elementary school, this did not protect her from pressures to assimilate. The aim of Jewish mainstream communal organisations, including Jewish schools and Jewish youth clubs, was to turn young Jews into good British citizens. The use of Yiddish was not allowed and Ruth, like other young Jews, soon abandoned her mother tongue. After leaving school, her intellectual and social horizons opened up when she attended the Progressive Youth Circle, which was part of the Jewish Workers' Circle.

The Jewish Workers' Circle, or Der Arbeiter Ring, was founded in the East End in 1911. Branches were soon established around London and in the provinces. Based first in Brick Lane, it moved to Circle House in Alie Street in 1924, where it remained until 1956. Then it moved to Hackney, and finally closed its doors just a few years ago. One of its primary purposes was to provide benefits, including sickness and burial, in the tradition of the Friendly Societies, and it was an alternative to Jewish mainstream organisations. Solidly rooted within the Labour

25

movement, it was committed to mutual aid, workers' co-operatives and education. Circle House itself became a cultural centre, with a reading room and library, its own school for a time, and classes, lectures, concerts, Yiddish theatre productions and art exhibitions. It played an active role in the anti-fascist struggle during the thirties. While women were always admitted as members of the circle, a specific women's section was set up by one of the divisions in 1931. Politically it was non-sectarian and included anarchists, communists, social democrats and Zionists.

Through her activities at Circle House, Ruth was exposed to a range of radical political ideas and in the late twenties she joined the Communist Party. In later years when her children were growing up and her parents becoming increasingly dependent on her, Ruth, like so many women, was torn between family and political commitments. The revelations about Stalinism after Stalin's death were deeply traumatic for many members of the CP. Ruth, like many of her comrades, left the Party in 1956, but her socialist politics have continued to be central in her life.

Like so many immigrants, her parents suffered a real sense of displacement. Their family and friends who had remained in Poland perished in the Holocaust. The whole family was devastated by what they learned of the fate of the Jews in Europe during those years. Although her husband remained a member of the CP all his life, the Holocaust changed the direction of his political work towards working exclusively with and for Jewish people until he died. For her parents, the pain and loss of the Holocaust meant that they became increasingly dependent on her in their old age. She has now come to understand them better, particularly her mother, and talks of them with great love and respect.

The seventies and eighties have been a marvellously exciting period for Ruth. She began her career as a writer and, later, a new and loving relationship with a man. Her family and friends, her work, her Jewish identity and her socialist politics are all still important in her life as she approaches her eighties.

I was born in London in Stepney Green in 1912. Early that year my father came from Poland; my mother and my older brother came later; my mother was very pregnant with me. When my father first arrived, he had 37 shillings and he bought handkerchiefs with it. My mother was very cross and said, 'If you've got £2, you don't buy only handkerchiefs, you buy this, that and the other.' Anyway, it worked! He sold the handkerchiefs from a little case on the pavement in the local market and then he bought other things. He was a timid little man, yet somehow he gathered the courage to do this in a foreign country, without the language.

When I was 18 months old, my mother took me and my brother to Poland to see her family again. Travel was very cheap in those days, and no passport was needed, or she wouldn't have managed it. The night we arrived, a fire broke out at my grandmother's house and everything they had was burnt down. They were left high and dry. They got going again eventually, but whereas before they had just been poor, now they were very poor.

My mother went for her health; she hadn't been well after I was born and the doctor said her own climate would do her good. When she was better, she wanted to come back to England but the First World War broke out. She couldn't get to England; my father couldn't get to Poland. After his army service, my father was scraping a living, and when he'd made enough money he sent for my mother and the children. But she came back only with me because the little boy had died, owing to the bad conditions in Poland because of the war and poverty. By the time we came back, my father had a barrow – this was really up-market! Later they got a shop, but he still kept the barrow and went to the market, because the shop did not yield enough to make a living.

My parents came from different small towns near Warsaw. I don't know if it was an arranged marriage but they certainly cared very much for each other. My mother was the leader, my father the follower. She was stronger than he was in character and initiative. The guests at their wedding were people from nearby small towns. It was too late for some of them to go home, so my mother spent her wedding night with her husband and with all these friends, who slept on the floor. Next day my mother went to my father's home town, to share his home with his old mother, who was sick. Their home was one room. They arranged the two wardrobes sideways on to the room and hung a curtain between them so they had that little bit of privacy. My mother took care of the old lady till she died and only then she became pregnant. How could she become pregnant before? My mother told me that my father had such a respect for her that he couldn't dream of doing 'that' to her. Whether this was the real reason or whether it was a rationalisation, whether he was too timid or whether it was the knowledge of his old mother in the second half of the room, I don't know. But nothing happened until the old lady died.

What I marvel at is that given those conditions and that start in life, they were each, in their different ways, so delicate. My father did unrefined things like spitting when he was in the street and spitting into the sink when he was at home, but in certain things he was very sensitive and aware. For instance, when my mother and I came back from Poland, my father and my uncle had gone to meet us at the station and missed us, so we came back first. There was a crowd in the room and when my father came in with my uncle, people asked me which one was my father. I remember thinking, silly fools, of course I knew my father. I'd seen a picture of him. So I picked him out – and he didn't dash at me. This is what I call delicate. He sat down and after a little while he beckoned to me. He was a nice-looking man and I went. He indicated his lap, so I sat on his lap and he produced a roll of Nestlé's chocolates, with red paper on the outside and silver paper inside.

Years later I had care of my father when he became senile. My mother was in hospital and I had to look after him. Once I took him to a station to wait for a friend of mine. The train was late and he was hungry so I bought him a bar of Nestlé's chocolate from a machine, and he took it as eagerly and gratefully as I had taken his chocolate when I was seven and a half. He was like a child then, so the roles had become reversed, as they do in old age.

His approach to me after that interval of six years (and he was crazy keen to see me and touch me) showed the restraint he put on himself. I've heard very different stories of soldiers coming back from the war whose children don't know them. My own mother's father came home in uniform from army service and embraced her violently; she fought and kicked and screamed. She had a little set of toy buckets and during the night he drove holes in them to punish her. It ruined their relationship until she was 16, when there was smallpox in her *shtetl*. Several people died of it and those of my mother's friends who survived were pockmarked for life. My mother also had gone down with smallpox, but she didn't have any pockmarks except for one in the small of her back. Her father had sat day and night by her bed, having tied her hands behind her so that she couldn't scratch, and he fanned her constantly to relieve the itching. She was so grateful to him that she began loving him and nursed him devotedly through his last illness till he died. So I do appreciate the way my father took me on. I've often wondered at this kind of sensitive awareness – my mother too, in a different way – when they had those really poverty-stricken conditions to start life with. My mother never went to school; my father went to *cheder* till he was 13. Yet you get people who are better educated who wouldn't behave well in those circumstances.

I don't think there was any such thing as a non-religious Jewish family in those days, but my parents left their religion when they became adult. They were brought up among Jews in a very closed kind of community. I'm certain that neither of them had a friend who was not Jewish. The tradition, the festivals, the Bible and the prayer books formed their culture. I consider that they were cultured by that tradition and religion. And when they left the religion as conscious adults not believing in God any more, their behaviour didn't change, their natures didn't change. They were still the same people as they had been before, but they thought differently. My father referred to God in a humorous way and he'd make me laugh, which somehow distanced me from God. He said, 'What is God doing now? Is he sitting and eating a nice supper?' He rather made fun of it; religion seemed to him a superstition.

I didn't observe *Shabbes* after I left Poland because my parents had a draper's shop which was open all day Saturday, longer than on other days. My mother's life was frantic. She was cooking with one hand and serving in the shop with the other. One of my memories is of her rushing into the shop and asking a customer to wait a minute. She'd go into the kitchen and turn the gas off and then go out and finish serving. And when the customer had gone, she'd come back and turn the gas on again under the saucepan. And that's how it always was. For my younger brother, born after our return from Poland, this division of her attention was a tragedy. She never had time to stay with him when breastfeeding.

She'd have the child at the breast and if a customer came in, she'd pull him away, go and serve, come back and so on. Eventually he lost interest and there were all sorts of feeding problems. I was nine when my little brother was born. I loved him, but I sometimes resented having to do things for him; I had my own concerns. I had to wash him on a Saturday night, when my mother was still busy in the shop. I quite liked doing that; I felt like a little mother. The shop was not shut till eight in those days before the Second World War. Then things had to be tidied up in the shop, and then they came in and had supper. By the time they'd cleared up it was 10, so it wasn't easy for her. Sometimes she would cook the night before. But you can't cook everything ahead of time and my mother was very keen on everything being freshly cooked. I regret that she didn't have time to develop herself. I feel that all her intelligence (and she had a very good intelligence) went into the cooking and the shop.

My mother missed the festivals and the celebrations. She always told me when it was a festival and when she could, she cooked on those occasions the appropriate foods to celebrate. She made up her own version of Pesach. Because they were not reading out of the *Hagodah*, my father would make a point of telling me and my younger brother the story of how Moses led the Children of Israel out of slavery. I remember the look on my parents' faces when, as a young woman, I said I wasn't coming to the Seder because we were going to a meeting addressed by Saklatvala, an Indian Member of Parliament who represented the Communist Party in the twenties.[1] We thought we were very advanced, and anyway we knew my parents' Seder was not the traditional one; it was just a nice occasion for getting the family together round the table and reminding ourselves what the Seder was about. Perhaps if they had felt it more deeply as a religious occasion and if we had thought we were breaking their hearts, we would not have done it. I think now that we shouldn't have done it even so, but young people do these things to their parents.

Now for the last 40 years I have gone every year to a friend who celebrates the Seder in the proper way with *alle pitshivkes*, all the little details, and I like it very much. I feel regretful that I haven't. got someone to celebrate the other festivals with – although I have no feeling for religion, only for the ethics that religion brings with it. But I feel sorry that we don't celebrate all the Jewish festivals, because we celebrate the Christian ones. It's inevitable, in a way, if you live in a non-Jewish country. They are public holidays, occasions for seeing your friends, so they get celebrated.

I remember my first day at school; it was all very strange. Things were happening round me which didn't register, but I don't remember being scared. A little cousin who was six was given permission to come from her class and sit next to me and translate what the teacher was saying. I don't remember having any difficulties with the language after that. At the end of the first year I got a prize in English. I spoke only Yiddish till I was seven and a half; English is my second language. For quite a while my parents and I spoke to each other in Yiddish. But then a teacher said to me, 'If you want to learn English, you must speak English, read English and *dream* in English.' When I told this to my father, he roared with laughter. But I took her advice and stopped speaking Yiddish. Then I spoke to my parents in English and they answered me in Yiddish. This is a very common story, not only among Jews. And so we got by until my parents began to speak English too.

I went to Stepney Jewish School.[2] We were a ragamuffinly lot, because it was the East End and there was a lot of poverty. Perhaps there was a little less poverty among the Jewish community, and this may be due to the fact that Jews, in those days at any rate, spent no money on drink. A new headmistress came when I was about 10 or 12, Miss Kate Rose her name was, and she wanted us to look like secondary school children. She didn't say so, of course, but I can now interpret it that way. She issued an edict that we were to have uniforms, navy-blue gymslips and white blouses. Well, I could go on for a week about the trouble this caused. How long can you wear a white blouse? Our parents didn't have the wherewithal to keep a stock of white blouses and give us a fresh one every day, so by the time Friday came, they were pretty grubby. The teacher would say, 'You should have clean blouses on, girls, even on a Friday.' But our mothers would say, 'It's the last day of the week; it's not worth putting on a clean blouse.' My mother couldn't face the expense of buying the new uniform so she made mine. She was handy with a needle, but this was difficult because you had to have three box-pleats in front. She found she didn't have enough material for three, so she made two. Imagine my agony, going to school with only two box-pleats – but I had to sweat it out.

I adored going on school journeys because it made me feel like those girls in the library books about boarding school that one got in those days. I thought it must be so wonderful to go to a boarding school, and for two weeks it was like being in one. I thought it was marvellous. We had to pay according to means and some paid very little. Yet my best friend couldn't go because her parents couldn't even afford that very little. We spent quite a time going up and down the market, after the stallholders were gone, in the hope that somebody had dropped a pound note. We searched the gutters but we never found anything. And so she couldn't come.

Stepney Jewish School was considered a poor school. I got up to all sorts of mischief because I was bored. However, I survived. I left when I was 14 and went to commercial school, which was free, for 18 months. I did shorthand, typing, book-keeping, a little arithmetic and a little French. And then I went to work at 15½, as a shorthand typist in a shipping office. I think I was earning 15 shillings a week. I had great big, heavy parchment bills of lading to type out with ever so many copies. It was so boring and I kept losing the place because I was typing from a manuscript. If you made a mistake, which I very often did, you had to rub it out on eight copies. Once I got right to the end of this huge sheet of parchment and found I had all the carbons round the wrong way – and the copies were blank.

I grew away from my school friends at Stepney Jewish School; I was more serious than they were. I made one friend at the commercial school who off and on remained my friend until a few years ago, when she died. But my more adult friends, that is when I was 16, 17, I made at the Jewish Workers' Circle. That's where I got to know my husband, Morris. I first met him at home but our friendship was developed at the Progressive Youth Circle in Circle House. But my closest friends, who have remained friends all the years, were in the Communist Party with me, until one by one we became disillusioned and dropped off.

My husband came to this country from Poland, where he had been a member of the illegal Communist Party. In the Progressive Youth Circle, which he and another comrade set up in the late twenties, there were all sorts of young people: communists, anarchists, socialists, Zionists, and non-Party people who were interested in political matters. We used to thrash things out in lectures and discussions. It was a marvellous time for me. Up to that time I'd been buried in books. When the two young men from Poland arrived, my future husband was 19 and his friend was 17. I was 14, in short socks, and didn't even notice them. They would argue with my father about politics but I didn't really listen; I was reading my eyes out. When they introduced me into the Progressive Youth Circle I was about 16 or so. A new life opened, an intellectual life, people hammering out their ideas. It was meat and drink to me. I'd veer between Zionism and communism according to who was speaking. I can't say now whether I was intellectually convinced that communism was the right way forward because of a dispassionate examination of the facts or because the two people I was in love with, one after the other, were communists. That may have helped to swing me over. At any rate, I became a communist.

With the little education and intellectual training that I'd had, my politics were absolutely emotional. I can see it now, though I probably would have challenged it at the time. What appealed to me was the idea that all men were brothers (which of course meant 'all men and women are brothers and sisters' – we didn't need to spell it out) and that we would build a beautiful world where everybody would be nice to everybody else and there would be no more war, no more poverty, no more disease, because socialism would put everything right. This was our nebulous ideal.

My parents didn't mind that I went to lectures and socials at Circle House. They had long wished me to stop reading and go to dances with my young cousin, but I didn't want to. I was too damn serious for my own good. I'm much younger now than I was then, in some ways. My parents approved of my going to the Progressive Youth Circle until there was a lecture advertised as 'Sexual Disease and Its Effect on the Youth of Today' and my mother saw me painting a poster for it. She was absolutely appalled, because she thought I was much too young to grapple with that sort of thing. I don't remember whether I went after all.

When I read now about youngsters having to be very careful at night, girls particularly, I remember that my mother was just as anxious then (and it was 60 years ago) about me coming home late down a dark street. Once there was a play in the Progressive Youth Circle which was a great success. The relative I'd come with wanted to go home before it finished because her husband played hell if she was late. I thought she was completely mad to think I could leave this enthralling drama. Not only the drama on the stage; it was during the course of the drama that I fell in love with my future husband, who was one of the actors. I was absolutely rooted. She was pulling at me and I said she should go home. So I got into terrible trouble because I was putting myself in this awful danger of coming down Stepney Green alone at night. I think that mothers particularly were anxious about their daughters, and they still are. I think this anxiety is built into parents.

When my periods first started my mother gave me a good talking to and said I shouldn't let myself be kissed and I shouldn't show my legs too far up. She actually said something which I think is very wrong, but she did it for the best. She said, 'Men are very bad.' She didn't have the language to say you have to be careful not to provoke men unless you want to get into an affair. Later I understood that it's very easy to get a man excited and unless you want it to go further, you shouldn't do it.

Our attitudes must have been affected by Party ideology, to some extent. We had ideas about 'free love' which were very much misused by some people, especially men. There were misconceptions that you could be as promiscuous as you liked. Those of us who were more serious understood that 'free love' simply meant that you didn't have to be officially married in order to love someone physically. My future husband and I became lovers a year before we were married and we only got married officially because we wanted to have children – at least, that's what we told ourselves. Whether this was a rationalisation and we didn't want to be too different, I can't actually analyse now, but it may have had something to do with it.

I knew about contraception when I was 17 or 18, though it was not very common for my age group to know about it. There were a few clinics dotted about and I went to the Walworth Road Mothers' Clinic, as it was called, because it was furthest away from my house and I wouldn't be recognised. When I found the street, I looked around to make sure that nobody was watching and dashed across to it. It was very hole-in-the-corner. There was a fine-looking woman doctor there and I said that I was going to be married next month. I hated having to tell her lies – because I wasn't going to be married for at least a year. She told me what I could do in the meantime and that after I was married I should come back and get properly fixed up. So I said thank you very much and took what she gave me. Then I had the business of giving it to my young man. I gave it to him in the dark because I was so embarrassed about the whole thing. We got by all right without my getting pregnant and then, two years later, it was time for me to get properly fixed up, as she'd said, which meant a Dutch cap in those days. I went to a different contraceptive clinic this time and lo and behold, there was the same doctor. She looked across at me and said 'I think I've seen you before'. I denied it. I felt I was perjuring my immortal soul, but I couldn't tell her that I had wanted to sleep with my man before marriage. I didn't have what it took to say such a thing. Now it's very different.

When I was about to get married my mother handed me a post office book, saying that they had saved all the money I earned since I was 16 and that it was for me to get my home furnished with. I didn't know if I was pleased or sorry, because I felt that it made nonsense of my feeling of having helped them. Every week since I started work I had handed over my salary. I thought I was helping to support the family, because the shop didn't bring in much, and was very proud of this. I wouldn't have put it in those words at the time, but it felt like a rejection. They didn't mean it that way; it was a gift. After all, they could well have used it; they were living in great discomfort. Perhaps she should just have given me the money and said, 'Do what you want with it.' But parents never know what to do for the best. In general, we try not to repeat our parents' mistakes, but we make new ones. So what can you do? You can only do your best.

My parents' friend the cabinet maker had given us a catalogue from which we chose our stuff. I hadn't the least idea how to furnish a home, but I didn't like some of the things in the catalogue and had to have a fight every time I suggested something different. And in the end I was unhappy with it, but didn't understand why till many years later. It was my ignorance and my inexperience. I realised then that it was stiff and conventional and formal, and it's much nicer when you just pick up oddments which don't have to match. But we were stuck with it. We didn't have the money to chuck it out and start again. My contemporaries after the war were usually people from much more cultured backgrounds and they knew what to buy. They would never get things the wrong colour or size or shape, and they appreciated the value of old things, whereas when I was a youngster, the great thing was to have something new, not secondhand. That was horrible; other people had used it. I didn't want it to be like my parents' house; and yet many years later when I was writing, I remembered very vividly our kitchen at home, which was a kitchen and a living room and everything else room, and it made me cry, because I realised it was very cosy, in a way that kitchens are not cosy now; they are just machines for cooking your dinner in. I found it very moving to remember the flames in the fireplace and a rug in front of the fire.

Before we were married, when I asked my husband to help choose furniture, he got very impatient. It wasn't important to him, but it was important to me, because I realised we'd have to live with it for a long time, perhaps for ever, and I cared more about the appearance of things. He thought I was getting too bogged down in this choosing of furniture. He thought I was reneging on the movement, spending all my time on these domestic problems.

In a way, this difference in attitude went on throughout our marriage. It began to impinge on more important things, like relationships with the children and with me. I thought, 'Why aren't I happy? I've got all these things: I've got a home, husband, children – a husband who loves me nearly as much as the movement.' And that was it. That was a very central thing in my marriage, my feeling that I wasn't first in his life. If he had had to choose, he'd have had to choose socialism, the movement. It was very deep in him, this need and wish to make life better for the great mass of people, and he sometimes forgot, I think, that I was one of the great mass of people. But he was a good man, a very attractive man, and people loved him. He never set out to seduce or to charm, he was just like that. People flocked round him.

He came from a religious family of 10 children, from a small town not far from Warsaw. He was born in 1907, so he was seven when the First World War began and 11 when it finished. He became aware of the struggle with poverty and he remembered hunger. One of his most painful memories was of being given a loaf of bread, which he knew very well he ought to share with the younger children but he started eating because he was very hungry, and he went on and ate the lot. He felt terrible about it. This memory haunted him all his life. He referred to it the night before he died. We were sitting round the table with friends and for some reason we each had to tell about something we had been ashamed of in early life and this is the story my husband told – eight hours before he died – and it wasn't the first time. Imagine carrying that guilt about with you. He should have forgiven himself, but he couldn't. It's terrible to be hungry when you're young and growing.

So, what with the hunger and poverty and anti-Semitism, he became a communist. It was illegal to be a communist in Poland at that time, when he was about 14 or 15. He used to go to illegal Communist Party meetings, and his father would lock the door. There was my poor husband locked out in the depths of the Polish winter. He went into the stable to sleep with the horse and cow until his mother, when she was sure that the father was asleep, would creep down and unlock the door and let him in. His natural rebellion was fostered at home and it stayed with him. It was a very strong motivation for him; everything in his life revolved around doing something for the movement. But he wasn't strait-laced, he could enjoy himself too. We used to go rambling and singing, having fun, having friends round. But the important things in life had to be measured against his contribution to the movement and to changing life so that it would be better for everybody. It wasn't very easy for me.

I married just before I was 20. My husband didn't have British nationality; he had a Nansen passport.[3] So I had to have an identity card like a foreigner, until a new law was passed and women born in Britain could get their British nationality back again.

I lived in Clapton after I got married till I was pregnant with my second child and couldn't manage the stairs any more. Then we moved into Hackney, where my younger son was born, and then to Willesden. When the war broke out, the children and I were evacuated near Northampton for two and a half years. During the Blitz my parents' shop and house were bombed and they couldn't go on living there. They came out to me and eventually found another shop in Northampton. The odd thing was that the shop and house were even worse than the one in the East End. They were there about five years. I nearly went crazy living in a little village with nobody to talk to except the children. So the children went to a little boarding school and I came to London and shared a furnished room with my husband. Eventually, when the war was over, we all got together again and bought this great house in Hampstead, which nearly killed me because it was so vast. We had lodgers and my parents and my brother, and we, my husband and I and our sons, occupied the ground floor. My father went to help my husband in his business, with dire results.

I had been my parents' child until I was 19, when I married. My parents were my children for much longer because they became emotionally dependent on me until they died. They lived in the flat above us in the house in Hampstead and I got very involved with their problems. Then, when we moved from Hampstead, they also came to live round the corner in Willesden. Because their life had been such that it had not been possible for them to develop a social life and make friends, and the relatives were dying off and the few friends they had were far away, they were thrown entirely on me and I found that very hard. It was the great tragedy of my mother's life in particular that she did not have time to develop friendships. In Poland she had had interesting friends, people who read and went to plays, but there was no such friend here except the cabinet-maker and his wife, and they lived at a great distance. They were the only non-family friends my parents had – or should I say my mother had, because my father was more withdrawn; all he wanted was a quiet life, because the life he lived was exhausting for him. My mother had a need for friendship and really didn't get it. The people in the family were on my father's side and all they thought about was the business or the cooking or both. My mother's family were in Poland till the Holocaust wiped them out. In her old age she was very lonely and that made problems for me.

It was very hard to take in that all those people had perished. It chiefly hit me when I read in the French Yiddish paper that my favourite uncle, who was a writer, had perished in Auschwitz. It brought it home to me. I had a very curious reaction – I wanted to have another child immediately. I dismissed it later but my instinctive reaction was that I must replace him. I also felt the Holocaust because of my mother. My mother's three brothers had all perished under the Nazis, in three different countries. She missed them very much and she missed her close friends, with whom she had been in correspondence until the war. This all rebounded on me in a way because she wanted me to be all of them. I wouldn't have put it like that to myself then, but I understood it later. All I felt at the time was that she was constantly making demands on me, not necessarily verbally but by continually coming down and staying and wanting to talk, and I had other things to do. I felt that she was clutching at me and I was going to be swallowed up. I had to withdraw and tear myself away. I had all these people making demands on me, and there was a houseful of tenants and the Party too. It was a hard time.

But as for losing people in the Holocaust, I can't take it in to this day. I was very sad and very angry. All these years since the Holocaust, I'm still asking myself how human beings could do this to one another. The question has been reinforced during more recent times by reading about people who are imprisoned and tortured in the South American states and also in the Soviet Union. A relative by marriage was taken to Auschwitz, and so were her husband and her parents. She left a little child behind with friends. Her parents she never saw again. Her husband was still alive at the time of the Liberation but it was too late to rescue him, he was too starved. She survived. She and two Frenchwomen had formed a trio of friends and saved each other's lives, over and over again, each one at the risk of losing her own. I was present at the wedding of the daughter of one of them, to which they all came. There was a beautiful table, set with nice things to eat, and I wondered whether they could possibly have imagined this when they were in Auschwitz; if so, it would have been the wildest fantasy. I also felt they had beaten Hitler because they survived to live normal lives. In the years after the war we heard terrible stories about the camps and the ghettoes, and everything that happened became part of my mental furniture for ever.

My sons identify as Jews, but not as much as I do and certainly not as much as my husband did. Their culture is English culture and I don't regret this. But I do wish sometimes that they were more conscious of their Jewishness. They are aware of being Jews and of anti-Semitism, and because they know what happened, perhaps what can still happen, they identify with other people who suffer discrimination. So their Jewishness has worked in that way. My children's consciousness of being Jewish came chiefly through my husband. When he first came to England he was a foreigner and his work lay with other foreigners who were Jews. Then he moved away from the East End and those people moved away too, and he was in the Communist Party. The Holocaust brought him back into the Jewish field as nothing else could have done. I remember him telling me of a meeting of Jewish comrades at which Willie Gallacher[4] appealed to them not to abandon their people, their culture, though some of them opposed his pleas on the grounds of Internationalism. Because of what had happened in Europe, my husband began to concentrate still more on work among Jews and in the Jewish Workers' Circle. All the contacts he made from this time on till his death were Jews. He had committee meetings in our house; journalists came from the Yiddish communist papers in Europe. Discussions were going on all the time and so my children absorbed this into their background, but they didn't want to remain in it. We were not Zionists, although we welcomed the State of Israel and what it could do for Jews, and we were not religious, but my Jewishness is very strong in me. I can't perceive of myself as anything but a Jewish woman who was born in England and soaked in all these tragedies of the past.

The Communist Party was great while it lasted and while we believed in it. I think it did a good job until the war, because it was in the forefront of the fight against fascism. And after the Soviet Union came into the war, the Party's chief function was to help in the war effort, in order to beat Nazi Germany. The Soviet Union was 'our gallant ally' then. But soon after the war all this finished. Then I began to wonder what the Party was for, and it became harder and harder to belong to it. We began to get the stories about what was happening in the Soviet Union; the labour camps, the shooting of the Jewish Anti-Fascist Committee and people we had known from there, Mikhoels and Pfeffer. Mikhoels was a great Jewish actor in the Soviet Union and Pfeffer was a colonel in the army and a poet. They headed the Jewish Anti-Fascist Committee in the Soviet Union and were sent out during the war to act as cultural ambassadors and to rally support for the battle to defeat fascism. They were among those who were killed. Why? They were Jews, they were 'cosmopolitans', therefore they were not to be trusted, and so they went.

We began to get all these stories and I began to wonder what was happening and what was true and what was not. And finally came Krushchev's speech in 1956 which blew the gaff. He told what had been happening under Stalin. It was a great watershed for me and my friends. Nearly all of us left either immediately or the following year, but the friendships remained. That side of it lived on after our attachment to the Party had been broken. Most of these friends were Jewish but not by any means all.

The divide among Party members in their response to the crisis was between the intellectuals and the workers. The intellectuals felt a sense of responsibility for what had gone wrong. They felt they had had an unwitting part in misleading people about the Soviet Union and so they felt the betrayal more. But there was an overlap; some working people felt as the intellectuals did and some intellectuals remained in the Party.

We had all had such dreams; everything came crashing down. The whole thing was such an enormous blow. We were spending night after night in each other's homes, trying to understand what had happened and why. These discussions often went on till two o'clock in the morning and when we went home we couldn't sleep because we were so upset. How could such crimes have been committed in the name of socialism? The betrayal of the peasants, the slaughter of hundreds of thousands of people, the betrayal of the Jewish Anti-Fascist Committee, the way the attitude to the Jews had changed from the early days of the Revolution. It was a terrible time. Any physical weakness people had came to the fore because of the mental shock. And there were still people who didn't believe what Krushchev was saying. My late husband found it very hard to believe until an article in the Jewish Polish paper convinced him. My husband and my younger son said there isn't a better Party and we must stay and fight for things to be different. My husband remained a Party member till the day he died. My older son dropped out around the time that I did, but my younger son remained in the Party for years as a critical and rebellious young Party member. But there were others who are Stalinists to this day, and who are still in the Party.

When my husband finally permitted himself to believe that things were indeed as Krushchev had said, I felt that in a way this would help our relationship. We used to argue before all this came out in the open – for instance, about books. I would try to read Soviet novels but I found them excruciatingly boring. I thought I ought to like them but I couldn't, so I would abandon them in anger and then have a row with my husband, because he would say it's an important book. Actually, it was on this very topic of literature that I often felt a great division between myself and the Party. The official attitude was that literature and music and art are weapons in the class struggle. I felt that they had quite a different function. At any rate, when all this came out, I felt that now my husband and I would be able to discuss things more amicably and not with the real hostility it aroused sometimes because we took such different attitudes. And in a way it did help a bit. But I had rather fierce arguments with my younger son, who said I had no right to criticise, only those still in the Party could criticise. But it didn't disrupt us as a family.

After we moved out of Hampstead to Willesden, I found I couldn't manage financially, so I went out to work again. I stayed at work for 14 years, until I retired. I really enjoyed my jobs. In the early part I was working for the Relief Committee for the Victims of German Fascism. During the war I was working for the Joint

Committee for Soviet Aid, as secretary of the Women's Committee. Then the war ended and the children came home and I started to rebuild the family. In 1951 I found a job in the Imperial College of Science, in the Mathematics Department (about which I knew nothing), but I was working for a very interesting man, Professor Hyman Levy, and we used to go out to lunch and talk our heads off. After that I got a wonderful job in Harley Street, as receptionist to a children's surgeon who specialised in congenital deformities, Sir Denis Browne. I really felt I was doing something very good by helping him. He was a Tory and a racially prejudiced man, but at the same time he was such a marvellous human being to children of any race or colour that I couldn't help liking him, though we had some fierce arguments.

I resigned when I was 53. I wanted to do three things; to learn to drive, to learn French and to write. I started to learn French first of all, but my husband died very suddenly and the shock drove it all out of my mind. I learned to drive after that and five years later, in 1970, when my parents were also dead, I started writing – nearly every day.

I had written before but under such difficulties, it was stolen time. I wrote short pieces for the *Guardian* Women's Page for quite a time in the sixties. Then I realised I was using up dramatic material which ought to be kept for some bigger, more serious piece of work, so I stopped. But one of my short stories took a second prize in a competition in the *Jewish Quarterly*. At the award-giving ceremony a publisher who had been on the adjudicating committee told me he really wanted my story to take first prize but he was overruled. He asked if I had any more stories about the same people and I sent them along.

His reader sent me a letter, asking me to come to see her. Imagine my feelings. I practically ran all the way. She said she'd loved the stories but suggested I write a novel. I said I couldn't write novels, I could only write short stories. She said I should go home and try. I thought I couldn't write a novel but what I would do was write a long story which would be an introduction to those I'd already written. When I began, I intended to write about the market, about Poland, about the Progressive Youth Circle, and suddenly I realised that it wouldn't go into a story, that it was a book. I wrote two chapters and sent them along, saying, 'These are so different from the short stories that I think they can't be any good. It's not what you would like, but it seems to be flowing.' She wrote back and said, 'Let it flow.' And that's how *A Family of Shopkeepers* got written.

When I started it, I had meant to get to a certain point. Although I've written two books now, I've not got there yet. Everyone asks about the third book but I don't know if it'll ever get written. My own life now has got complicated in a very nice way, by getting a companion. It takes a lot of emotional investment, which would perhaps otherwise have gone into the book. And there's the question of physical time and space. I took up with him when I was 68 and I had all the same sensations as when I was 18. Absolutely everything – the excitement, the joy, the fear, the doubts. When I knew he was coming, I'd fly up the street to meet him as if I was 18. It was marvellous.

To this day I feel I can't look my mother in the eye (her picture is by my desk) until I've written the third book, because it's about what happened between her and me in her old age and in her last illness. I can't do it because I feel that it's too sad. I loved her very much but our relationship really went wrong in her old age. When she finally went into hospital, I would have torn heaven and earth apart to help her, but there was nothing I could do. Since her death she has grown in stature in my mind. Through being a parent and a grandparent, I understand more about her. She had some great qualities. I've often spoken about her to my friend; he's practically fallen in love with my mother. He said, 'I would have liked to know her. What would she have said to me?' I said she would have called him '*a voiler goy*' – I know she would have said that – a nice goy. So the third book remains in the back of my mind. Sometimes I've thought perhaps I'll write the sad part as the first half of the book and about this wonderful love affair in the second.

I wrote my second book, *Beginning Again*, and sent it to the publisher of *A Family of Shopkeepers*. I was very miffed when they wrote back and said they didn't want it. I was so disappointed, but after the shock had worn off I didn't mind so much and started sending it on the rounds. But when it had been round seven publishers and refused, I thought I'd have to put it away and give it to my grandchildren to read when they were grown up. Then I saw the announcement of a literary competition called 'Woman of the Eighties'. I wrote to the literary agent June Hall and said I had a book ready but it was not about the eighties, it was about the forties, so it wouldn't do for the competition but perhaps they would read it. She said I should send the first chapter. I rang her up and said that I had a dream that I was in a publisher's office and he was reading the first chapter and then the last chapter and then one in the middle. He gave me a cheque for £100 and said, 'You're on.' So she laughed and said, 'All right, send me the last chapter as well.' So I did – and then she wanted to see the rest. After that she asked whether I could change the period to the eighties. I said no – everything would be different 40 years on. The woman in the book would have had a Hoover and a refrigerator and a washing-machine and she'd probably go to a women's group. She knew I was interested in another competition and she said I'd better go in for that.

Then suddenly one day June rang up and said she didn't know what I'd think of them, but could I let them have it back. All I had left was my final copy, horrible and tattered and not very clear. I sent it in and then one day she said I was on the shortlist of six. I can't tell you how I felt. She told me the result was expected in September and I said it would be nice if she could tell me the result on my seventieth birthday.

On my seventieth birthday I'd had a party given the previous night by my sons, and part of my Dutch family were sleeping all over the floor. The phone went and June said I'd got it, I'd got the prize. I nearly dropped through the floor. I was sure she was making a mistake, it couldn't be true. But she said she was sure and I was to get my manuscript back from the other people. The award meant a big money prize and a promise of publication within a year. I was on a high. And that was that. My book took the prize – 'Woman of the Eighties'.

(Both *A Family of Shopkeepers* and *Beginning Again* were subsequently published in paperback by Coronet [Hodder and Stoughton], in 1985.)

AFTERWORD

I enjoyed the interviews. How nice to be encouraged to talk about one's life and thoughts without being considered egocentric! I hope they will convey to some extent the background in which I grew and developed, and the ideas and attitudes which left their mark on me and my close contemporaries. At the same time, reading the transcript made me aware of the limitations imposed by this form. I therefore welcome the opportunity for an afterword about my late husband and parents.

In speaking of my husband I should have emphasised that he was brought up at a time when men expected to be waited on by women, even when their womenfolk worked full-time outside the home. He was in fact ahead of other men. He helped me to some extent when he was at home. My difficulties, partly physical and partly emotional, arose from his being so little at home. He was driven by the intensity of his need to take part in the movement for a juster, more equitable society. While I shared largely in his hopes and beliefs, for me the family had to come first. I was often in conflict with myself about this. My husband had no such conflict. But he was a caring person and during family crises he did his best to share the burden.

The lives and characters of my parents, and particularly of my mother, were also inadequately expressed. She was a wise and original person with an ironic sense of humour; to this day I find her quotable. This lively, sociable and quick-witted person found herself in old age burdened with a senile husband and socially isolated for reasons referred to in the interview. Her dreams, nurtured for many years, of further education and culture, were hopelessly frustrated. It was no wonder that she came to lean on me more heavily than I could bear. She became obsessional about cooking and about her troubles with my father. Yet she was never bitter or petty, and always tolerant. Both she and my father found some consolation in the birth of first my children, and after a long interval, of my brother's. These latter, and family celebrations and festivities, to some extent brightened their difficult old age. Both of them were unusual in their class and generation. In my childhood I took them for granted, as children do, but with the perspective granted by my own old age, I count myself lucky to have been their child. And lucky too to have been granted the opportunity, through these interviews, to introduce them to a wider public.

NOTES

1. Shapurji Saklatvala was first elected as a Labour MP for Battersea North in 1922. He was elected as a Communist candidate, supported by the local Labour Party, in 1924, the year the Labour Party banned dual membership. In the 1929 election he was dropped by the Battersea Labour Party.
2. Although the Jews' Free School was by far the largest and best known of the Jewish voluntary schools, there were, and still are, several other Jewish schools in London, as well as in other major cities. Stepney Jewish School was founded in 1863. It was situated to the east of Whitechapel, the centre of Jewish population in the East End of London. The majority of the children were English Jews, whose parents were themselves born in England. In 1969 the school moved, with most of its teachers and pupils, to the outer suburbs of London, and is now the Ilford Jewish Primary School.
3. Large numbers of people became refugees and displaced persons after the First World War and the Russian Revolution. In 1922 the League of Nations issued Certificates of Identity to stateless persons who did not have the right of return to the state which issued them. The documents were introduced at the suggestion of Dr Nansen, who was High Commissioner for Refugees at the League of Nations, and were called Nansen passports.
4. Willie Gallacher was MP for West Fife from 1935 to 1950. He was the first Communist MP to be elected without first having been a Labour MP.

ROSE KERRIGAN
'We Just Want to Get Something for the Working Class . . .'

Rose was born in Dublin in 1903. Her parents, Rebecca and Benjamin Klasko, were both immigrants from Russia, who had met and married in Glasgow. Rose is the second of five children. Rose's only sister died in infancy, and her brother Willie died in 1914, at the age of 14. Moses and Davie were her surviving brothers.

The Klasko family returned to Scotland from Ireland, settling again in Glasgow when Rose was six years old. Glasgow had a comparatively small Jewish community; in 1902 there were 6,500 Jews living there, mostly new immigrants who had settled in the Gorbals. Rose's parents were engaged in two 'immigrant' trades there, tailoring and cigarette-making. Jewish workers had been brought to the city in the second half of the nineteenth century specifically to work at these occupations.

There was high unemployment in Glasgow and the Klaskos lived a precarious existence. Benjamin was an active socialist and his political work lost him at least one job, in Dublin. Rose shared her father's politics. Through her exposure to the anti-war movement, which was very strong on Clydeside, Rose became politically active. The war led to increased prices and rents. At the age of 12, in 1915, Rose took part in the Glasgow Rent Strike, initiated by the women of Glasgow. Mass demonstrations by the women and the munitions workers of the Clyde led to the introduction of rent controls.

The First World War made the fortunes of some in the garment trade, because of the enormous military uniform contracts. Benjamin was not one of them, and he was made bankrupt during the war, a trauma from which he never recovered. The family's brief moment of prosperity had passed.

Rose and her brother, radicalised by their father, attended the Socialist Sunday School, which exposed them to completely secular values. This, and the devastation of the First World War, led Rose to reject her religion and cease being a practising Jew.

From early on Rose resented the unfair burden of domestic work imposed on Jewish wives and daughters. She challenged her father – he was a radical and yet he did not help in the house. She was and remains passionate in her defence of the rights of herself and others: the right of women to work, the right to control our fertility and have nurseries for our children. Rose was a founder member of the Communist Party, and remains a Party member. She has worked for most of her life in the garment trade and has been an active trade unionist throughout her working life.

Now in her eighties, Rose is still an activist, fighting for pensioners' rights. She is chairperson of both Lewisham Pensioners' Action Group, a campaigning organisation, and Lewisham Pensioners' Forum, which brings together all the pensioners' groups in the borough. She is also on the local council's Pensioners' Committee, and is on the editorial board of the Pensioners' Gazette. Throughout her life she has remained true to the conviction she came to in Glasgow as a young woman: 'I learned that some righteous people accused the working class of being shiftless drunkards, and claimed these were the reasons they were poor. I knew from personal experience this was not true. My parents were hard working, honest and had ambitions for their children . . . I resolved to struggle to improve our lot, knowing that we could only do this by joining with others to achieve it.'

(Extracts are from Rose's autobiography, which appeared in an anthology, Childhood Memories, privately published and circulated by Marian and Hymie Fagan and Margaret Cohen.)

My mother came here quite young – 19 when she came to Britain. She was born in Vilna. Her own mother died when my mother was about 16, from cholera. Two years after, or less, her father remarried a young woman and my mother didn't want to stay. In those days, because she was underage, my mother had to have a ticket of leave from her father to go abroad. It was a permit to leave the country and stay away for a year. With this she went to Berlin. She was a glove-maker, but to keep in work she learned cigarette-making as well. She stayed there more than a year but because her father wouldn't renew her ticket of leave – he wanted her back – she defied him and came to Britain. She had a friend who went to Glasgow and this friend sponsored her to come over, and that's how my mother came here.

My father was born in Tobolsk, in Siberia, and never knew his mother or father, as he was reared by his grandmother, who by all accounts was a most remarkable woman. During the Polish-Russian war[1] around the 1860s she was living in her Lithuanian town of Vilna and she earned her living by baking and selling rolls. On her rounds she discovered a man hiding. It is never quite clear if he was a deserter from the Russian army or an enemy Pole, but he was starving and she fed him. On being discovered she was deported to Siberia. There is no record of a husband, but she had a son who married at the early age of 19. His wife was under 17 when my father was born, in August 1876. The son caught a cold which was neglected, due, no doubt, to the excitement of the new baby, and he died of pneumonia when Benjamin (my father) was only 3 months old. His grandmother, whose name was Rasalia (I am named after her), decided that her son's wife would no doubt marry again as she was so young, and that she, his grandmother, would take responsibility for Benjamin and bring him up. As Rasalia was Jewish and there were very few Jewish people in Tobolsk, she worried about the child, Benjamin, not getting a Jewish grounding. She made up her mind to return to Vilna so that the boy would be educated and know his own people. Without a permit or the necessary papers, she hired a driver and a wagon and proceeded from Siberia to Vilna. My father was then 8 years old and the journey took several months. One story that stands out was that it took a whole day to come through Moscow because the driver crossed himself at every church and there were as many churches there as pubs in the Gorbals!

My father was sent to a Jewish school in Vilna and at 12 was apprenticed to become a tailor. He got involved in an apprentice strike in Russia when he was 14! His grandmother had the wind up after her own experiences of being sent to Siberia for less than a strike, and sent him away.

He landed in London and went straight into the East London Hospital, because he came on a cargo boat, travelling steerage, and was very sick when he arrived. He was coming to an uncle who lived in Hackney – his only relative here – who had lived there for a long time. I don't know *how* my father got in touch with him. In hospital, without any English and very helpless, his name, which ought to have been Klatchki, was spelt Klasko. He kept it like that until the end of his life and we were known as the Klaskos.

Tailoring was such a precarious trade that he worked in almost every town in Britain before he came up to Glasgow. His uncle had gone there because he was a cigarette-maker and worked in Mitchells factory. My mother also worked there. My uncle invited her to his home, where she met my father.

They married. My father was always boasting of the fact that he married without a *nadn*. In those days that was something! They never had anybody that fixed up the wedding for them. And he went to work in Edinburgh. The firm that he worked for, B. Hyams and Co., wanted him to start a workshop in Dublin, and that's how I came to be born there, in 1903.

My father was a first-class hand tailor. There was bespoke tailoring, when a suit was ordered, and piece-work tailoring. My father did everything, but he didn't like making trousers, so he was considered a jacket-maker, ladies and gents. When he taught me some of the trade, I learned to make skirts and waistcoats – which I hated. I was never a good sewer, because I didn't like it! My mother never worked after she married, except for one period in my life when I think things were very, very rough and she tried to go back to the cigarette-making. She got a job cigar-making for three weeks, but she really wasn't able to keep up with the speed of it.

My father followed the jobs. A man who could do the whole thing like he could, he was a natural! He could cut his own patterns. He could measure a man and make him a suit. So he would make one for someone who could afford to pay for it – a private job. My father always said to me, 'Never keep a workman waiting for his money. The landlord can wait but workmen you must pay.' Because we suffered from that. If he made a suit we would be waiting ages to get paid for it.

The family lived in Dublin for seven years working for Hyams. My father was a manager. Of course, he was always a workman first, and everything else afterwards. He always stuck out for his rights, and for the proper wages for his staff. He was always quick-tempered. In the end, there was a dispute about wages and conditions, and they put him out. My mother always said, 'Oh, your dad, he must speak his mind!'

When we came back to Scotland, we weren't as well off. My mother was always very regretful that they had had to leave Dublin. She had a nice home there and a girl to help in the house. She had had children there and there was a Jewish community. She was happy. We came to Falkirk first, and my father worked there for a while. I started school there. Then work dried up. There was no unemployment benefit or anything like that in those days, and he came up to Glasgow to look for work.

My father came out of Buchanan Street Station and he walked up to the Cowcaddens, which was a real slum area. He saw this building, and there was a notice of a flat there with a room, a kitchen and a bathroom. A bathroom! He couldn't believe his eyes! He got that flat, and we lived there for four years, nearly five. Everything around about us was decrepit. The other flats, which were larger, took lodgers in for the Royal Theatre round the corner. I spent my childhood watching the ladies in their fine dresses going to the opera.

We moved in 1913, because father realised that it was not the kind of area to bring up children in. We lived in what was called a 'high back' in Scotland – the yard was one stair up because we were above the shops. You had to come upstairs from the street into this yard, and walk across to the entrance to the flat. Well, it was a bad area. Drunk people would be lying on your steps sometimes when you were coming up at night, or would try to get into the flat.

We had to live and we had to eat. If my father wasn't working, no matter what, we were always fed. The result was that we were always in debt. The main person that we were in debt to was the landlord. In Glasgow in those days there were no council buildings, it was all private landlords. The man who used to collect rent from us was an old chap called McNab. When McNab found that we were about to be taken to the court for not paying, *he* paid our rent. So we owed the money to him. When my dad couldn't pay him, he would end up making him a suit to wipe out the debt. He was very fond of my father, who was an armchair philosopher and had opinions about everything. I suppose it was a mundane job, collecting rents, meeting all kinds of people. People who wouldn't pay, people who didn't pay. He knew that we were in genuine poverty when my dad had no work.

My dad was so *honoured* that although he was a poor man himself, he could walk into the Gorbals collecting for someone in need and nobody would say 'Who is this money for?' My dad just had to say, 'I need something for someone,' and they'd never question him, they'd give him the money.[2]

My people were very anxious to keep up our religion, even though my father was a radical. He didn't really believe in it all, but he always went to *shul* on the high days and holy days. He went to the Gorbals, where the working people were. When I was 16 I gave up religion; I accused him of being a hypocrite. He turned round and he said to me, 'These are my people, and that's where I meet them. If I didn't go there I wouldn't meet them. And they listen to me and they respect my views.' I now know as I'm older that he was right and I was wrong. When you're young you only see the black and white and you don't see the grey shades in between. You think you're seeing it all so clear.

My father scoffed at silly laws. You know, in those days you used to have someone come and light a fire on a Friday, or light the lamp.[3] My dad said, 'This is nonsense. You can switch on the light, the electric. When that law was made, it was work to start a fire with flints.' He questioned things.

I was taught my religion by my mother, who was very devout and very kosher. She didn't go to *shul* much. She was never very strong, she was often ill. I always remember this. I must have been about eight years of age, and came *Shabbes* evening and my mother lit the candles and we hadn't finished the work. So I said to my mother, 'But you've not finished, and you're lighting the candles.' She said to me, 'Yes, I know we're not finished. God knows we're not finished. He knows why. You know, and I know, but nobody else needs to know.' That was the essence of it, that you satisfy yourself and God. It's a religion that can satisfy almost anyone, satisfy yourself. I once heard *mitzvah* defined as doing a favour without hope of what happens to you, and that itself secures your place in heaven.

My mother wasn't able to do anything, but she farmed me out to everybody. The woman on the top floor from us had twins. I was only 14 or 15 and my mother sent me up to her. Every night I went to help put the babies to bed, because my mother said that's what must be done. There was an old lady lived above us and she was stuck in bed, and the place literally stank. I hated to go in there, but my mother made me go in. That was a Jewish thing. So you were brought up with the idea that you were badly off, but other people could have even less than you and you must help them.

My father was very keen on learning English. He read Dickens, he read Jack London . . . Comics were forbidden in our house. That wasn't English, that wasn't good enough. So we were brought up to read and we were brought up to question things. He spoke English always with an accent. When other children used to mock, because he had an accent, I used to say, 'You don't know half the vocabulary that my father has; you're not half as intelligent as my dad.' My mother and father spoke Yiddish to each other and to us. I could understand a bit, but I could never speak it very well. My father's native tongue was Russian. Although he left there at eight years of age, it's the first language that counts. He didn't hear any Yiddish until he was nearly nine. That I never learned Russian really breaks my heart. My mother's Russian wasn't so good, because she was brought up in a Jewish background.[4]

Up till I was 10, we lived in an area where there were very few

54

Jewish families. In the school I was in, there was one other Jewish family. The Jewish boy was the best in the class and I was the best girl. A good job we were, because some of the teachers were very anti-Semitic. We were waylaid quite often coming home from *cheder*, especially on winter nights. My mother hid in a doorway one night when we were coming home. We'd come home crying 'cos these boys had hit us. We were running from them and my mother came out with an umbrella and gave them such a fright that they never came back!

My parents' attitude towards my education was no different than towards my brothers'. As I said, my dad was a radical. He was hot on education. It broke his heart that I left school at 14.

My dad never did anything about the house! That was the thing that I challenged him about. I was very proud of my father – he supported the suffragettes, but he never did a bloody thing in the house! The two things didn't equate. My mother had a big say, though – he was never that kind of man. He believed that women were oppressed. It wasn't because of him that she didn't go to work or anything like that. She wasn't very well. They were good pals. My father never did anything without discussing it with her. They respected each other. That's why we had to come away from where we lived. My father said we were getting too old and seeing too much rough life and drunkenness there.

In Glasgow there was a very divided community of Catholics and Protestants. When they found out we were Jewish . . . 'Well, you killed Christ!' I was told several times that I was responsible for the death of Jesus. When I came into my father and said, 'Who was Jesus?' my father said, 'Jesus was a rebel of his time, a man who stood up for his people and he suffered.' He always had an explanation for everything, and that is really how we were brought up.

Our *cheder* teacher came back from university. She took an interest in us children and she put me in a Purim play with another girl. My father sneered terribly at this – he thought she was do-goodish, doing it for charity. My dad was terribly against charity; he would never go to the Board of Guardians for anything.[5] She produced a dress for me with a blue sash. My mother said to him, 'For goodness sake, let the child enjoy herself!' I can remember it to this day. The other little girl was blonde. She had a pink ribbon on, a pink sash and a white dress. I had a blue ribbon, black curls. It was one of the highlights of my life at the time! I thought my dad was going to stop me being in it, and my mum stuck up for me for once.

Why did my brothers never get asked to do this, that and the next thing, only me? Whenever there was a quarrel and my mother would come into the room, we would all be fighting, but she would ask no questions and batter me. A girl should be different – that was her attitude, with no explanation why.

I had to help with the housework. The Jewish attitude was that boys weren't asked to do a thing. The only one who helped me was Willie, who was younger than me, and then he would only help me to do the brasses. We had a copper kettle, a brass fender, we had brass candlesticks, we had a brass jelly pan and we had brass fire irons, and I had to clean them every Friday. How I hated the smell of Brasso! My mother was so ill that I had to clean the floor when I was *six*! She would sit on a stool and wring out the cloths and I would wipe the floor over. I did *all* the shopping.

My mother taught me how to recognise fresh fish, all the names of the parts of the meat, and *all* these things. I also knew how to make food kosher, how you cooked it. You never had to mix the milk with the meat. The Pesach pots and dishes were all locked up in a cupboard and brought out every time Pesach came. My mother had iron pots. You took the hot poker out the fire, and you put it in the pot, and you cleaned it that way.[6] All these things I know.

My mother had four children who lived. She lost two babies. In Glasgow particularly women all had their babies at home, because there was only one maternity hospital and a big Catholic population. A lot of women lost their babies because of that. So at that time, the agitation was to get women into hospitals, because they did not get good attention at home. Also women with a new baby would also have two or three small children, and be up and looking after them and the baby. It was a small family if you had four or five children; some of them had nine or 10.

People can't see today that this was how it was. My mother-in-law once said to me, 'We've just to take what we get.' She once used the expression that you use nowadays about animals, that you 'serve' your husband. Her idea was that you did it because you wanted these children. Can you imagine any woman ready to go out, or do things, with five or six children – or even more, as some of them had? What chance had they to break out? None at all. So they took what they got. Later, when I was married, I could say when I was going to have children. My mother thought this was marvellous for me. She was astounded by that.

My little sister died at 14 months from a severe attack of whooping cough. My mother also had at least one miscarriage. As a child you didn't know that, it wasn't spoken about. The funny thing was that you lived in a room and a kitchen! The boys slept in one room and I slept in the other, the same room as my mother and father, until I was nine years of age. I was sleeping on top of a hamper. I finally fell through! Then she got a chair-bed for me. Later, when we went to live in Stockwell Street, I had a front room, which was the parlour. There was a 'hole in the wall' bed there, which you could close with a door.

The war broke out in 1914 and I was 11 years old. My dad, who was a keen student of politics and events, was against the war from the start. Yet the only work he could get was contracts from military uniforms. At this time he had his own workshop, with about 12 to 14 other workers, depending on this work. Although he was a good tailor and manager, he was a poor businessman. Within two years he was made bankrupt, and our good home was impounded for his debts.

My dad never really recovered from this traumatic experience. Willie, only 11, got a job delivering rolls in the morning before school. After a week or two he said that the butcher asked him to work for him, offering a shilling more. He suggested I took on the rolls. So we became helpers in the struggle to survive.

My father sneered at the stories put out about why we went to war to save little Belgium, and assured me it was to capture markets and carve up Europe. He often said how lucky he was that his boys were too young to fight.

We used to go to Glasgow Green, Willie and I, to hear the men talking. It was like Hyde Park Corner. And we'd get into arguments against the war. My father had it all sorted out, right from the beginning. As it went on, the people were getting very disillusioned with the many, many casualties. In Glasgow a lot of people were particularly anti-war. So during that time, meeting all those people, we found out about the Socialist Sunday School, and my brother and I went and joined.[7] One of the main directors of this enterprise was a local businessman called Tom Anderson, who put a great deal of effort, and his own money, into the running of the Sunday School. He played a very screechy violin, to accompany our singing socialist songs.

In 1915 they raised the rents. We were all with private landlords. Things were going up in price, because the war had been going for a year. The women of Glasgow protested. They were not organised, but the initiative came from them, and the cry went out: 'Pay the rent without the increase.' So I said to my mother, 'Pay the rent but not the increase!' I was only 12. By this time I was already going to Socialist Sunday School and I knew all the things that were going on that my family did not know about, because I heard them talking about it there. I went up to all the tenants and got them all to agree to withhold the rent! I said to my mother, 'If you're worried about debt, we'll put it in the bank.' And we never ever had to pay that money because the men in Glasgow were prepared to fight for it. They threatened to strike over the issue and they needed the men to make the munitions. It was a very important place for engineering at that time. So they brought in the Rent Act.

We were all voracious readers. At that time we were gaslit and we got my mother to put in electricity. We had an inside WC, with an electric light in there, and I would read my book! Mother called it the library! I was reading a lot and I began to question my religion. I really had a heartbreak time of it. I used to go to sleep at night wondering whether I was doing the right thing.

My main thing was that I couldn't understand this God, who was so omnipotent, as my mother and everybody told me. Here was this God to whom the Germans were also praying! And we were praying and everybody thought he was on our side, but he was also on their side, and yet he let these casualties happen.

I couldn't equate that, and that was really where I gave up my religion. But I had great heartsearchings over it. I used to lie awake at night and really worry myself sick, between the ages of 14 and 17. At 16 I was convinced, but then, when it came to Fast Days, my friends would go up town and have a meal and I couldn't. I had to stand up for myself, so I argued it out with my family that I didn't believe in it any more, and I wasn't going to fast and I wasn't going to do anything like that. Yet when I was so upset about the Israeli invasion in Lebanon, I fasted myself in this house on the Day of Atonement, because I was so angry with my people for doing that. It was a sort of protest in my own individual way.

The war convinced me and I've never looked back on it since. Only, over the years, because I've got older and met people and I know now how everybody needs to have something to hang on to, I'm not so antagonistic now as I was. My attitude is, if it's good for them, it's good for them. But it's not necessary for me. I can sort it out with my own conscience. Really, if I believe in a religion at all, it's in 'Do as you would be done by'.

The Jewishness may be as a national thing with me. I recognise that people have a nationality and have traditions and have a history behind them, which makes them what they are. But when my sister-in-law, who's a Christian and very, very religious – she was a missionary in Africa – wrote to me, 'How lucky you are that you're one of God's Chosen People, Rose!' I wrote her back a sneezer, because I said I didn't believe that any father or mother should make distinctions between their children! I wasn't happy to be a chosen child if that was how others were going to be treated!

When I left school I applied for a job in an office. I was called for an interview. I was only 14. And I walked up and the boss looked at me and said: 'Are you Jewish?' and I said, 'Yes,' and he said, 'I am suited.' He did it so blatantly that, by Jove, he got it from me. I can tell you that at 14 I wasn't the least bit inhibited! My English was good enough to put him down there! Glasgow was not known to be very anti-Semitic, though. It was pretty good in this respect.

My first job was in a departmental store, the Iron House. The wages were eight shillings a week. One of the girls I worked with had a brother who was a conscientious objector, on the grounds of religion. He was an evangelist. One Saturday night when we were having tea – we were allowed 15 minutes at 7 p.m. – one of the girls was taunting her about her brother, calling him a coward. This girl was in tears and I defended her brother. As there was only a curtain between us and shop walkers having their tea, I was tackled by my boss, who called me a pro-German. When I tried to defend my point of view he was furious, and gave me a week's notice. He was a territorial, who came to work on Saturday in uniform. So I told him, 'You are only a weekend soldier, and not fighting in France.' When I came home and told my parents I had got the sack, my dad said, 'You will have to learn to be more diplomatic!'

After one or two dead-end jobs I went to work at the office of the Socialist Labour Party.[8] I was partly office assistant and partly helping in the bookshop. They had a small printing-press and produced a weekly paper called the *Socialist*. I was in charge of the record of the comrades all over Britain who received the paper to sell, and were subscribers.

I worked for the SLP for a year, then my mother got round me. My dad had opened this little shop and she said that he was too lonely by himself. I used to do everything they asked me to do. So I went to work with him until we couldn't get any work. Things were bad in the twenties. So I went door-to-door selling, shop jobs and then I came back to the clothing trade again.

I was terribly naive. I never had any flirtations. My husband grew on me. We were pals, went hiking. I was frightened to be kissed. It was silly; nobody told you anything. I only learned when I was married that some women had had abortions. Backstreet abortion was not talked about. I was terribly scared when I had my first period. My mother did not explain to me that it was a natural thing; friends told me. She never gave me anything to keep myself comfortable; she only gave pieces of towel. I was at school and honestly I nearly had something come out on the floor, till a friend of mine said that these days they had towels with loops on that you washed. I was in a desperate state – 13 when I had my first period. I didn't connect it with births. I only had a real explanation when I read Marie Stopes' book *Married Love* and then I was in my twenties. That was quite a usual thing. Another thing which kept me from having anything to do with boys was that I read a book called *Damaged Goods*. It explained all about VD. I thought this was terrible. But I have never had any experiences and I have only been with the one man for 51 years!

It was a terrible stigma to be pregnant before being married. It was kept under the table. But last year I had a letter from a relative in which she told me, quite openly now, that she discovered a child whom she had given away, a boy who was born to her when she was about 17. I never knew. My family never mentioned it. He was looking for his original mother. He was put in a well-off Jewish family.

My mother and father never came to my wedding. And yet my father was radical, as I told you. I only had a civil wedding. I got married in the registry office and Peter's mother and father came and stood as witnesses. My mother and father didn't come and the day I was leaving to get married, my mother was crying the whole morning. Yet she went to my flat and made all the cushions and prepared my bed.

My auntie blamed me because her daughter married out. She said it was the example that I gave, which was nonsense – they weren't even in my circle. Me and my husband stood for them, but then, to please her mother, they had a Jewish wedding afterwards.

I think that the feeling was that if a Jewish man married a *shikse*, if she was willing to become Jewish, good enough. But if she didn't, they didn't care so much about the man that went out of the religion as they did about the woman – because she carries on the race.[9] So a woman going out and marrying a gentile was a bigger crime than a man who married a gentile. My parents did not dislike my man, they just did not want me to marry out of the faith, because it was tradition. But they were very fond of him.

As for me, it was not a question of 'I did not want to live with a man unmarried!' It was a question of my children being legal.

The marriage certificate could go to hell if a man did not treat me right.

In years afterwards, when my father became paralysed, my husband – not me, mind you – said, 'They can't look after themselves. They have got to come in with us.' And he took in my mother and father. My auntie said about him, '*A sheygets aber a mentsh*.' 'A gentile but a gentleman!'

I read Marie Stopes' book in 1924 and I married in 1926. Birth control was a secret thing and the clinic was a little backstreet place. I attended it because I had my mother and father to keep and I was afraid to have children. I put off getting married and I must say my bloke was very patient. I kept him waiting for two and a half years – no compensations. A very virtuous woman I was! Also there were so many unemployed, and I was determined I wasn't going to get married on the dole. I knew that I had these responsibilities: my father was paralysed and my brother Mo was idle. The other, Davie, buggered off and we never saw him again. I was determined I would have a place of my own and I wouldn't marry before, so that's why I was interested in birth control.

They wouldn't treat you first of all if you had never had any children, of course, even if you were married. So then I explained I had the responsibility of my mother and father; it wasn't that I was afraid to have children. The clinic fitted me with a cap. I used that all my life. When I decided to have my baby I came and told them and so the doctor, Amy Fleming – she was a first-class obstetrician – attended me with my first child. She said, 'I will do your confinement if you go into a nursing home.' You couldn't get into the maternity in Glasgow, unless you were a real bad case. I said I couldn't afford to pay – I knew she was a specialist. 'Nonsense,' she said. I paid her what you would pay an ordinary doctor.

In *Married Love* it mentioned several things that I really didn't understand. I was terribly green. I was a woman of nearly 50 years of age before I knew anything at all about homosexuality. In our day these things were never spoken of – nobody knew anything about them.

I was 29 when my daughter Rose was born. At that time I had a little shop and I thought that I would be able to pay for help.

My mother was living along the road and I thought she would be able to help – I worked it all out. But my baby was born on 4 April, my father died on 9 April and my mother died on 13 April. My mother died of the shock of him dying. She looked after him too long. The two of them got the 'flu and I was rushing after them. I was having the baby in a home. I said 'Why has my father not come to see me?' and nobody would tell me why. Then the girl who helped me in my shop said, 'Oh, isn't it terrible about your dad!' The matron of the home was afraid I would lose my milk with the shock of it. I never even went to my father's funeral. So there you are: you can't always plan everything. I did plan my children, though.

Before I got married I worked in a salesroom shop near the station at Queen Street. People from the country used to come up and see it. The man who ran the shop was a Londoner and Scottish people did not understand him half the time. He had this idea that if we could restock something, we should sell it for *any* profit, even if it was for less than we should have got for it. You had made a customer who would come back. I had been working for him for about two or three weeks when he said to me, 'I thought I would never keep you here because you used to blush if you weren't telling the truth.' I said, 'I never blushed for myself – I blushed for you. The stories that you told were so unbelievable!'

I was good at sales. If a woman, come in for a fur coat, could pay the price for a fur coat, I sold it to her. If a poor man, come in up from the country, had 25 shillings to spend on a suit and the suit was really 30 bob he got it for 25 shillings. If he went up the road and had work to do I would shorten the sleeves or the trousers for him and the boss would not know anything about it. The customers used to send other people to me and the shop was really doing well.

One day came the question of marriage. Down here in London people married and they worked, women went cleaning and did all that sort of thing, but that wasn't the custom in Scotland. You got married and you stayed home. Nearly always you had a family before you could look round. I said, 'I have to work to help my family. If I got married would you keep me on?' 'No,' he said. 'You couldn't look after my shop if you got married.' I was 18 months married before he found out. I was on holiday, and the stupid girl in the fruit shop next door let it out. 'If you could deceive me about that,' he said, 'you could deceive me about anything.' He gave me a week's notice because I got married.

When I married my husband, first of all he worked for Brown and Poulson – that's the people who produce cornflour. Then he went off on a course and he was away for several months. That was when I had my family to look after and the Means Test was on. I had my mother, father and brother, and the government only allowed me 11 shillings a week for them.

I had my own shop then. I opened it as a place for doing sewing repairs and odds and ends. I worked it up and did quite well, and kept the family until Peter came back. If the family had had a household of their own they could have got money. So when Peter came back I got them a little flat and I guaranteed the rent for it. We all ate the midday meal at my mother's and I paid for that. They were getting a proper allowance of 30 shillings, so they were better off than staying with me.

I gave up the shop. I was having Rose and one of the women who used to come to the shop had a daughter, Mary, who was only 14 or 15 when she came to work with me. She used to look after Rose.

Once the baby came off the breast, I worried that Mary would lift her out of the pram. The shop was not doing so well that I could afford to put someone else into it, so I closed it down and came home. Rose was nearly a year at that time. I used to make food for my husband, myself, Mary and my brother, all in the back of the shop, and serve the customers as well. A terrible life. I never went back to work until I went to a job in London during the war.

When my husband came back from his course he was given the job of working as an organiser for the Communist Party, and he worked for them all the rest of his life. He died in 1977. He never earned as much as he would have if he had worked as an engineer! Many a week he got no wages at all. I was always behind him. When we had no wages I used to gather together anything and sell it down the market and that used to push us through the week. We lived from hand to mouth but never starved.

We went to the Soviet Union in 1935. We stayed there for nine months. Rose was three at the time. My husband was representative to the Comintern.[10] We had a large room in a hotel, a beautiful room with a parquet floor; men used to come in and polish it.

At that time there was the very first Gastronom – a big food store with different departments, with everything. There was no interpreter for me. They came for two days and took me shopping and on the third day nobody came, nor on the fourth. So I said to Rose, 'Let's go. We'll go ourselves.' By this time I had mastered the money. I was walking around and all of a sudden Rose got lost. She didn't appear. I didn't know the language, I didn't know anything. I frantically went looking for her. When I found her she was standing watching the coffee machine operating and she was fascinated by it. I got hold of her and gave her a shake and suddenly there was a crowd around me, all telling me off. You don't treat children like that!

Whilst I was in the Soviet Union there was a woman called Maggie Jordan who used to broadcast to Britain. She was on Moscow Radio two or three times a week. First of all I was asked if I would go to the Arbat market and see what I could buy there and write an essay about it, as a stranger. She was going to do the talk. Then, because she had laryngitis, they sent for me at midnight. It was about nine o'clock in Britain, and they asked me to do the talk. It was quite an experience.

By this time I had got a job and Rose was in kindergarten. I read all the letters from Britain and marked in pencil all the things which they asked. If it was something we had to answer over the air, it was marked a certain way, and if it was books, I sent them. I was really enjoying myself, for the first time for a long time. All these things happened in the month before we came away. We were supposed to be in the Soviet Union for a year, but Willie Gallacher won the election and became the MP for Fife. So we had a holiday in the Crimea and then came back. Peter said that the constituency needed to be looked after. I was very cross about that; I would have learned that language if I had been left there for a year. That was the year of the Seventh Congress and all the interpreters were taken up, so there was no one to teach me. I only had five weeks' tuition, but everything has stuck with me to this day.

So there was all this disappointment about not learning the language, and about losing the job which was very interesting. When I did the talk, they thought I came over very well. Another disappointment! When we came back we decided we should have another child because we thought it was wrong to have only one.

Peter went to Spain in 1936.[11] He looked after the men, and he used to go on the firing line and bring them their letters. When the thing broke out we were on holiday in Arran. When it came to December he said, 'The Party would like me to go to Spain.' At that time they went illegally through the Pyrenees, they couldn't get the passports to go through legally. He went on many of these journeys with the men.

Peter's brother was a chemist and he went to Spain to help the medical staff. Peter went out there in the December and they came back the end of March the first time. Oh my, did he look ill. First of all they never got fed properly, but that wasn't the worst of it. It was having seen so many people die. Peter was grey before he left but he was white when he came back. He was really queer for the first few days. I could hardly get him to speak.

He went out again when Sheila, our new baby was 15 months. He was the correspondent for the *Daily Worker*. He was at the front, not actually fighting but training them. He had been a soldier himself in the First World War. Peter and I both worked on the illegal paper that they produced in Spain called *Mundo Obrero*. We raised money for it to become a weekly paper, just before Franco died. I did all the clerical side of it and he did the appeals. We raised about £1,500, just our two selves. I have been a member of the International Brigade Association ever since.

We moved down to London at the end of 1939 because of my husband's job. Peter was too old to be called up to fight in the Second World War but he was called up to work, and gave up his job in the Communist Party. He went to work at Napiers[12] as an engineer. He was conscripted to do work but they didn't want him when they found out who he was. When Russia came into the war on the Allied side in 1941, he appealed to be released. Then Napiers didn't want to let him go because he was such a good worker.

When my children were evacuated I got a job with the Prudential Insurance. I couldn't stand doing nothing at home and them away. We hadn't long come from Glasgow, so the Glasgow authorities were willing to evacuate them for me. They sent them to Dunoon first of all. Rose was very unhappy there, and I wanted her to be with someone that I knew. I knew a lot of people in Arran, so I asked for them to be evacuated there.

My kids got ringworm. They put it down to the cattle. It was a really traumatic experience for me. I had to go to Edinburgh with them. Glasgow at that time had only one place where they could give them this X-ray treatment for the ringworm. I had to put their names down, and it was weeks before it was done. A terrible time we had! This treatment left them completely bald, with no guarantee that the hair would grow back. Can you imagine how I felt? It had to be done twice for Sheila as it didn't take the first time. For over a year Sheila was walking about with this Tammy on her head, and very little hair, and the boys used to pull it off.

I spent all the money I earned on running up to Scotland to see them. I would go off on Friday night and travel through the night. If you knew what travelling in war-time was like, when they shunted the trains backwards and forwards! It would take 12 hours to get up there sometimes. There was only one Sunday boat from Arran. I had to come back, get on the train, and be at work on Monday morning.

When we left London and went back to Glasgow, my husband talked me into having another child. He thought he would get a boy next time. I was approaching 40 and I said it was a bit late to have a baby, but I decided to go along with it. We had come down to London again to live. I was only a couple of months from the confinement. I came down the middle of October and the baby was born in January, in Berkhamsted, in the grounds of this Tory hideout where they had evacuated me! It was really a military hospital, with a piece put aside for pregnant women, but it belonged to a well-known Tory.

I had another girl. When I was young I used to say, 'I don't want to have girl children. I don't want it on my conscience to bring another girl into this world.' My mother used to say – this was a Jewish curse – 'You should have six like you!'

When Jean, my third, was born, Peter never made any fuss, because I told him that if he did I would never look at him again. That's the only reason I agreed to have the baby. I said, 'I don't object to having another child, but you pull a face if it turns out to be another girl and I will never look at you again!'

I was almost 41 when she was born, in 1944. I never had any preferences one way or the other. In fact, I was anti-boys to a certain extent. I was brought up with three brothers and I thought I would never marry. I couldn't be bothered with men. They got away with murder and I had everything to do in the home.

When Jean was nine months old I got myself a job. At that time women could do some kind of war work. When they need you, they can provide the means. During the war the government opened nurseries up for the women because they had to get the women to come and work. I was listening to the radio and there was an appeal for women to go and work at the post office. We were living in Colindale at the time and it was very, very hard for us to live on the Party money. Peter never got a big wage at any time.

By the time I started work the children were with me again. They were at school. I went to the post office, and said that I could come and work for them from 11 to 3 without a lunchbreak. I loved that job. But soon they said they didn't really need me.

Because it was war-work I had got Jean into the nursery and having got her in, I had to have a job or I wouldn't have been able to keep her there. I was very disappointed, so I went into the local tailor and asked him whether he could do with a hand, and he gave me a start. The tailor's shop was right next to the nursery. On a summer's day when the door of the tailor's shop was open, I could see the reflection of the nursery in the glass doorway. I worked for this man for over a year and then he didn't have enough work. By this time Jean was very well established in the nursery, so I wanted to keep her on there. I got another job with a tailor in Hendon Central. She was in that nursery from nine months old till when she was 5, when she went straight to school. They gradually did away with nurseries, and how did they do it? They charged so much that women couldn't afford to pay. They also made out that there was no need for them. They wanted women back in the home so that when the men came out the army they could get the jobs. We had a lot of fights over them doing away with the nurseries.

After that, I worked in a clothing factory. I organised a union. There were different rates of pay for women and men and one thing the unions did, they raised the wages. I worked in places where there was no union, and the money for things was scandalous.

Women did the finishing, the buttonholing and the handwork. Men did the main machining and women did pockets and parts, and then it got joined up by men. Nowadays there are more women in the trade than men. Men now mainly do the cutting. Finishing was partly the felling;[13] if something is handmade the linings are always felled in by hand. The other thing a finisher did was the padding of the lapels, which all had to be done by hand, and buttonholing. That was a real terror, and it is still done by hand in Savile Row and in places where you pay hundreds of pounds for a suit.

In later years, I worked at the International Dress Company in Burnt Oak and I brought the union there too. First of all we had a sympathetic manager who wanted me to build a union really. I knew him personally so he turned a blind eye to the thing for a while. I first of all tried it on one or two people, who could understand that a union was necessary, and after I got them in I would tell them, 'You try and get so and so.' I divisionalised them. They would say, 'Oh, I can't talk like you, Rose!' 'It doesn't matter,' I said. 'All you need to do is tell them that you have joined the union!'

There were very few men in that factory; they were only the cutters, and one who was a presser. Two cutters served the whole factory. The rest were girls. Three particularly were first-class workers, and were quite militant, because they fought for the money. They could turn out things much quicker than the other girls. They fought for a higher price per piece, because they realised that other girls were not as fast as them. But because they had fought for the price they thought that they did not need the union. That was why it was so difficult for me.

I got off a machine and on to a job where I could move about the factory, and the manager used me to fit into places where a girl was sick. Now the girls were on piece-work, and they were always having difficulties with the office. A girl wrote a chit when she gave them a bundle of work, but she could make a mistake. There was no way of checking, and girls were always fighting with the office, and then they would look at the slip and see they had the wrong number to the wrong name. I worked out a system when I was in charge. When I noticed that the person's number was wrong I went to the office about it and sorted that out. So the girls had confidence in me after that.

The manager was sympathetic to the union. He was a socialist, but he was stupid in many ways. On a terribly hot day in summer, these girls were on piece-work. If they didn't work they didn't earn. It was so hot, with the machines as well, that they slackened down. So he sat down and he worked on this machine. I never saw anything so stupid in all my life. 'I showed them,' he said to me, 'that you could do the work.' I went up and I said to him – he was Jewish – '*Chochem*, smart lad! I suppose you think that was a good thing to do? These girls aren't earning any money if they don't work. It's too hot for them.' 'Well, what could I do about it?' I said, 'Power off for 15 minutes. Out in the yard! In the canteen you can get cold drinks and they would have gone back to work.' The next day it was hot and he did just that, and it worked.

I was a good shop steward. By that time they had faith in me, that I was out for them. They all joined finally, all except the pressers, who were working a racket! I couldn't understand why they wouldn't join the union. In fact, they were making money on stuff they weren't working on. How can people not fight for what they are entitled to and then do a thing like that?

The factory closed down because the administration went bankrupt. If the women hadn't been in the union they wouldn't have got a penny. As it was the union got them their holiday money and more. We got 150 girls into the union. That was a good, organised shop.

The closing down of the factory coincided with my going into hospital to have an operation on my knee. When I came out I was five weeks idle. I had to get work because we could not live with just what my husband earned at that time. The children would have had to come out of education: one was at university and one was still at school. So I walked into this factory – the Bijou. I came to the door one day and asked if they had any work, and the girl said to me, 'We are not taking anybody.' So I said, 'Have you got a passer?' 'Oh, wait a minute,' and she went to ask the boss. I had never done any passing, but I had enough experience. Passing is examining the work. If it is wrong, then you have to take it back to the girls. If they were on piece-work, they did not like you very much for doing it, but you had to see that the work could pass.

I got this job and I was really timid about it when I got into the place. They started me because the passer was off sick and work was piled up. I started in and I wondered what I could let go and what I must go back with, and I didn't go back with anything unless it was really bad. A week went by. The manager had come out of the RAF, an English upper-class sort of type, and he ran this bloody factory like the army. After two weeks he gave me a rise.

Then I went to work with the East German Trade Delegation – I was there for 16 years. I was '*hausfrau*'; looked after the staff, sat in on the telephone, kept the place tidy, did the post. I was woman Friday! I learned a lot of German. I was 70 when I left. Then I got a job with Debenhams. I was feeling a bit fed up. Peter was home – he had retired by this time as well. I thought, we are going to be knocking into one another with nothing to do. So I saw this ad for Christmas work at Debenhams and I went along and asked for a job. It was October to Christmas. I got one of these papers to fill in, where you have to put your age. I looked at this girl and I said to her, 'Do I have to put my age or is this just for knowing about national insurance?' 'Oh no,' she said. 'We would like to know your age. It is only us that will see it.' So I said, 'It's not that I don't want anyone to know my age, but if you know my age you might not give me a start.' She looked at me and said, 'We are more concerned with experience than that.' So I put down I was born in the 1903 and this was 1973. At that time my hair wasn't grey the way that it is now. I tinted it. I didn't look at all like my age. She said, 'You could have fooled me.' They put me into the coat department. The woman in charge was very pleased with me. I can make sales.

Christmas went by, New Year went by, the sales went by and I still was working. All the other people who had been taken on for Christmas had been given the sack. One day the supervisor came to me and said, 'Rose, I would like to see you. They wanted me to sack you, but I wasn't getting rid of a good saleslady like you without a fight.'

I gave up my religion but I didn't give up my people. My daughters all knew I was Jewish and that they were half Jewish. Then again, what was stronger in our family was that their father was an atheist and I was too. Peter was terribly annoyed when Rose went to school. First of all he said that she wasn't to have any religious teaching. I argued with him. I said that as children we had had prejudice for being different, mainly for the fact that we were allowed to come in half an hour later for school, because we went to *cheder* at night. That was where the teachers knew we were Jewish.

When the children were evacuated, I said, 'Peter, you won't be behind her to tell her this is wrong and all that sort of thing. Just let her get it in school.' He knew he couldn't do anything about it. Rose was evacuated when she was 12. She wrote us a letter, and she said, 'You will notice that I have got a good mark for scripture, but that was to keep my average up!'

My relationship with my daughters has been that I never stopped them doing anything that they wanted to do. They do not entirely agree with me politically, but it is mainly about methods of how to achieve socialism. I feel they are conscious of the real aim for a better and more human and equal society. Sheila in particular works unceasingly for peace, and I am a member of CND. So we generally have a common aim.

The Twentieth Congress was a terrible eye opener to us.[14] People say that we must have known all along, but it's not true. There were rumours, in fact, when we were in the Soviet Union in 1935. Kirov had died and his funeral was at that time.[15] I saw part of the funeral from a window in Gorky Street. That was at the beginning of what was happening, and various things happened afterwards that people questioned, but they never thought that Stalin had become so megalomaniac.

I didn't question whether to continue in the Communist Party, though it was difficult to be in the Party after the Twentieth Congress, and after Hungary as well. Even at the moment there is quite a bit of controversy in the Party. But it is a party that I was a foundation member of, and every party and every organisation has made mistakes and will go on making mistakes.

I consider that I am doing my Party work working with the pensioners and making people aware that they mustn't sit down to things! Certain jobs I can't do that I used to do when I was young. I sold pamphlets, stood in the street and sold the paper. I couldn't really do that now even if I wanted to, because I can't stand for a long time. Considering my age, I still do a lot.

With people who have a different political outlook to you, find where you agree on something! And then they get to know you and they get to like you and they realise that you are not a communist with horns, and that you are meaning for the best. We want to get something for the working class. I've lived through the years that we gained things and now we are losing everything under this Tory government. What is the use of spending your time arguing with people that you must get this policy sorted out, or you must get that policy sorted out? You antagonise people. You should win them!

Even in our pensioners' group you have to learn how to approach a thing and win something. We are a non-political organisation in the sense that we are non-party political. Our pensioners' group accepts everybody. But there is no such thing as pensioners fighting for their rights being non-political. They are being political, but they don't see it that way.

Every time I have been asked to go to a group to speak, I've gone out to do it and I've done it. Take me there and I can do the job. My brain is still the same. This question of ageism – the truest saying that is ever said is: 'You are only as old as you feel!'

Because some people are old at 50 because they have no outlook. All they have is an inlook, if you know what I mean.

AFTERWORD

I feel that my mother and father brought me up to give a helping hand when needed. The Socialist Sunday School taught me that we have an obligation to each other. This aroused a feeling of solidarity and made me understand my life in relation to others.

I went on from that to meetings and lectures on socialism, and because the First World War was on, on peace and the economics of war.

After this grounding I joined the Communist Party, when it was formed in 1921 in Glasgow. I was 18 years old. All my life I have taken part in all efforts to make our society better for the ordinary person who works for his or her living by hand or brain. My main aim has been to change to a socialist society: 'To each according to his efforts'; and ultimately for Communism: 'To each according to his needs.' On the way I have been a trade unionist wherever I have worked and helped to make living better in my tenants' association, and generally to raise the standard of living.

Now, in my eighties, I am active for a better deal for pensioners, who are being treated like second-class citizens. My generation fought and won a free Health Service, the shorter working day and week, and holidays with pay. We saved this country from Hitler and Mussolini, a war which was only won through struggle. Although not producers now, we produced those who are producers today. I spend my time reminding this present government that we deserve a better deal. Now we are surviving longer, we want to live, and not exist. I feel in my small way I have tried to leave the world better than I found it.

NOTES

1. The Polish uprising against Russian rule in 1863.
2. The immigrant Jewish communities carried on the tradition of mutual help and support central to the ethics of the religion.

3. It is forbidden to do any work on the Sabbath, and in orthodox households a gentile would come in to light the lamps and stove.

4. The vast majority of Jews in the Pale spoke Yiddish as a first language, but as Benjamin had been born and raised in Siberia, his first language was Russian. The Russian census of 1897 showed that only about 3 per cent of Jews had Russian as a first language.

5. The Board of Guardians for the Relief of the Jewish Poor had been founded in 1859. The Board and its provincial counterparts were essentially Anglo-Jewish in character, and their patrons and members were the Jewish middle and upper classes. Because of Anglo-Jewry's ambivalent and sometimes hostile attitude to the immigrant poor, as well as the Board's association with general philanthropic 'do-gooding', many immigrants did not want to approach the Board for funds.

6. During Pesach no leaven (grains that are capable of rising) is allowed in the house. A different set of pots and dishes are used, or else utensils are specially cleaned and made *pesachdik*. Special crockery, cutlery and cooking utensils are used which have not been touched by leaven, while all leaven must be banished from the home.

7. The Socialist Sunday School was a non-Party, grassroots movement, with branches in many parts of Britain. It 'gave children an ethical outlook on life without involving them in religious creeds' (Jack Jones, *Union Man*, p. 19, Collins, 1986). Children were also taught a secular 10 commandments at the Socialist Sunday School, which in Glasgow was founded by members of the Socialist Labour Party.

8. The Socialist Labour Party was a Marxist party founded prior to the Communist Party, whose branch in Glasgow was set up in 1921. Most founder members came from this party or two others, the British Socialist Party and the Independent Labour Party.

9. A child born to a Jewish woman is Jewish, regardless of the father's religion.

10. The Third International (the Comintern) was formed in

Moscow in 1919 to promote world revolution and coordinate the efforts of national communist parties.

11. During the Spanish Civil War, the struggle between fascist and Republican forces. The International Brigade was founded in November 1936 to defend the Republican cause. Franco's victory in 1939 led to the establishment of dictatorship in Spain.

12. An engine manufacturer.

13. On handmade clothes, linings and interfacings are stitched in with tiny, invisible stitches, a technique known as felling.

14. Stalin died in 1953. Three years later, during the Twentieth Party Congress, Khrushchev made a seven-hour speech in a closed session in which for the first time Stalin's terrible reign was openly discussed. The text of the speech was circulated to some communists outside the USSR, and soon became widely known.

15. Sergey Mironovich Kirov (1886–1934) was a Politburo member and Leningrad Party leader. He was a close associate of Stalin, and it is widely suspected that Stalin was behind his murder in December 1934, which served as the pretext for the show trials and purges which followed.

ENA ABRAHAMS
'I Had This Other Life . . .'

Ena was born in 1924 in a nursing home in Stoke Newington, North London. Her parents, Millie and Abraham Ruda, met in this country. Abraham, known as Alfred, had come to England from the Ukraine as a boy, around 1900; Millie was brought here somewhat later as a babe in arms by her parents from a town near Cracow in Poland. Millie's older sisters were left behind in Poland, to be brought over when their parents had established themselves. Both parents began earning as children – Alfred in order to survive on his own, Millie to help feed her family – and became highly skilled workers in the garment trade.

Tailoring was one of the 'immigrant trades', so called because of the method and scale of production, as well as because immigrants worked at them. Cheap clothing was produced in bulk. The tendency, particularly in a city like London, where the price of land was high and labour was cheap, was for manufacturers to contract work out to small workshops rather than to build factories. Demand for clothes was seasonal and it was more profitable for bosses to employ casual workers from week to week as they were needed. Only a few highly skilled workers would be kept on retainer between seasons.

Ena's parents were part of this huge, underpaid workforce. Many women worked in the industry, often at the 'unskilled' end of the trade. Ena's mother found it easier to get work than her husband during the 1930s, when Ena was growing up. In general, women commanded lower rates of pay and were therefore used in preference to men during the Depression. Millie Ruda, though, was such an exceptionally skilled craftswoman that demand for her standard of work was probably less affected by the slump.

77

Ena's account of her childhood vividly conveys a sense of living between two worlds – the poverty and warmth of home, where Yiddish was the mother tongue, and the 'Englishness' of school, where pupils like Ena were discouraged from talking about their backgrounds.

In spite of her alienation at school, Ena later became a teacher and educationalist. She retired in 1984 from her job as Primary Adviser in the London Borough of Haringey. 'I think there is a move in the country towards educating ourselves to understand difference ... I never ever wanted to expose myself, and I think that is very, very true of my generation. But nowadays I do, and I take pride in my roots.'

My mother began her working life as an embroidery hand – hand embroidery, of course, not machine. My eldest aunt was already in a workshop, and there was a vacancy. My mother used to go home for her midday meal, and my grandmother, who had a great struggle, used to provide a meal for two of the other girls who were working there and they used to pay her a couple of coppers a day. Then after that she went into a tailoring establishment, a workshop owned by the husband of my father's sister; and this is where she met my father.

My mother was a *couture* tailoress and dressmaker. She made the outfit for the late Duchess of Kent for the Investiture of the Prince of Wales.[1] She was of that calibre. The only thing she wouldn't have done was cut it. She wasn't only a wonderful crafts-woman, but you see she also worked with her brain. She was bright. She had a *feel* for materials but, of course, she never really had a chance. She was a very independent woman, and in fact she worked to the day she died; we think she was about 78. The sad thing for me to recall was that the older she got, the less opportunity there was for her actually to use her skill, because of mass pro-duction. In her latter years, because she so insisted on working, the jobs she got were *way, way* below her competence. Also, of course, as she got older her wages dropped as well. That was a very bitter pill to her, because she couldn't *bear* what she called 'slop work', and wherever she went they used to tell her that she was too good. You see there was no call for her standard of work.

My mother was the third child – in a family of 10, originally.

Two died. She went to St Paul's School, Wellclose Square, and was taught by Anglican nuns. It must have been because of where they lived that my mother went to a Christian school. Lack of knowledge of the system too. My grandmother used to tell the story that when she went to register the children, they asked her name – it was something like Engelchik. The headteacher asked her to spell it, and of course she couldn't, so she said 'Well, my husband's a *cohen*, let it be Cohen.'[2]

My mother got a scholarship to go to grammar school, but of course she could never go. In fact, it was only the younger members of the family that ever had any educational chances. My mother was *bright* but she didn't ever have any opportunities. She had to go out to work. It wasn't only that – first of all they lived in very bad housing conditions; secondly, of course, there were all these children coming along, and their father was also a semi-invalid, suffered with his chest, mostly because he became a presser over here.[3] And so the three older girls were always having to help at home. Certainly my grandmother falsified the ages of the three oldest girls when they went to school. My mother must have started work before she was 14 years old.

I have no knowledge of my father's parents. His mother died in childbirth when he was about 15 months old. He came over with his father, and his younger sister was brought up by his eldest brother and his family; they came over to England in 1901. It's quite a sad story really. His father had remarried, and went back to collect his wife and bring her over here, leaving my father in the care of some friends. My grandfather died, and my father was orphaned here at about the age of 10 years old. People that knew him, tailors, took him in and let him sleep on rolls of cloth underneath the cutting table. My father died in his early sixties from emphysema, and there's no doubt that the origin of his very bad chest went back to these early days, because he always said that he could never remember a time when he didn't have a very bad cough.

From that early age he did various things. He said he pasted insoles into shoes in a factory somewhere – must have been in the Spitalfields area. He had thruppence a week and did what he could. People were kind to him. And then he worked as a lad in a fish and chip shop; of course in those days people just converted the front room of their house. Then, because he had no home, he joined the British army. He must have been about 17 to join, I would have thought. It's difficult to tell because he didn't really know how old he was. There were no birth certificates. My mother didn't exactly know how old she was either. He joined under a false name – Isaac Levy – because he was afraid of being known as a Jew under his own name. You see, he couldn't read or write at that stage, and obviously he had little knowledge of English-sounding names, so he just chose another one; in fact it was more Jewish-sounding than his own! He left the army later on, and when my aunt was settled here he lived with her, and that was the first real home he ever knew. They lived just off the Whitechapel Road.

My father went to work in the workshop his brother-in-law owned. He learned the tailoring trade. He was as talented as my mother, and used to design, but he was absolutely dogged by ill-health. He set up so many times on his own as a master tailor.[4] When there was work he was ill, and when he was well there was no work. They were very hungry years, the twenties, the thirties.

My parents initially lived at the top of a shop in Hackney Road. They lived in two rooms, right up high, on the top floor. I lived there as a child. I remember that there was no water, and there was an outside toilet which was about 80 steps down, at the back. We didn't move until I was about six years old. And that's where they actually set up home.

Because of the tremendous slump, you see, my mother could always get work, and she was one of that rare generation of working women. I reflect on it a great deal, because I think that although it was adversity that forced my mother out, in fact it was because she went out to work that her horizons were widened. She actually became very much a woman of the world. And independent. She had very, very high standards. Although we were very poor, our home was *absolutely immaculate*. When I think that I remember her working till seven or half past in the factories or workshops and then coming home . . . There were always little touches there. She was a good needlewoman, as I've said. We had embroidered doilies, we always had lovely tablecloths. Even when she couldn't afford flowers, she would go out and gather grasses. She herself, in her own appearance, was always immaculate; she might have had cardboard in her shoes, and that was *very* often, but she always looked as if she came out of a bandbox. Her mother was just the same, and all the girls in the family too. When I think about my grandmother's circumstances I think that's tremendous.

I don't know *how* my grandmother lived. In the latter years, she lived virtually on the few pence that her children could give her. All her sons went to America. Subsequently one or two drifted back here; they had a hard time there. They sent her something when they could. We actually gave up our two rooms in the Hackney Road and went back to live with my grandmother, who lived in a tenement, because we were badly off and she was literally starving. So my parents stored their furniture and we went back to live with her for a period of time so that we could survive.

Women of her generation were slaves, there's no doubt. You know, they were always pregnant, and heaven forbid they should have a doctor either! Apart from not being able to afford a doctor, women ministered to women. I remember we used to go and collect the live fowls, put them in these straw bags, take them to be ritually slaughtered and then take them home. The place would be full of feathers, from all the plucking. Women would think nothing of bringing three or four fowls home and doing this. When you think of the size of the families. And everything had to be brought in *every day*.

I remember the very small dairies in the East End, where we used to go with a jug and buy our milk. The milk was warm – I'm sure it was full of bovine TB! And also, what were called the dumb cows, brass plates in the wall in the shape of the head of a cow. You used to put your halfpenny in, press a button, and the milk would come into your jug or glass. So instead of buying sweets, sometimes on the way home from school, if you had a halfpenny – it could have been a farthing – you used to go and buy a glass of milk, or half a glass of milk. I certainly remember going to the baker's and buying a farthing's worth of cake crumbs, and shopping at the corner shop to buy a *cup* of jam, or *half* a cup of pickles, because you couldn't afford to buy anything else. Very small quantities. The market, that's now called Hessel Street, but in the days

I remember was called Morgan Street market, where almost all the shopkeepers and storeholders were Jews. It used to be very exciting! A treat would be to go into the shop that sold dairy produce and buy a glass of *smetana* topped up with cream. No wonder we were all so fat! That was a rare treat. And, of course, the Lane. That was wonderful. I remember the wet fishmonger's – the freshwater fish would be swimming in tanks and you could choose the fish that you wanted. When the people came from Russia and Poland, all the fish they ate, unless you lived on the seaboard, was freshwater. So that was the fish people were used to, the pike and the carp. They would be boiled, plain, eaten cold with jelly. Delicious. Or chopped, or chopped and stuffed back into the skin. Tremendously skilled cooking, when I think about the quantities that people had to make. Many people didn't have gas cookers, they just used kitchen ranges.

Part of Thursdays used to be spent in the bakehouse, so it was very good communally for women. They would make their cakes or their bread, and they would be baked in the big ovens, but of course they would be talking to one another. You mixed the dough at home and took it covered with white cloths. The same with the Saturday meal. That would be taken all prepared, put in the ovens on Friday and just collected on Saturday. When we lived with my grandmother, I remember that she used to pay the woman on the ground floor a halfpenny for the use of her press. She had a big press, it was like gigantic rollers, and this had pride of place in her bedroom. She used to hire it out and all the bedlinen used to go through. So there were communal things going on, but although people lived in tenements, they lived quite private lives within their own rooms. I suppose in many ways, although conditions were bad, they might well have been better than in Russia or Poland, in some of the small villages. So possibly it was an improvement.

We were always well clothed, for obvious reasons. All my clothing was made by my mother and father. I remember, it was quite a custom at the time, people would have lengths of material, the 'cabbage' that would be left over. They used to pawn this, and if you wanted a piece of material you bought the pawn ticket, redeemed it and got it for next to nothing. Any possession of any value my parents had, which was largely as a result of when they got married, with the exception of three little pieces which I actually still have, was pawned. *Everything* was pawned and never redeemed. Even little trinkets. I remember I had a locket, I think it was a gold half-sovereign, and even that went. The only thing that my mother ever redeemed was her wedding ring. That was not unusual, by any manner of means. This is how the pawnbrokers grew rich.

My mother was a woman of great strength, there's no doubt about it. Of course, the *helpful* thing was that I was an only child until I was nearly 10. My father used to say that the bigger the family, the less affection. Whether this is true, I don't know! And she worked. People used to say, 'Poor Millie!' You see? 'Poor Millie goes out to work!' I think that there were other families who were in similar circumstances who in many ways rendered themselves helpless because it was frowned upon for the women to work. I mean, it was a real disgrace! You were looked down upon. My mother didn't care about that. We always had something coming in, however little it was. It was a big problem, of course, when my sister was born. My mother had to give up work for a while and it became imperative for some money to come into the house other than the Relief system.[5] We never applied for that, you know, they had too much dignity. You could starve. My mother brought a girl over from Wales who was probably in worse circumstances and she lived with us as one of the family, and she looked after my sister so that my mother could go back to work again. Of course, my father was working intermittently. But times were bad.

There are incidents I remember. For example, on Saturday he used to go to get his pay. You would have to 'shop' the work. I used to sit on top of the barrow which he, or a shop boy – who used to bring the cloth from the manufacturer and take back the garments – would push. I used to ride on top. You couldn't get your money on a working day. One particular manufacturer he was working for had his place in Artillery Lane. There used to be the most terrible battles, physical battles and rows, there on a Saturday morning, because the outworkers used to go and collect their money, and when they actually used to look at the wage packet, as often as not it would be less than they would expect. The manufacturers just willy-nilly used to cut pence off the garments. There were no firm contracts, it was all word of mouth. There was nothing that you could do about it. I remember the pleading and the arguments that used to go on, on Saturday mornings, when they used to go for their money. It was all out-work, you see, and piece-work. Of course, the working hours were very long, as you would expect. It seems another world . . .

My father was a complete atheist. And my mother – how can I put it? They weren't religious but, of course, the religion determined the way in which we lived. All the festivals were kept up, we had a kosher household, but it was mostly based on superstition, rather than an understanding of the ethics of the religion. We didn't ever discuss religion in our household. Except for my father to say that he believed it to be all hogwash. My mother didn't ever commit herself either way. As she got older, certainly after the war, and because she worked with non-Jewish people as well, she came further and further away even from keeping the festivals. They became much more token. But as I say, religion was a way of life. It affected us.

They couldn't *really* keep *Shabbes* because if you worked, Saturday morning was a working morning. Only the governors kept *Shabbes*. The festivals were a great problem because you didn't get paid. I remember as Passover approached, people used literally to batter their heads against the wall: where are they going to get the money from for all the stuff? And, of course, in many trades, they didn't get paid for the national holidays until after the war. So it wasn't only Jews. But it was particularly difficult for Jews, in fact. Because many governors knew that if you were a practising Jew you wanted to finish early on Friday and didn't work on Saturday, and my goodness me did they exploit their work people! So, if you were working Saturday morning, I mean you couldn't keep *Shabbes*. That was an end to it! But we always had candles on Friday night, and we always had the traditional meal. Don't ask me when my mother ever cooked it. My recollection as a child is of my mother being up till one, two in the morning as a matter of course, cooking for the next day. Washing, tidying, you know, getting everything ready. My father was very helpful in the household. He always used to do all the ironing and help with the cleaning. We had these high standards, you know, everything that could be brass was brass, and everything that was brass you could see your face in!

The older I got, the more work I did in the house. There was no compulsion for me to do anything, or an expectation. I think it was a responsibility that I increasingly took on myself as I understood the stress that my mother, in particular, was under. I used to do all sorts of things to surprise her; for instance, come home from school and do the washing. Not on a regular basis – perhaps on a Friday, to take a lot of the burden off her, really. She used to leave everything ready for the evening meal, even to the potatoes being peeled, so that it was just a matter of putting it on. My father used to lay the fire as well. But, of course, until I was of an age when my parents felt I could be trusted, I didn't actually light it. It used to be cold in the house until one of them came home and lit it.

My first school was called Teesdale Street, which is in Bethnal Green. It was not a Jewish neighbourhood. I remember children coming to school without shoes and I remember the teacher sending me home with paper patterns of children's feet, to ask my mother – because I always had shoes – if there were any that I'd grown out of. If the weather was bad and they had no boots, then they stayed home. I must have been well into my forties before I realised that the fact that we had mid-morning milk in school must have been *solely* due to the fact that the teachers provided it. They must have paid for it out of their own pocket. Because it was the days before school milk. I remember we used to have to take a cup with us – mine was orange. I think that *must* have been provided by the teachers, *warmed* by the teachers, *washed up* by the teachers ...

I was possibly the only Jewish child in the school. I left that school when I was six, when we went to live with my grandmother. After that I went to Fairclough Street School. There, they were nearly all Jewish children. We used to do a double session on Friday, finish early and my grandmother used to meet me at school. She used to carry with her a straw bag with food in it, and we used to go *straight away* to the cinema, either to the Rivoli or the Palaseum; the place would be full of children and grown-ups, mostly grandparents or mothers. It was terribly noisy, because we used to do simultaneous translation! In *fact*, most of us were bilingual. I would read the captions in English – it was silent you see, the talkies were only just coming in – and translate them into Yiddish. The grown-ups used to bring food in case the children died of hunger, so everybody was eating. The place smelt of oranges, and I remember that as you stood up you used to crunch peanut shells on the floor!

My parents spoke English to one another, smattered with Yiddish, and Yiddish to my grandmother; everybody spoke Yiddish to my grandmother. She could speak a bit of English – well, she could speak a fair bit eventually, but she chose not to. We conversed in Yiddish to her, and in the latter years a mixture. She would speak a bit of both to me, but increasingly I lost my facility. I think that's sad. It's important to maintain the mother tongue, not just because it's a pity it should wither, but if you're made to feel that your language is second-rate it does something to your self-image, which probably takes you the better part of your lifetime to recover from.

At school, the norm was towards anglicisation. It was done by covert means, because you were never encouraged to talk about your own country or background, and inevitably, there grew within you a feeling that you came from a sub-standard culture, although you probably couldn't express it. I certainly remember going out with my grandmother, my mother and an aunt, and one of my aunts who was at the tail end of the family, who had better chances in education, used to say to my grandmother when we were out, 'Speak English, speak English!' in case anybody heard us.

People were very keen indeed to give their children a good education. The number of children who learned musical instruments is quite phenomenal, when I think about it now. You know, somehow people seemed to find two coppers for this, and certainly there were always the coppers for Hebrew classes, for the boys in particular. I only had one night of it. I went to Hebrew classes when we went back to live at my grandmother's, and I obviously came late into the class. Because I didn't know something when I was asked, I remember actually being yanked out of my seat and shouted at! Some of the Hebrew teachers were real sadists. My husband recounts that he had one that he vowed he would kill when he got older, and he always says that it was his good luck that he died before he could get his hands on him! My father came to collect me. I was obviously very upset by this; I *distinctly* remember him going in and getting the teacher by his collar! That was the first and last bit of my Hebrew education!

Jews in London tended to move north if they could. Stoke Newington was a place to aspire to. It was the first step out of the slums and the terrible conditions that I remember in the East End. Certainly we had bugs crawling about in the summer in the walls. You couldn't help it, because there would be wallpaper on wallpaper, put on with flour and water paste. The landlords didn't do anything. We used to go around with candles and paraffin [to try and get rid of them], and if the weather was very hot, we used to sit outside. So anything was one up from those conditions.

When I went to Northwold School, in Stoke Newington, there was a fair-sized Jewish element there. Most of the children did not live in slum conditions. They were poor, but the actual housing conditions were better.

The school just didn't want to know about differences in cultural background. And this is true when I went to grammar school as well. You took part in all the rituals of the time, the communal rituals like Empire Day, and Christmas. I think parents didn't want to make you any different, so they allowed you, whatever their thoughts, to take part in the Christmas festivities, and all the rest. They wouldn't have done so in a school in the East End of London, because there were more of you together and you could say, 'Well, we don't want this.'

I don't think it created conflict between parents and children so much as conflict in the children, in terms of their *adaptation* to the English school system. You know, there were things that were *mysteries*, and things that you didn't talk about. Certainly I remember that well, when I went to grammar school. Although it was a school that obviously had thought quite seriously about the small number of Jewish children they had – or maybe it was because it so happened that the chemistry teacher was Jewish. She used to provide a separate assembly for Jewish children. But the children stayed at school for dinner and there was no understanding that there was a need perhaps to have kosher food. So I think there was conflict as far as the children were concerned. Certainly, when I went to grammar school, which was very English indeed, the typical girls' grammar school, a *complete* contrast to my life at home, and where there was no understanding at all of the economic hardships that some of us were experiencing, I think there was great alienation, in many instances. I had a behaviour problem myself, when I was at grammar school. And I look back and I realise now that it was because of the gulf between the school for young ladies and my home circumstances, where there was this massive struggle for survival – and also to get the school uniform – which made me resentful. I remember that when I first went to grammar school, everything had to be got from the school tailor. The fact that my father made garments *far* superior was neither here nor there. So they had to beg and borrow to get me a coat from the school tailor, when he could have made me one.

When I got a scholarship, you were given a list of schools that you could apply to and for most of them you had to take a separate entrance exam. My mother wanted me to go to the City of London. So I sat the entrance and I passed; and then we were called to the school again. The headmistress spoke to my mother about our circumstances, what my father did – my father was unemployed at the time. She said to my mother that she didn't think that I could *benefit* from that type of school, because my background would be so different from the other girls that it would be impossible for me actually to *integrate* into the school. I remember we came away from that school and we crossed one of the bridges of the river. I remember my mother crying all the way across the bridge. I remember it clearly, holding my hand and crying. Because she felt that disaster had overtaken us. The headmistress said to my mother that if we went to Dame Alice Owen's School, they had more girls of my . . . *class*, is what she was really saying, and they might take me, you know, graciously. Graciously. And they did.

I remember going to the school dressed in a very nice, plain, dark-red dress that my mother had made for me. I had silk socks with clocks up the side, black patent shoes and white gloves for the interview. I have a great friend – we've been friends since we went to Owen's together. She remembers, the day when we both happened to go for interview, saying to her mother that I must come from a very wealthy family because I had on such a very nice dress.

I often think there's a parallel when I see clothes that people of Caribbean origin wear here today; the accent on fashion. The Jews did *exactly the same thing*. If you live in poor surroundings, if your life chances are not very great, I think that one way in which you can actually develop any sort of feeling of self-image is likely to be through your clothes, through externals. Things that make you feel a bit up.

I always felt different. And I think that's why I behaved differently as well. I think it was probably a way of saying 'Here I am, I'm here.' You see, I had tremendous responsibility when I was a child. My sister was nearly ten years younger than me. For example, when she started to go to school, my mother found a woman living opposite the school, who, for 5s a week, looked after her in the morning until school began, gave her dinner – there were no school dinners – and gave her a cup of tea and a sandwich and looked after her until I came for her. I used to set off very early in the morning, it must *easily* have been round about seven. My mother had to be in work at eight, and my father. I would take her, walk with her to this woman, which was a fair way, walk all the way back, and get on a tram to Old Street Station, and from there get on another tram to take me to school at the Angel. Although I could have gone all the way on the 73 bus, it saved a halfpenny if I went on two trams. Then after school I used to have to do all this in reverse. Go back and collect her, bring her home – my parents used to come home late – wash her, get her ready for bed, get the dinner on, get all her clothes ready for the morning. Then we used to eat, which was about half-past eight, at the earliest. When everything was done, *then* I used to start my homework. Of course, I also used to mind her in the holidays. In many ways I was responsible for a lot of her upbringing.

Then war broke out. The school suddenly found I had the strength of a *lion*, because I was so accustomed to responsibility; it was nothing to me. I was in my matriculation year then, and what started to happen was that the teachers began to lean on me. A most *tremendous* change came over me, because I think the school suddenly saw something that they hadn't known existed. That I had this other life. Most of us were resilient. Only the resilient survived. That made a very big difference in terms of their attitude to me, as teachers. They weren't fed up with me, in other words!

We were evacuated to the Midlands on the Friday before war. War was declared on the Sunday. When war broke out, all the schools in London closed down. That's why, for many people of my generation, their education stopped. If they didn't go away, they couldn't go to school. Well, it was matriculation year, and also my mother and father were very nervous, and so we went.

People weren't prepared for us in the reception areas, they didn't *want* us. I remember the trauma that I suffered when I first had unfamiliar food, and, of course, the people we were staying with in the Midlands had no knowledge of Jews. There was an assumption that Jews carried knives, and the old stories of the ritual slaughter were still *very* prevalent indeed. I didn't exactly encounter hate, but rather suspicion. It was the *strangeness*, because obviously for the first time they came across people who came from a different cultural group. It was really ignorance more than anything else. It wasn't overt anti-Semitism. There weren't so many of us who were Jewish.

I think there were a lot of strange assumptions covertly, until people met my parents. They used to come and see me quite often; of course they were aliens, so they used to have to register with the police when they went and when they arrived and before they left, which was a great palaver.[6] My mother used to send us food parcels regularly, whatever she could manage. It was difficult, but it was a way of saying thank you. She also used to supplement the billeting allowance, send half-a-crown a week, in a postal order. I think the billeting allowance was about 7s 6d a week. The rationing was very sparse.

I seemed to take it in my stride; that was the situation, I wasn't really used to a pampered life, although I was very protected. I didn't *like* it. My memories of living in the Midlands are horrible ones. The people I went to originally were nice, but the lady of the house had a very bad heart, and she died during the war. So we had to move after about a year, and we went to a really awful place, absolutely dreadful. Our experience was not untypical of what was happening then. We were strangers, they didn't want us, and we also had to work shifts at school. We shared premises with Kettering High School, and we had the bad shifts, early morning half-past eight to half-past eleven, and then half-past three to six – in winter, with the blackout, we used to go home in the pitch dark.

At first, in the middle of the day most of us were just wandering about. They didn't really want us back in the houses. Eventually the school managed to get hold of a hall and British Restaurant[7] dinners were provided. We used to go to this hall in the middle of the day, for homework and things, and then go back to school again. So it was really quite difficult, especially the afternoon session, which ended so late. The blackout was *really* a blackout. We all walked, of course. I lived quite a distance from the school. It was easily a walk of three-quarters of an hour.

My sister came with me. She was six when war broke out. That was a *big* responsibility. She wasn't with me through the whole of evacuation, because I knew that I would be leaving and was very anxious for her to become settled.

The people in her first billet were downright unkind. They wouldn't let her in the house until a certain time, so she was out in the cold. She was only little. They had a child of their own, who was very resentful of her, and they generally didn't feed her properly. We had a terrible place together at one time. I slept in a cot bed, and my sister shared a bed with the girl of the house. The lady of the house had very recently come out of a mental institution and the man was *horrible*. In fact, he was such a lecherous creature that I had to put this cot bed up against the door at night before I got into bed, because I was *dead* scared of him. We had no proper coverings, only cotton sheets in the winter. We had one kettle of hot water to share between us in the evening, and I remember that I used to come home from school in the middle of the day once a week and do the washing in cold water. I used to have chilblains all over my fingers.

I went away when I was not quite 16 and I came back when I was 21. I got a Major County Scholarship, which could have taken me to university. My father said to me, 'Don't go to university, be a teacher. You'll never starve.' *That* was *really* true. 'Take the known, and the security.' I wanted to do it anyway, it was no great hardship. When I went to college, we were evacuated all over again. It was a London college but it was evacuated to Huddersfield. We were out in billets; I was never a resident student anywhere.

I had the very best education in the whole family. In the war my aunts used to try and pressurise my mother to take me out of school; they used to say there are so many very good office jobs, I could earn such a good living. She would never listen, so I had the very best education of any of them – and my sister, of course, afterwards. We were the two members of our *whole* family. Remember, my mother was one of eight; she missed her own chance.

My teacher training college shared premises with Huddersfield Technical College. We were on shifts, and certainly the situation was far from ideal. The course was an excellent one. It was just two years then and we had to do some work of national importance, so in the middle of the day I worked in the Coal Board. We used to do that free, gratis and for nothing! If you weren't up to standard every term you had to leave college and, of course, you had to go into the forces. So we didn't have much leisure time really, apart from Saturday and Sunday. There was no *student* life, for lots of reasons: the blackout, the lack of facilities, the fact that we had only restricted use and shared premises. You had to make the most of the time that was allocated to you. I got a scholarship so I had no fees to pay directly, and I got a grant. It was ever so small. I've got a feeling that I got £27 a year, £9 a term. But I was very fortunate – not many students had that. Most students had to borrow from the local authority, and it restricted many from going, obviously. That's why you got a very middle-class element in all the colleges and places of higher education. Many students had a real financial millstone round their necks.

There was no Jewish community in Huddersfield at all, and I shouldn't think even 1 per cent of the students were Jewish. When you think about it, in Jewish families there was no great expectation of the girls taking advantage of higher education. If you were wealthy enough, the goal was for your daughter not to work at all. My father would have been quite happy about that situation. Well, he would and he wouldn't; it's a protective mechanism, in a way. There was never any expectation that I should ever contribute to the family finances; that's what it amounts to, really.

I think that was relatively common. You see, we were a small family. In my mother's family it was very important to get out to work as *soon* as possible, because that was a big family. I don't know whether expectations had changed because I was the next generation, or also whether as families became smaller, therefore there wasn't the *financial* push – although we were still badly off. Of course, war brought employment, that's the sad thing. As a family, we became better-off financially, because there was work. I don't think my parents found it the financial stress that they were accustomed to by the time I went to college, though I'm not saying we were well off.

I think it was just the expected thing that I would marry a Jew. Nobody every really discussed it. Although I didn't come from an orthodox background – we weren't synagogue-going – they would have been very shocked if I had wanted to marry out, and certainly wouldn't have countenanced it. I might have been tempted, but I don't think I would have done it in the end.

Nobody spoke about sex. No, absolutely not. I only found out about periods after the event. I think that was common practice. When you think about it, people living in cramped housing conditions in big families must have been exposed to the facts of life very early, but there was a modesty in the household. My mother always used to tell me, at home there were four girls and four boys, so they used to have to have a very carefully worked out rota of baths and dressing and beds. A modest way of life.

But we weren't foolish, and, of course, I was always a reader. So we weren't unexposed, in a secondhand way. I never ever heard my mother discussing pregnancy, even with her sisters. Not ever within *my* earshot. There was a dichotomy really between the realities of life, which pushed people together, and the things they actually spoke about. But, of course, my mother's generation *and* my generation were very reticent about their emotions. People just didn't speak about emotional things that were troubling them. People were very self-contained in a way; they tended not to speak to one another about intimate matters concerning their lives, even to their closest friends; unless mine was an unusual experience. I think there were taboos, unspoken taboos.

If a girl became pregnant she would be completely isolated – not just in Jewish families. I mean, they must have suffered *unbelievably*, unbelievably. It would have been covered up in some way, if possible. And, of course, there were many more children available for adoption than there are now. That was really quite dreadful. Of course, contraception was practised. There must have been some word of mouth. But nobody ever spoke about that sort of thing. I remember before my sister was born, I only knew that my mother was expecting a baby shortly before, and I only picked up that information because she brought home napkins. You had to hem them in those days, and she was sitting and hemming and I put two and two together, but nobody every really told you. Perhaps when families were much larger, like my mother's family, maybe – but I'm doubtful really. I think babies just appeared. I mean, children are sensible. They observe things, and therefore they teach themselves really. I think it's not right to say they didn't know what was going on, but they knew it in a very oblique way, and, of course, there were many misunderstandings.

The tremendous change in the generations in quite interesting really. For example, I well remember my father, who was wonderful with children, wouldn't be seen dead pushing the pram. In my lifetime, housework was a woman's task. Men just didn't do that. My father was very good in the house, he used to help and do whatever he could, when he was able. But I don't think that was very common. My mother-in-law waited on my husband's father hand and foot. I mean, he never actually did *anything*. He never made himself a cup of tea, till she became incapable of making it. And I think she wouldn't have liked him to have done so. That was *her* province, that was her domain, and the men had other business. I think women, particularly working-class women, carried the brunt of the household, in a very real sense, because they were generally responsible for handling all the money. They were the ones who paid the rent and worried when there was *no* rent. They handled the family finances, besides all the responsibilities of child-rearing. Although the men worked very long hours, in bad conditions, in many ways I think they never suffered the same stress as women. I think women's lives were very hard, very, very hard indeed. Lack of domestic appliances, continuous childbearing, how to find the next meal on the table. Many of them went without adequate food themselves; they certainly fed their children first. There's a whole generation of women who didn't sit down and eat with their families, their families were so big. I never remember my mother-in-law sitting down and eating. She always served everybody. How could you sit down with your family? I think it was fairly general really, not particularly Jewish. There's a life of servitude in all sorts of ways, and yet within Jewish households, I think the woman was all-commanding.

It was a way of life, and although I was evacuated all those years, it never really left me. When I came back, it was really almost as if I'd never been away. I think the feeling of family and the way of life were well and truly ingrained by the time we were 15. I was part of a very large family network, and weekends we used to meet at my grandmother's house; people used to drop in on one another, come in and play cards – her girls, and the boys, when they eventually started to get back from the States, one or two would come with their wives and their children. We always spoke politics. I think many Jewish families were politically conscious. To come away from their own homes was a conscious decision taken as a result of oppression, and obviously this would heighten political consciousness. Many had been very active Bundists and they brought that away with them.[8]

I grew up within this atmosphere. I was always a reader, and a reader of left-wing books, when I could get hold of them. I used to live in the library. I suppose it was just part of me really. When I came back to London I joined the Communist Party just before the 1945 election, when it worked with the Labour Party, to elect a Labour government. Of course, there was a Labour landslide in 1945. When I think of the mess they made of it!

My father could never afford to become naturalised; I believe it was about £5 in those days. When war ended, he applied for naturalisation and he was turned down. The only thing that we could think of was that I was very active in left-wing politics. We used a room in our house as committee rooms in the run-up to the 1945 elections. You never ever knew the reason, but it was logical. And we think that was why. So he never could become naturalised! He lived practically all his life here, and he didn't ever do anybody any harm, he was never involved in anything. I mean, he had no police record, he was a gentle, kind man. There was no doubt that people were watched and records were kept. There is no other possible reason whatsoever why he should have been refused naturalisation. So in fact he was stateless and didn't ever have a vote.

Many of my generation were very interested and very involved in politics as young people. And in a very active way. I would go out and sell the *Daily Worker*, once the ban was lifted; it was banned during the war years. We would go out and sell on the knocker, going from house to house, and wouldn't come home till we'd sold them all; or stand and sell them outside cinemas. Hold street-corner meetings – I was never a street-corner talker! – but people variously had different responsibilities, I think we felt we were part of a Labour movement then. We used to go to the Labour League of Youth.[9] They had a Youth Hostel at Broxsbourne, and we used to go there at weekends and actually walk, hike and talk politics. There was a tremendous political consciousness. I think it came from London and my own particular background, but it was by no means unusual for young people of my generation to be *interested*, to be concerned about the political scene, either actively or passively. It was because of the years of the Depression. Of course, the most important thing that did heighten our political conscience was the rise of Hitler.

We knew there were concentration camps in the 1930s, but we didn't know about the wholesale execution of Jews, the murder, until war was over. There were rumours, and whisperings, but nobody really knew. I remember the Youth Aliyah,[10] some of the children coming over. One of my friends' family had a child from Germany, and I remember asking my mother if we could have one in our house, and she was ever so sad, I remember that, and she said, 'Yes, we'd love to have one, but we can't feed ourselves . . .'

I started work in 1944. I actually took the first paper of my final examination on D-Day. That's how I remember it so well! I remember that when I came out of the examination room – we knew there was going to be a D-Day, but not when – and when we came out there was such excitement; the newsboys were shouting in the streets. I was taken on by the London County Council. I was immediately evacuated. It was the time of the flying bombs, the V–1s and the V–2s. The children were still evacuated, so we did three months in London and three months in a reception area. We were backwards and forwards the whole time, in fact. That's what teachers had to do. Teachers who were newly appointed and worked for the London County Council had to work a certain amount of time in a reception area with evacuees, and then they brought us back to London to do a stint here in the bombing, and sent other people out. I didn't come back here to work permanently in London until 1945.

We were given a choice of areas, so I chose Lancashire, and found myself up the road from my cousin! *So*, I actually lived there. I began teaching London children – we had a room like a church hall in a Church of England School. Probably still exists. That was a nice little school. There I was introduced to real professionalism among teachers. In fact, it was there that I joined the National Union of Teachers, which I never left – I'm the past president of the East London Teachers' Association.

In the other Lancashire school I worked, it was a very, very different matter. I only taught London children, aged five to 14. I had 53 children when I began. Talk about anti-Semitism! I went to work in this school, which was in the middle of a very, very highly populated Jewish district, *then* and *now*. There I came across the most dreadful anti-Semitism I'd ever come across in my life. There used to be collecting at school, national savings collections, for the war effort. The Jewish children could never do right. If they brought money, then the Jews had all the money. If they didn't bring it, the Jews weren't supporting the war effort. This was from the teachers, in an area where I think the majority of the children in the school were Jewish. Here I came across *overt* anti-Semitism.

I was out on a limb; I had the London children and I was never a cohesive part of the staff, because we were transient. I didn't feel I was able to say anything to them. I think if somebody else would have been with me . . . I felt very *bitter*, very bitter. It worried me. That was the first time that it was *really*, really overt. Certainly anti-Semitic remarks, which may or may not have been meant, I'd always found very hurtful in the past. I think as Jews we tend to be very sensitive, hypersensitive. No, I don't think we *are* hypersensitive, I think racism in any form has to be combatted and is always hurtful. It was a great shock to me.

In 1945 I came back to London and remained. The doodlebugs were still coming over. We used to have to take the children down into the shelters. I worked in Hackney. Schools were still all-age schools. Although there'd been the 1944 Education Act, it took some time for that to be implemented. I was sent to my first permanent appointment, which was in the annexe to Craven Park School, in Stamford Hill.

I left teaching for a little while, after I married, for about a year. Then they needed somebody to work at a school in Stamford Hill, to help train the girls who had come from the seminary at Gateshead[11] as teachers, but had never had any secular training. It was a Jewish school, orthodox, still in existence, the Yesodey Ha'torah School.[12] I went in there for a while and helped part-time. They were Hebrew teachers actually. They didn't have trained teachers, in fact, so I went in to help them with methodology and curriculum. That was very interesting indeed.

The head of the school's husband was one of the leading lights of the Agudas Yisroel[13] congregation here. That was the first time that I'd seen separate assembly, with a sheet in between the girls and the boys. There was a lovely family feeling in the school. There were girls' classes and boys' classes and never the twain did meet. That was a real difference. Of course, there was a real emphasis on Hebrew education, you know, and also the study of the Bible for both the girls and the boys. The aim was to educate. The principal aim, of course, was education *in* Judaism, but they were obviously also concerned about the secular side, or they wouldn't have asked me to come in. I couldn't ever completely reconcile myself with such an orthodox way of life, but then, as now, I think they've got a lot going for them. They've got a very clearly determined set of values. It's not the sort of life as a woman that I would like to lead. I certainly wouldn't want to have the number of children that they often have; they lead a very close life, but there are compensations. I suppose there are unhappy marriages; marriages aren't made in heaven among the orthodox any more than they are anywhere else.

It was a very interesting experience for me, particularly as I hadn't had any specific Hebrew education myself. It educated me in a way that I hadn't been educated before. Their values may not be mine, but I think they have clearly defined boundaries which perhaps don't subject them as much to the emotional traumas that people who haven't got them are often subjected to. On the other hand, heaven help you if you kick against the traces! There's the two ways of looking at it. The closeness can be very supportive and very destructive. Both ways. Both ways. I think, for women, it wouldn't be the life that I would choose. I would find it claustrophobic. In the new, young movement certainly, the girls are educated – there's no feeling of not educating the girls. I think that's gone, that's past, really.

This is my second marriage. I got married for the first time in 1946, but my husband died in 1957 as a result of his war injuries. And I married again in 1960. So in fact we just last year celebrated our silver wedding. My first husband was a political activist, no doubt about that. We actually met in the run-up to the 1945 elections. He studied to be a teacher when he left the army, but unfortunately he just became progressively more and more ill, as a result of injuries. He died of kidney failure. He was only 39. So, that was the war.

In fact, I've never stopped working. I had two years off when my daughter was a little girl, and then I went back because my first husband went to college to train; I had to because there were no grants at the time. Since then I've worked continuously. When I retired in 1984, that was 40 years of work; in that time I only just had that short period out. I started as an assistant teacher. I've always taught infants. I became the deputy head, then I became head teacher in 1958. I was very young in those years to become a head. I was appointed head just those few months after my husband died, in 1957.

I was the head of the school that the ILEA built for the Festival of Britain, in Poplar. Whilst I was there, they seconded me from my school to run courses for married women who were returning to the profession and graduates who wanted to teach young children, at the time of the shortage of infant teachers because of the bulge in the population. During that time I had an offer to join the staff of Goldsmith's College. I was there until 1971, when I was appointed Primary Adviser to the London Borough of Haringey.

I've had a wonderful professional career. If I had my time over again, I would not choose differently. I've been very fortunate. To retire without a sour taste, that's extreme good fortune, isn't it? I've worked hard, but I've loved it, every minute of it.

Since I've retired it's been a sad time for me, professionally, because I've seen the goodwill of teachers *deliberately* eroded. I've seen teaching becoming a less and less attractive profession actually. It's also an undervalued profession, because there's no doubt that salary and status are two sides of the same coin. Anybody who says that it isn't is just living in cloud-cuckoo land. I think as long as I live I'm never going to get education out of my system. I'm an enthusiastic educationalist, and I hope I shall always remain one.

The older I get, the more conscious I am of my Jewish identity. I'm prouder of it now than I've ever been. I think that has happened because of the general climate in the country at this moment; the fight against racism, the attempt in education to encourage children to value their cultural roots. When I was at school, we didn't actually speak about difference or about similarity. I've no reason to believe it was not true elsewhere. To be different meant that you were a bit of a freak and so you never discussed the differences. They were there and you felt different inside yourself, but you never actually spoke about the fact that you were Jewish, what it meant. You always felt as if you were a bit peculiar. My world has been a world of education and so I like to think that we've been in the vanguard, in the area where I was working, trying to implement anti-racist policies in schools. I think there is a move in the country towards educating ourselves to understand difference – that to be different is desirable and that, in any case, there is not a universal culture in any country, and that even if there were one, culture is a dynamic force and inevitably changes.

It worries me that fighting anti-Semitism isn't a tenet of the anti-racist movement. It's focused on black groups – I can understand that, because the greatest disadvantage of all in contemporary society in this country is to be black. But certainly, if there's a rise in fascism – there is a considerable fascist movement here – the Jews won't be excluded. Neither *are* we excluded. There's been desecration of tombstones, on the Jewish cemeteries. You can't get into a synagogue now, there's such tight security. What's also concerned me is that the Jews themselves haven't spoken out as a body. The Jewish Board of Deputies[14] haven't really made any statements. That's *bad*; they need to come out and speak as other groups speak.

Of course, we were always encouraged to be inconspicuous. My father used to say, 'A Jew mustn't do anything illegal, make a fuss in the street,' draw attention to himself, in fact. Because then all the Jews will be castigated. Certainly in my early forties, I wouldn't have dreamt of speaking to colleagues about my Judaism. I was in my mid-forties before I could speak with any confidence about it. I never ever wanted to expose myself, and I think that is very, very true of my generation. But nowadays I do and I take pride in my roots. I've always felt different. I've always been in the minority for two reasons as I've risen – can't think of another expression – in the hierarchy of education. As my responsibilities have become more varied, I've been in a minority because I've been a woman – the higher up the hierarchy you go in education, the fewer women there are – and also certainly because I am Jewish. In my very early days an inspector once said to me, when I was a class teacher and he was encouraging me to apply for a deputy headship, 'You know, you're a very good teacher, but what you really ought to think about seriously is changing your name. Because it might be a great hindrance to you.' That was the very reason that I've *never* changed my name, never even thought about it. Because I've been in education, I've always worked in a non-Jewish atmosphere; I've always said to people, 'You may think I'm the same, but I'm not. I know how I feel inside me.'

NOTES

1. Later to become Edward VIII in 1936.
2. Your family name need not be Cohen, or a variant of it, to be a *cohen*. Fixed family names were adopted or assigned to Ashkenazi Jews from the seventeenth century onwards. Jews often did not have a choice in the name they were given.
3. Working long hours in hot, damp conditions in an atmosphere laden with fabric fibres broke the health of many in the tailoring trade.
4. To set up as a master tailor meant either becoming an employer and subcontracting out work or setting up independently. In both cases, although little money was needed to set up, profit margins were so slim and the trade so uncertain that many soon went under.
5. A form of benefit that was extremely harshly means tested.
6. Government policy required all 'enemy aliens' (for example, German, Russian or Polish nationals) to register with the police on arrival and departure when travelling, to keep track of their movements. The policy made no distinction between Jews and gentiles.
7. The government set up British Restaurants to provide cheap meals during the war, when very few restaurants or factory canteens remained open.
8. The Bund (General Jewish Workers' Union in Poland and Russia) was a Jewish socialist party founded in 1897. It originated in the North-West of the Russian empire, where there was a large Jewish proletariat in cities like Vilna and Minsk. The Bund believed in Jewish national and cultural autonomy in a socialist society, within the diaspora.
9. The Labour League of Youth was an organisation founded by the Labour Party before the war, and the forerunner to the Young Socialists.
10. The Youth Aliyah was formed to rescue Jewish children from hardship and persecution and give them a better life. Part of the Zionist movement, it began work just before the Nazis took power and saved the lives of many children, organising transport out of occupied Europe and looking after the chil-

dren in youth communities modelled on the kibbutz. Some of the children went directly to Palestine, but the majority could not get the right immigration papers and so were sent to western European countries, in particular Britain.

11. Gateshead was established as a centre for Jewish learning in the 1920s by a group of scholars. As well as a *yeshiva*, there is also a teachers' training college for women, a school and kindergarten there, all extremely orthodox.

12. Yesodey Ha'torah School was founded in 1942 by Austrian refugees. Extremely orthodox, today it has nearly 1,000 pupils, including children from many different Chassidic sects.

13. Agudas Yisroel, the Union of Israel, is an ultra-orthodox political and religious organisation, originally founded in reaction to trends towards assimilation and secularisation in European Jewry in the nineteenth century.

14. The Board of Deputies was established in its present form in the nineteenth century. It is the official representative body for British Jewry, with elected members from synagogues and communal organisations.

RITA ALTMAN
Conflicts and Contradictions

Rita Altman was born in 1922 in Germany, the eldest of three children. Her parents, Manya and Morris, were from Lodz in Poland. The modern Polish state was established after the First World War and although protection of minority rights was written into the constitution, the new Polish state, and in particular the army, was fiercely anti-Semitic. This precipitated a new wave of immigration from Poland, especially of young men of army age. Rita's parents entered Germany as illegal immigrants in 1919. Her childhood and early adolescence in Germany were shaped by the experience of being a daughter of Ostjuden. At 17, she too became a refugee, fleeing from Nazi Germany. These two flights from persecution in the space of 20 years made her twice an outsider, first as a Yiddish-speaking child, separated not only from German society but also from the more assimilated German Jewish community, and later as a refugee from Nazism in England.

Life in Germany for the family was both a desperate struggle for economic survival and a coming to terms with displacement and separation from family and traditional Jewish life. Rita's story shows her sensitivity to the painful consequences for those who left their families and communities in Eastern Europe to make a new life for themselves.

It was not until the thirties that the family achieved some small measure of economic security. As one long period of difficulty and distress ended, so a worse one under the Nazis began.

By various means Rita's immediate family were all able to escape from Germany and come to Britain, but most of her relatives in Europe perished in the Holocaust, which has left her with a profound sense of loss and of anger.

Rita herself entered Britain on a domestics visa, as did thousands of young Jewish women who came from Germany and then Austria in the late thirties. Some of those who provided domestic employment for Jews did so in order to enable them to get a visa; others used the situation to help solve the ever-present 'servant problem'. Women's experiences as domestics varied enormously, but for most of them it was an unhappy and humiliating time. The majority left their positions fairly soon to take up other employment – though perhaps not as quickly as Rita did.

The interviews with Rita took a somewhat different form from most other interviews. Rather than using a chronological narrative as a way of talking about her life, she uses stories and anecdotes to explain and illustrate what she sees as being the themes of her life story – the conflicts and contradictions, the loss, the sense of being an outsider. But she believes that stories on their own are not enough; they may evoke sympathy but they allow both us and the gentile world to stay stuck in patterns of self-pity and anti-Semitism – in all its many forms.

Rita is now devoting her energies to renewing her relationship to her past, to redefining her Jewish identity and to educating herself about Jewish history. She is passionately committed to knowledge of our history rather than a sentimental attachment to being Jewish. She shows great resilience and assertiveness in setting herself this task at a time when many of us cling to memories as fading and untouchable treasures.

My parents came to Germany from Lodz – like everybody else, illegally. They crossed the border in their hundreds on false papers. It was 1919. It's such a lovely story. I really got to know my father when he told those stories. They were a *shidduch* and they left Poland an engaged couple, not yet married. (He told me that with some trepidation.) They crossed the border with 300 other people and when they got to the other side there was a resting place. They walked through bogs in their *shtievel*, their boots. He described this beautiful scene: my mother's boots were full of mud and he knelt down and took them off and cleaned them. Such a tender little scene he described, very affectionate, very nice. He said, 'The people round about knew we were only engaged; they looked sideways at us.' It was too close physically. Isn't it wonderful? I just love that story.

My father's brother was Chassid, so I'm a stone's throw away from all that. I don't think my *zeide* on my mother's side had *peiyes*; there are so many grades of *frumkeit*. My father was already proud that he didn't have *peiyes* and a beard, that he was a modern Jew. All these grades are within and the conflict is very great. The conflict certainly was in me. My father used to have a phrase; he used to say, '*Ikh trug nisht kein burd un Ikh khap nisht Got bei di fis, ober Ikh bin a Yid.*' [I don't wear a beard and I don't grab God by the feet, but I am a Jew.]

Bubeh (my mother's mother) was still alive when my parents left Poland. The *bubeh* said to my father, 'Look after Manya. She's a good girl.' On the deathbed, my father claims it was. There must have been awful scenes; one says it half-facetiously and romantically, but it must have been quite awful, people just leaving. My mother never saw her mother again. Imagine the guilt of it. That's why we had to be such good children, because they never were – not because they were bad, but because they couldn't. My family left their parents behind and they put their guilt on to us, saying, 'You've got to be good to your parents, you've got to respect your parents.'

The sadness I find now, and I'm not alone, is that whenever I asked 'Tell me, Mummy, tell me about your bubeh,' she'd say, '*Ikh gedenk nisht.*' [I don't remember.] So I've got to pull the things together. It's the roots thing, isn't it? My father was the same. Later in life I learned how to question him. He used to say, '*Farvus vilstu vissen? Freg nisht kein sheiles. Freg nisht.*' [Why do you want to know? Don't ask questions. Don't ask.] There was always this element of reticence. He hadn't really quite come to terms with himself. And then, much later, when he was more relaxed and I had learned a little more and I didn't quite reject my background so much, he was very cautious with me. I had read the New Testament – very suspect. He said, '*Du veist, di velst noch vern meshiggeh ven du klerst arein zi fil in di zachen. Di velst vern meshiggeh.*' [You know, you will end up going mad. If you enquire too much into these things, you'll go mad.] How about that?

Finally, I learned how to ask him and he told me the most wonderful stories. I used to go on a Friday afternoon sometimes. My mother was already not doing the house or anything. He was retired and had taken over. He was marvellous. He was standing there with his apron on, broom in hand and I'd say, 'Tell me, Daddy, tell me about those days. What happened?' *'Gey avek. Ikh makh Shabbes. Gey.'* [Go away. I'm making *Shabbes*. Go.] He couldn't resist it, though, because he was such a wonderful story-teller and a bit of an actor too – Mother used to call him Meyer Tzelniker[1] – but he'd look at the clock: you've got to make *Shabbes*; it doesn't come on its own, you've got to make it. So he's looking at the clock, saying, *'Gey avek.* If you want to know, *kim nisht Erev Shabbes.'* [Go away . . . don't come on Friday evening.]

I asked my father to tell me what was it like, 14 of them in two rooms. He made it sound hilarious – one on top of the table, one under the table, one on top of the stove (the East European sort). Whatever furniture there was was used as a divider for privacy. The extraordinary story he told me with great hesitation was that his two sisters left home – shocking in 1915. He told me with great shame that they left home to live near the factory in Lodz, where they were seamstresses. What he couldn't explain exactly was that they were teenagers and there were all these sons around. When the girls grew up it must have been absolutely hideous for them. He couldn't quite say it. My father told me very late in his life, 'You know, *z'iz geven a shande, a shande, az di maidelekh unzer zeynen avek getsoigen.'* [. . . it was a shame, a shame, that our girls moved away from us.] They moved away into rooms,' – and then instantly the apology 'We had no choice.' That was the awful thing about that generation. They couldn't separate what wasn't their fault and what was a moral wrong. So all these stories they used to tell with reservation. I always had the feeling that it was an inhibited way of telling me, a little bit shame-*afdik*, shameful.

I was born in 1922 in an attic. When my parents came to Germany and found this room in a lovely little house, it appears the landlady said they could have it, but she wanted no children. Poor Mummy, *nebbish*. Daddy told me much later that with the first pregnancy she threw herself down the stairs. She managed to abort it, but willy-nilly I came along. Anyway, they weren't thrown out. We lived in that attic for six years. Those were bad years. They had to go from door to door selling soap, which was illegal. They put the rucksacks on their shoulders and they sold soap. My mother and father both went out peddling and I was left with an old woman downstairs – well, what to me seemed an old woman.

The contradictions were terrible. She was Christian – and at Christmas there was the Christmas tree. She appeared one Christmas morning with a sheet over her head, right to the floor; she disguised her voice and came towards me, saying, 'I'm a little angel. You've got to promise me to be a good girl.' My parents were standing behind me. Can you imagine my father saying, 'Yes, promise Totzel to be a good girl. She's very good to you.' I was all of four, but I could see it was phoney. They were grateful for her looking after me; I had to participate in this game of her 'being an angel', but I saw through it.

Peddling was very hard work for the parents, especially when mother was pregnant with me. They became a little better off when they began to sell shoes, also with rucksacks. The parents would talk endlessly about those days, consoling each other as it were. Eventually we moved from the attic to a ground floor flat with a tiny little shop. Daddy then became a *shiester* and repaired shoes, while mother sold new shoes in the shop. We had a nice big room with a kitchen and access to a courtyard. They actually bought furniture, not big but nice, painted white with black beading, a mirror in the middle of the wardrobe, a washstand, an ottoman sofa with a plush cover thrown over it, a radio. How happy mother was then. I remember her making gefilte fish, bringing a carp home from the market, still alive, and pursuing it on the table. '*Oy, kim aher! Oy,*' she'd say, '*Kim aher! Ah!*' [Come here.] And she'd knock it on the head, poor fish. I was still an only child and I remember she dressed me nicely, in navy-blue pleated skirts with blouses buttoned on to the waist. That was just a brief period.

I was certainly the only Jewish child in my class. I think I must have spoken Yiddish when I went to school, because in the early days school was difficult. There must have been some problem in communication because I always remember being totally alone in the playground, never playing with anybody; always watching, outside. I think my youngest brother, born and brought up in England, had the same problem. The parents spoke only Yiddish – 20 years later nothing had changed for them except countries, they were still refugees – and so he went to school speaking Yiddish in England in 1947. I remember him saying, '*Mamale, mein shatzele*' [Mummy, my apron;] and something went 'click': that must have been what happened to me. I suspect that was the isolation, the language barrier. So school was difficult and the teacher was terrible. He hit me when I didn't know the answer to a question. He probably made a good Nazi.

After school my mother made me help her in the shop. She had little black overalls made for me with white collars and I was her assistant. She'd say, 'When the customer comes in, you smile. And when I tell you what size shoes, you go up the ladder and you hand them to me.' So I learned very early on how to be practical. I loved it. I didn't learn about life through pretend games; it was the other way round. Once I disappeared for a whole day. The parents looked for me all over town; they told me they had the police help them look for me. I was found – and I remember it well – with my nose pressed against a toyshop window. Did I get a hiding! I fell asleep exhausted from it all, sitting by the table, my arm bent, cradling my head. I don't think the hiding achieved much. It was about my disobedience to them and not about my safety. Dangers were not defined or explained. Poor mother, all her life any reference to sex made her blush to the roots of her hair. My childhood was littered with sexual abuse, from Totzel's nephew Karl to the odd workman my father employed part-time, to the last and most traumatic, an uncle by marriage (my mother's sister's husband) a prolonged affair.[2]

This ruined my first marriage in so far as it was unconsummated. I was a smiling virgin till I was 39 years of age. The suffering was compounded by pressures from family. Why did I not have children? What was wrong with me? Oddly enough, these comments came from women. My husband was never questioned, all this was my responsibility. I found a perfect alibi. 'When the war is over, I'll have children' – with the result, I never wanted the war to finish! When peace did come, there was such a mighty thump of fear in my heart; now I couldn't put off having children any more. Women pushing prams – I envied them and feared them.

One day my husband pushed me through the front door of my parents' home and said, 'There's something wrong with her.' Then it all came out – the abuse, the blame. I screamed at mother that she hadn't looked after me properly; she screamed back at me, 'What more did you want? I fed you, I clothed you, I bled for you.' (My mother always did have a touch of poetry in her.) Then came the denials. I told them of the first abuse by an uncle when I was four and we still lived in the attic. They said it couldn't have been because the uncle in question didn't live in Germany at that time. In that case I must have been even younger than four. '*Di host dir dus ausgetracht.*' [You imagined it.] In my despair I wanted to punish my mother. Now I am sorry for all of us.

What made me remember that particular event was my mother's voice. The parents were out. Suddenly I am awake and the light is on. I'm in the double bed and next to me is my uncle, resting his head on his elbow, looking down at me. He is wearing a trilby and his genitalia are lying outside his trousers. Then I hear a piercing shriek from the street: 'Stupack, what are you doing up there?' He jumped off the bed as if catapulted. His fingers shook while he was buttoning up his trousers. He switched off the light and scuttled down the wooden stairs. The alarm in my mother's voice . . . I knew he did a wrong thing. I remember the moon was out; the leaves of the tree made shadows on the wall.

My husband has often said that there must have been something about me; that *he* had seen me watching workmen, flirting. I have said to him, 'So, when boys watch workmen, they learn, but when girls watch, they flirt!'

If the telling of these experiences sounds fluent, it is because of years of going, on and off, to therapists. It took an age to pry away the guilt till suddenly it came away. My secret, my guilt, my fault – implied in the furtive smiles, the hurried movement, eyelids dropping, a sudden noise making both of us jump. I was caught. Guilt, fault had been transferred.

In a way, I think anti-Semitism works like that. Jews have internalised Christian guilt – their wrongdoing towards us. Why should Jews have to apologise for mentioning the Holocaust? Since my amnesia from the shock of being a Jew in Germany in the thirties has been cured, I do mention it when appropriate. Why should we feel embarrassed about what Christendom has brought about?

The treatment for my vaginismus was barbaric, but I had to

a. Ena Abrahams

Ena Abrahams and her grand-
daughter Jenny, 1989.

Ena's great-grandmother (right)
and her great-aunt, with her
children c 1890, near Cracow,
Poland.

Ena's mother Millie in the early
1920s, wearing a satin dress and
overskirt made and hand-
embroidered by herself.

A trip to Southend or Westcliff. In deckchairs (left to right), Millie, her mother Leah, Aunt Sophie; on the pebbles, Ena between her cousins Colin and Cyril, with her father Alfred.

Ena with her young daughter.

b. Rose Kerrigan
   ### (née Klasko)

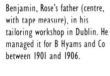

Benjamin, Rose's father (centre, with tape measure), in his tailoring workshop in Dublin. He managed it for B Hyams and Co between 1901 and 1906.

Rose as a young girl.

International Dress Company, Burnt Oak works outing to Portsmouth. Rose is front row, second from the left.

Rose with her first daughter, Rose.

Rose and Peter on a cycle trip in
the Campsey Hills, Scotland, 1925.
'A great thing, to be wearing
anything like that on a bicycle.
The children used to run after me
and call me lassie boy!'

Rose Kerrigan, 1989.

c. Elli Adler (née Goldshmidt)

Elli, winter 1939.

Elli with her parents
Albin and Maria, 1928.

A page from the family album, 1929.

Elli with her best friend Ditta.

Elli with her eldest daughter.

Elli Adler, 1989.

submit. Internal examinations were a nightmare. Muslin soaked with ether was put under my nose as I was asked to open my legs. My vagina was stretched and the gynaecologist said afterwards, slapping my bum, 'Now a horse and cart could go into you,' and then added the threat, 'If you don't let your husband in, he'll divorce you.' It was no use. None of the treatments helped. The crux of the matter was that I couldn't – by that time, wouldn't. Artificial insemination was proposed, but instead I built up my business.

Then one morning I woke up crying, and I cried for a week. Again it was me who was ill. I pleaded with the consultant at Colney Hatch[3] to speak to my husband as well. 'No,' he said, 'I see no need.' I was drugged to the eyeballs. Despite this, a friend gave me books to read, including *The Second Sex* and *Fear of Freedom*. The more alive I felt, the more he [the consultant] tranquillised me. He forbade me to read, saying, 'You think too much; you read too much. You are not a genius.' I was fighting for my survival. Shock treatments were suggested. I screamed the place down. Of course, he thought I was mad. The nurses looked meaningfully at him. His last attempt to tame me was to hand me various sizes of glass penises: 'Practise with those.' If you can imagine me, lubricant in one hand, glass penis in the other, legs open – and trying. As my mother used to say in moments of stress, 'as God is my witness', I did try. Sweat poured from me but I didn't succeed and he gave me up. As I left Colney Hatch, he sidled along my bed, his eyes focused on the bedside table. 'You've lived without intercourse for a long time [18 years, in fact], you'll come to no harm, you're used to it. But why don't you try oral sex?' Despite my early experiences, I had lived a sheltered life and didn't know what he was talking about. At this time I walked out of my marriage.

A year later I fell in love. I wanted to be normal. I went to a gynaecologist to have a Dutch cap fitted. She was an old lady, crippled with arthritis. Needless to say, I couldn't do it myself and explained why. She unravelled the mystery with one question, 'Did you have an orgasm with your uncle?' Her question was so straightforward, so natural. She made an orgasm sound like an utterly commonplace phenomenon. 'Yes,' I said. I was able immediately to insert the Dutch cap.

In 1927 my first little brother, Herbert, came along. I am sure now that my mother had a post-natal breakdown, though in those days they didn't know. It all got confused with a quarrel with her brother, and we moved town. It was a bitter quarrel about a gold watch, a going-away present from her parents. Her brother, with the help of his wife, claimed it was meant for him and there was talk of theft. Ever after my mother used to say, 'Families are all right until the strangers come.' The feud was never resolved even unto her brother's death. All that period of my childhood was about their belief that families should stick together because they had left home, but when they were together the reality was different, they were *broiges*, they fought. So all my childhood is about how you must help your family – and the contradiction that they were always *broiges*. It was a tremendous tearing apart of what I saw was the truth and what they fantasised about.

My mother only saw her father once more before he died. He came to Germany from Poland after my *bubeh* died, with a view to staying. I came home from school one day to find this old man in my parents' bed, sleeping on his back with his long white beard arranged over the feather bed. I remember running out of the room terrified. No one had told me of his visit. It must have caused a great upheaval. All his children were in the same boat, living in one room with children – it was the story of all refugees then – so grandfather went back. Thank God he died before the war.

Blooma was the only one of my father's sisters left in the end. She was in Auschwitz; her two girls were snatched from her arms in the camp and gassed. She knew that somebody in the family had a picture of them and after the war she wrote all round the family that was left, asking for it. My father was too afraid to send it to her. He couldn't cope with the responsibility of what she might do to herself. They wrote to each other regularly, addressing each other the way all that generation did: *'Mein teirer lieber brider.'* [My dearly beloved brother.] Whenever Blooma wrote to him, my mother used to mock, saying, *'A brievele fin dein teirer lieber shvester.'* [A letter from your dearly beloved sister.] Who knows what lay hidden in that mockery? They so romanticised when they separated, but when they were together it was terrible. I think that probably it comes from a real sense of displacement.

Of course, they talked constantly of *der heim*; it was a constant flow. They'd just left when I was little, so it was inevitable. They were displaced. They talked about people I didn't know, the feuds in the neighbourhood, the streets in Lodz, my grandparents' *frumkeit* – and I used to listen. Those are the memories. I remember absolutely nothing of *frumkeit* when I was little, only from 11, when we moved to Ludwigshafen. They were very restricted for space. They lived for six years in an attic in one room, so I wonder how good a Jew can you be if you're that restricted? At what point do you say, '*Ikh ken nisht*' [I cannot]? Also, perhaps, it was the sudden freedom from the orthodoxy they had left behind.

But when we moved town we had three rooms, and from that time on I remember mother making *Shabbes*, baking *challah*, making her own *lokshen*, making cakes, cheesecake, all that sort of thing. She became a very good *baleboste*. There was a stove like a primitive Aga that my mother used for cooking and baking. Then Hitler came into power – I remember hearing it on the radio – and soon after that, or so it seems, there was the boycott. Father's tiny shoe-repairing shop had 'Jude' inside the Star of David written on the window and soon after that it was closed. His workbench was moved into the kitchen and on *Erev Shabbes* it was covered with a large sheet. Father raced through his work to finish for *Shabbes*. It was such an odd time – religious observance seemed to rise in our house at the same time as Hitler.

My father's Seders were magnificent. I think he made up for all the times he couldn't do it. I remember it was very festive: he wore a white *kittel*, and the cushions, and everything *bezoigen*. They didn't have enough money for two sets of crockery and cutlery; they had to kosher, with *opbrein* [scalding].[4] My mother's ambition was to have a gold-rimmed dinner service for Pesach – it had to have a gold rim – and she saved, penny on penny, until finally the jug was full and she bought it. And all the year round it just stood – her *tsatske* in the kitchen cupboard.

My father did the whole thing about Yom Kippur. He blessed us, the tears falling on our heads, just before going to *shul*. All the inside felt so holy and good, and he'd call the children to him and he'd put his hands on our heads and make his little speech: 'Be good, *zei gitter kinder*.' [Be good children.] And as he was talking,

113

the tears were falling on his hands and on to our heads and we all cried. I can't actually think about it properly without getting quite peculiar. I have to laugh; if I didn't, I'd cry. It's very evocative, that sort of thing. And then we'd all go to *shul* together. That was good. That was already in Hitler's time. Many things were good – the duty and the love. It takes a life to sort out one from the other; you never finish.

His funeral was not so long ago. I was standing there with my head bowed and all these marvellous things being said about my father – surviving Dachau, coming here, having to adapt. And I thought, 'Umm.' Just as I'm thinking, being cynical, that's not all of it, the rabbi says, 'Let no one cast a stone.' And I thought, good correction. One is so brittle and cynical; one says, ah yes, all this stuff. But it's clearly thought out, the ritualisation of it all, when everyone comes and shakes hands and says, 'I wish you long life.' It's a very good way to leave, isn't it? I'm beginning to accept many things that I rejected and was so brittle about. A lot of it, of course, was shame – never knowing properly, never understanding really, no one really answering questions, and me not knowing what to ask. It's a lot to do with that. I would say to the future generation: you must know your history.

The Jewish education I had as a child consisted of ritual within the family. I didn't go to *cheder*; there wasn't time, and also I wasn't a son. So I was the one who got the *shissel* for the *bentshing*[5] – at the Seder the girls brought the water, didn't they? There was just ritual, going to *shul* – an aura, rather than a knowing. It was the tradition. And now that I'm an elderly lady, I'm angry because of how ignorant one was kept, I'm angry because ignorance is no defence for anything.

The first time I ever read the Bible was when a young woman who worked for me in my first shop answered questions I had always wanted answers to – questions like why we Jews were called Christ-killers. It was a real shock when she pointed to chapter and verse in the New Testament, that his blood was on our hands. She was probably the worst anti-Semite I had ever known. Her own story was appalling. She was a young Polish Jewish girl and she became a Jehovah's Witness on a transport from Auschwitz to Belsen. She told me this story many times, the miracle of her conversion. On a packed lorry full of people bound for Belsen she heard people whispering and pushed closer to hear. They were quoting scriptures – this world was of no consequence and they looked forward to their resurrection. She believed her faith made her survive (Jehovah's Witnesses were good survivors), and when she came to London she was baptised. She nearly had me baptised too – but I couldn't give Christendom or Hitler a posthumous victory.

I was in my twenties and she was the first one to answer my questions. I read some of the Old and some of the New, but always for pointers towards the Christ thing. I never read it as a book – which, of course, interests me enormously now. I find it very exciting not to approach it from the religion to find God, but to find how the law was forged, the birth of conscience. And to interpret for myself, not walk along the ghetto wall, being ashamed of the *peiyes*, but find that possibly one's ancestors might have had a point, that I can actually walk with my head up.

As a child, I always asked, 'How did the world begin?' Father would laugh and say, '*Z'iz shoin tsi klig. Ikh hob dir gegeben geld dafir; z'iz tsi klig fer mir.*' [She is already so clever. I gave her money for it, she's too clever for me.] It was almost a rejection, not understanding what the question was about, what my needs were. I think that was what was wrong in my childhood. They were too busy, they were poor, they were hard-working, they were working class. A gentile friend I had in the fifties said, 'Rita, what you are describing is working class, it's not particularly Jewish.' She had the same experience in Yorkshire, the same rejection. The strength of ignorance; when you're in it, you can't break out. Finally, I had to break out with a nervous breakdown. It wasn't a break-down, it was a break-out. But in ignorant circles, you have to do it like that. Intellectual needs are not understood. If it's recognised, you're accepted; if you ask unusual questions, you're odd, you're put down. There was no one in my environment to say, 'Read this!' No one, not a sausage. When my first husband and I were already separated, I was curious and finally asked him, 'Tell me, when I was reading, why did you object so much?' And for the first time he gave me an honest answer. He said, 'With every book you were reading you were going away from me.' And that's what it's about

115

– the male fear of the woman knowing more, or being more intelligent. He could hardly cope with me being better at cutting hair!

It's well known now that when the *Ostjuden* came to Germany, German Jews thought, my God, they're spoiling it for us now. The division was very clearly felt; my father went to the *shtiebel*, to the *shul*, and they went with their high hats to synagogue. Much later, after the war, when we lived in the country, a man turned up at the house with a friend of somebody's and we discovered that we both came from Ludwigshafen. He asked my family name and I told him. Then he asked where we lived. I could see he wanted to make a remembrance of the whole thing, but I was very brittle then about those memories and wanted to hurt. I asked where they prayed. He said, 'What do you mean?' I said, 'Where did you pray?' He said, 'Oh, in synagogue.' And then I said that we couldn't have known each other. We felt it very strongly, that division. It's like chapel and church, isn't it? It was very much like that.

Some German Jews most certainly denied that Hitler meant them and said, 'Ah, Hitler means the *Ostjuden*, nothing to do with us.' When they came for the man I worked for, on the Kristallnacht[6] he actually told the thugs that he fought for the fatherland – and they went wild. Poor man, he couldn't understand, he had no comprehension that they could mean him; and, of course, he was taken off to Dachau.

There was a certain closing of ranks and unity in that time. Also, with the German Jews, the divisions closed as the problem got bigger and bigger. But not with a woman I worked for; she was extraordinary. I already had my visa and I was going to England; it was imminent. I worked as a domestic there because you could only work for Jews. I was a grade lower because I was an *Ostjudin*, so the hierarchy was all in order. Her son had already gone to America and we were just packing up all the goodies for the Nazis – the silver, the gold, the bracelets, all the valuables – into those coffers. And she said, 'When you go to England perhaps you would send, as a memento, to my son . . .' and she picked up a little bracelet and a gold chain. Her hand was half-way between her and me and she looked at me and sighed very deeply, and she put it

116

in the coffers for the Nazis. I thought, that's very interesting – never to be forgotten. Couldn't quite trust me. It's a real division, isn't it? Not bad enough that the Nazis saw us like that, but there was confirmation on all sides how horrible we were. But even then I didn't take it personally; it was a collective insult.

But in the end it came together. I had a friend here in the summer who lives in Germany now. She's German Jewish and she survived the camps. She told me when she was in the camp there was an *Ostjudin* who said to her, '*Di bist nisht kein Daytshe. Di bist mein Yiddishe maydele.*' [You aren't German. You are my Jewish girl.] Isn't it lovely? So the reverse is also true. '*Di bist nisht. Redt Yiddish tsu mir.*' [You aren't. Speak Yiddish to me.] She taught her Yiddish and she took her under her wing. 16, she was. It's interesting that it's on both sides, the prejudice. That's how the Polish Jews started calling them '*Yekkes*'.[7] It's lovely, isn't it? So we equalise; nobody can be proud.

It's funny how one could be happy. This photograph of me with my friend Trudel, who perished in the Holocaust, was taken in 1937. Look! We're happy, laughing. We had such a good friendship. She was much older than me and we had a good thing going. It was a happy time, intermittently. And, of course, one had the Habonim.[8] That was a great joy; you identified and it gave hope. I went to the *hachshara* and all that sort of thing. You danced the *hora* and it was lovely. There was one incident when we went camping. It was over Christmas and New Year in the mountains, with lots of snow. We had a little stove, the fire was glowing and we were singing Yiddish songs and Hebrew songs. Suddenly there was a bang on the door. We had the most terrible fright when two stormtroopers burst in on us with the revolvers on their hips; but they were so pissed, they slid to the floor and slept there all night. And we just kept on singing very quietly. We were a little frightened but we carried on.

My father was taken off to Dachau[9] by accident. Although an *Ostjude*, he was stateless, so by a quirk of history we weren't shipped off to the east;[10] we remained in Germany. Later we got papers from the English family to come to England and he came out. There were some things I simply can't remember. For instance, the memory that is absolutely gone (and I've tried very hard to think about it consciously) was the period when the thugs came, the Kristallnacht, and we had to move into a Jewish house. There was just me, my mother and my brother. It's like the shutters came down. I was 16, yet I have no recollection. All I remember is Daddy coming home from Dachau. That was in the new place and that's where the story picks up again, where I remember.

He came home in the night. They did strange things like that – they didn't let skeletons travel by day! Oh, you've got to laugh. There was the front door with the glass inlay. We heard the bell upstairs and I came down to answer the door. There was this man standing there, a skeleton. I knew it was my father, but it was a skeleton. My legs went to jelly and I ran upstairs and I said, 'The key!' My mother said, 'But the door is open!' I said, 'No, I can't open it!' And I ran downstairs again. It happened twice. I ran backwards and forwards and the door was open all the time and I couldn't open it, and there was this man desperate to get in. Fear, isn't it? Finally he did come up and and he didn't want anything to eat; he wanted nothing, only to leave Germany. He talked all night in the dark – he didn't want the lights on – and subsequently never mentioned it again.

That was the only time he talked about the experience until much later, about 10 years ago, and he told me in quite a different way. He was safe and he could extend the story more and talk about his personal feelings. Everything was very normal until Munich, when they changed trains. They were normal civilians until then and treated like ordinary passengers. 'And then,' my father said, '*Ikh hob balt gevist*, but not *di Daytsche Juden. Ikh hob balt gevist.*' [I knew at once, but not the German Jews. I knew at once.] He knew from the pogroms. They started hitting with the truncheons – '*Raus, Jude, raus!*' [Out, Jews, out!] And it was like hell let loose on those trains to get them to the other train. Young men just jumped off the train; and my father said with pride, '*Ich bin doch noch geven ying*' [I was still young] and I jumped. But what about the old men? They couldn't jump, you see. By that time he'd thought about it and didn't just think about himself but thought about somebody else. He'd been reflecting.

When he had to survive, he sussed out exactly what the score was – to watch the guard, not the people who were falling dead beside him. That was his policy and thus he was all right. Oddly enough, he came home quite a healthy man – until he came to England. Then it all came to the fore again and he used to have blackouts and nightmares. Terrible. But he was a survivor and a very lively spirit, was Dad. Vulgar, wonderfully vulgar! He survived and in the end he got his *shul* and was happy. But that was a bad time for him.

My grandfather wrote cards and letters to the cousins here. Of course, they hadn't seen each other for 40 years, like most Jewish sagas, and family feeling had to be evoked. And so my grandfather, my *zeide*, wrote, '*Ah, rateve mein zin, mein einzigen, ibergeblibiner zin, fin gulas.*' [Save my son, my only remaining son, from exile.] (Though my father was not in fact his only son.) He was a *soifer*, so he wrote these beautiful Hebrew cards – and, of course, family feelings were evoked. One cousin – I called her *tante* because she was much older – she sat at Bloomsbury House[11] day after day after day to get us out. Years later we always used to say, 'Ah, wasn't Tante Esther good? Wasn't she wonderful! She sat at Bloomsbury House so patiently, she was so good.' And one day, something snapped. She couldn't bear it any longer and she said, '*Zei nisht kein nar.* [Don't be a fool.] I wasn't good; it was the slack season.' It's wonderfully cynical, isn't it? There was nothing to do at work, so she might as well sit. Really, I love that story.

You know, I don't know to this day what happened to my mother in the six weeks after I left for Britain. What did she do? She had the papers to say she couldn't stay in the flat. Who did she go to? Most of our friends were *Ostjuden* and they'd been deported. Isn't it funny how there are certain things that aren't brought up again? She arrived three days before the war started – just made it.

I had two visas, one organised by my father's relatives in the East End, one as a domestic. My lovely little brother, Herbert, was 11 when he came here on the Children's Transport.[12] We did what we could; it was late in the day; it was urgent. Before he left Germany, he said, 'I want a picture of you to take with me.' I thought it was very sweet, touching, you know. But what he did with this picture was extraordinary. He was in Birmingham for a bit and he went round all the Jewish families and said, 'This is my sister. She is lovely. She can cook. She can sew. She can clean.

You have got to get her out.' And he did. He found a Jewish family in Dudley, Birmingham – the last place God spat on. They lived in the Victorian era still, and me not speaking English. It was horrendous. I was the ungrateful refugee – a fortnight and I was gone. They went to all the trouble. Oh, I was miserable. But he did get me out, my brother. And then I came to London to the family in the East End.

Who could take my brother? What could my poor father do? He's got no home, no *parnoseh*, no anything. We had one room in a relation's house. So the child is looked after by a rabbi in Stoke Newington – and he grew *peiyes*. My *zeide* would have been delighted with this little boy having *peiyes*, but my father, he was already a modern man and for him it was a terrible problem. And how did he deal with it? In the most awful way. Herbert comes home for a weekend and he can't bear to look at him and cuts off his *peiyes*. He goes back to the yeshiva, and the *rebbe* says, 'If you want that, you've got to take him away.' Then we got a little flat in north London, and Herbert came back home. Then he was so *frum*, he used to lift the lids off the pots and ask if it was kosher. It drove my poor mother mad. Conflict, fights, it was unbelievable. There was a war on, and she had a baby coming – 50 she was, and a baby was coming. It was horrendous for her but my father was proud as a peacock. So you can imagine, it was difficult.

After I arrived in London, I met a boy I'd known in Habonim. In Habonim days everything was very puritan, and here I was, not tarted up but I certainly wore make-up, eye black and lipstick. I was walking along Whitechapel Road one day and he tapped me on the shoulder. I turned round and the first words he said to me were, 'I always knew you'd wear lipstick.' I was attracted by glamour and he sensed it. I've never seen him again from that day to this.

It's a curious thing, when I think about it now, that we came away from traumatic experiences and yet when we met we never pursued things and asked what happened. So strange, a kind of negligence almost. I don't understand it. What plagues me now is the callousness. Dreadful things were going on and one didn't seem to be interested. It really didn't occur. One was too busy making one's way. The biggest tragedy in the world seemed to be when two cousins in England were getting married and my aunt was making me my first evening dress and the wedding was cancelled. That was a major tragedy. Imagine! Hitler's Germany all faded into the background. I often wonder. I suppose it's survival, isn't it, or amnesia. Now I feel a guilt of unawareness. It remains a strange and unresolved thing in my life. I doubt whether one can make amends.

Before the war my mother's sister Lotte and her six sons lived in Luxembourg. The parents fantasised that you could smuggle over the border, as they did in 1919. Well, nobody else came up with a better idea. That was in 1938. So a brief correspondence started with my cousin René; we were the same age. We asked each other what we did. He told me he was a *'damen friseur'*, a ladies' hairdresser. I thought that was very glamorous. I wrote back to say that was exactly what I wanted to be. We corresponded briefly, and then I went to England, and soon after that the war started. After the war we heard they were all wiped out. So it was brief, the correspondence, the relationship; everything was temporary. Relationships started and came to nothing. From that came the obsessional nostalgia, the longing to know.

I think that's my resentment against the world – you couldn't develop any relationships, everything was transient. I internalised my anger, got rid of it, 'forgot it'. I fantasised like children who have lost a parent. They romanticise about them, and then inevitably they make them bigger than they are. Family and friends grew in my imagination. I don't think you get a grasp of reality that way. And then the reality of the Holocaust became so enormous that I went from one extreme to another: to Jewish self-hatred.

I learned to be a hairdresser in the East End. The favour they did me – to take me on and to charge me so little for the premium. In those days you paid to learn. There were very strict rules about apprenticeship: for six months you earned nothing and then you earned 5s a week and tips, and when you earned 10s – mmmh! Working all night Christmas and all that. But I learned a lot there. My father was interned in the Isle of Man,[13] so I was the only earner. We lived with family and it was a question of handouts or me, so I had to set to. There I was – 17, 18 – and my mother used to wait for my tips to buy bread. I used to go home for lunch and she'd say, *'Di host epes gelt gekrigen?'* [Have you been given some money?] When my father was released, he got a tiny job, illegally, in a Yiddisher firm. They employed him, but tiny amounts of money. On a Friday night we'd put our wage packets on the table, with great pride. Soon my wage packet was more than his. I worked hard and thought I deserved 15s. It was Dickensian, like Oliver asking for more. I said one day to the boss's wife, 'I've got to keep my family. I need to have a raise. I'm doing all the things an assistant does.' And she shouts downstairs to her husband, 'She wants more money. Tell her to go!' End of story, I went.

It was wartime and there were the air raids. We lived in a shelter for a year and a half, under Lex Garage, if you please. Imagine! A thousand people under petrol. It was in Brewer Street, in Soho. We lived in Berwick Street till we were bombed out. We had one room to have breakfast and supper and then go to the shelter. We had no furniture, not even a bed, because we didn't sleep in the room. It was because I was in the shelter that I got my job in the West End. A receptionist who worked in a West End hairdresser's had the next bunk to me. It was Lena, my dormitory friend, who got me a job for five more shillings. It was very convenient to be in the West End and I worked there for five years, right through the war.

In the old days a hairdresser did everything: cutting, setting, perming, tinting – a one-man band, if you like. An assistant did everything too. It's not arrogant that I say this, but when I left the East End hairdresser I had just learned how to perm, and I considered myself a *shtickel* assistant, and that's why I wanted more money – he was plain and simply exploiting me! Each perm cost 15s and I did six on a Saturday, so I reckoned I was entitled to a little more money. Not at all! He was doing me a favour, that he was letting me, you understand.

In the West End girls washed the hair and passed the pins; men in double-breasted suits cut and set the hair. The *women* hairdressers were in the suburbs. In the West End there was specialisation, but because of the war and men being called up, girls had a better chance, and I became the perm girl. I hated the frizzy perms that were done then and I innovated big, loose curls. I loved my own hair free and flying about. I never understood this thing about lacquered hair and reckoned if I didn't, there must be other women who didn't. As I couldn't speak English very well, I invented a language to express what I meant. I would tip my head down and ruffle my hair with my hands to demonstrate. Before the cold perm there were thin metal rollers and clips which heated up on electric bars. To make a loose curl, I used to put crepe hair and cotton wool around all the rollers – it was wartime, you had to innovate. Because equipment was short, anyone using the rollers after me had to undo all the crepe hair if I was busy. It was a constant source of conflict, but I wasn't deterred. It's called determination, isn't it? I stayed all hours of the night. The sirens used to go and I was still in the shop practising. I would practise in the shelter – they slept in the pin-curls and in the morning I'd comb them out.

My clients loved the loose curls. And when a client asked for me again, it was such a thrill I can't tell you! I ran home, 'Mummy, mummy, somebody asked for Miss Rita!' Oh, I knew I was good! I was fighting my way out and my takings went up and up. One day when I was combing out a client's hair, the boss walked by my cubicle twice and looked in, and I knew that I was going to be promoted – and I was right.

Then I met the English Jewish boy at a tea-dance. 'What is a lovely girl like you doing in a dump like this?' was the opening line. I wanted – it was unconscious perhaps – to be British. He did me a favour too, marrying a refugee. Very cruel, you know. Never mind. I was lovely and quite talented; it was a favour. 'It didn't matter to me,' my first husband, Bernard, used to say. 'She was a refugee and very poor when I married her.' I had no defence against that. I used to hear those words. It's like when you read English literature; you hear anti-Semitism and your ear gets used to it. Like a bad smell, it passes. I think survival is stronger; it's not the time to hear. And so I didn't hear my first husband either. But it was later that I realised what it all meant. 'Great pride in marrying a poor girl.' It's hideous. I would understand better now about humiliation and pride.

I should have known that he wasn't my partner. I told him I came from Germany. 'Oh, Germany' – vaguely interested. And I told him a story about a Nazi I encountered. I told my stories – I don't know what the impulse was; perhaps I thought people understood. And that was the story of the Nazi who hit me in the street a few days before I left Germany. We had already had the Kristallnacht, Daddy had been in Dachau, he'd come out, he'd already gone to England. Now my papers had come. I'm ready to go. My mother still hasn't got her papers. So I'm out in the street and there's the man from the Gestapo headquarters. I knew him because we had to go for papers and signings and all that sort of thing. He was one of those bald, thick-necked types. I said, 'We had a letter this morning from you which said my mother must leave the flat at once. I'm going to England and I want to know that she's all right.' Did he give me a *mishebeyrekh*! 'What do I care where your mother is? She can sleep in the lavatory for all I care!' I said, 'But it's a Jewish house. I thought it was still allowed that Jews could live in Jewish-owned houses.' He just picked up his hand and slapped me right across my face. And Bernard says, 'Didn't you stick up for yourself? I would have done!' He's Jewish, he's supposed to understand. Shouldn't I have taken the whole bundle of me and run? Isn't it absolutely marvellous? 'Didn't you speak up for yourself?' – no comprehension at all.

When I got married to Bernard, it was at Stern's in Aldgate – most East End Jews had their wedding at Stern's. I paid for it; my father really believed that he made the wedding, but never mind. I had to give it to him, didn't I? You can't humiliate people. In the end I was a good girl. There was no choice, none whatever. I wanted to be free and live, but on the other hand I was the only one there was. The English family were poor, so they couldn't help – not wouldn't, couldn't. And so it was a question of *kein breira* [no alternative]. I resented it terribly and I wasn't happy about having to do my duty. It was very painful, because I had no time to live. There was always something wrong – and there was always only me. My father was ill from the camp. When he came to England he had frostbite in his knees, so for two years his knees were bent and he couldn't walk. He was in hospital for weeks, months. Who was there to take him? Me, who else? I was trying to work my way into the world, my career, and a phone call would come and I had to excuse myself and go. So you can imagine, I wasn't that good, I was very irritated, but it had to be done. And

I was responsible with money and setting them up in all kinds of other ways. Much later, when all was said and done, I came to the conclusion that thank God I had to do my duty. I would have been a monster otherwise, because mostly human beings' response is to be selfish. I didn't do it *all* right, but I haven't got the guilt that I didn't do this or I didn't do that. I did it. I was not always nice about it and there was conflict, but I did it. I was responsible. I'm beginning to appreciate that kindness has to be legislated. You can't rely on people's spirit to move them. It never does, or rarely. So I am very happy to have had to do my duty. I think I'd have been an unbearable human being now and unable to live with myself.

I live with my parents a lot now, looking through the Hebrew dictionary. The whole of my childhood is in front of me, recognising Hebrew words, remembering what they said and how they expressed it. Of course, the parents spoke Yiddish only, but I never realised how rich the language was and how much Hebrew there is in Yiddish. Although we were working class and very poor Jews, the language was rich. Hebrew is an old language and it had not been refined to the modern idioms. I've got to learn Hebrew properly to read original texts. I'm reading the Bible from beginning to end. I've got to know what it was that I was going to be clobbered for by the Nazis – and Christendom, for that matter. One didn't know and one always felt an awful sort of shame: they were right to clobber us, we are peculiar; those people with the *peiyes*, they do look strange. Chassidism was my background, and I moved towards assimilation – 'Nothing to do with me' sort of thing.

During the war, after I was married, we had a wonderful holiday in Cornwall away from the bombs. We made friends with people staying in the same inn and had a wonderful time. We joined in all the talking, but kept the Jewish thing to ourselves; we never split the whole time we were there. They used to say, 'But you're so different. Who are you? What are you?' and we never said because we didn't want to spoil it, the assimilation was so good. But after the holiday, we exchanged postcards and again they said, 'We had such a lovely time. But you were different; what are you?' And self-consciously we said, 'Well, the thing is, we're Jewish.' That was it; end of story.

After I was married, I earned more than my husband, who was also a hairdresser. That didn't make for a happy life, I can tell you. I had to pretend it wasn't true, but people knew, they could see. After the war I thought about all the money I was taking and thought, 'I can do this for myself.' I started plotting to have my own business. We looked for premises in the West End, but we didn't have the money. The only alternative was to go to the suburbs. And in those days the suburbs were really the suburbs. For me, it was the end of the world. It was 1947 and that winter was horrendously cold; I nearly went bankrupt with the power cuts. But such is women's tenacity for looking beautiful, they used to come with hot-water bottles and blankets to have their hair done. After frying the fish on Fridays, they had to have their hair washed and set. My clientele was mostly Jewish, and did they lead me a dance. I hated every minute of it. I reckoned myself to have style you see, and they didn't know what I was doing. They'd come in and say, 'You know, I've been to the West End,' and at that I should drop dead! Oh, it used to hurt in the depths of my being. They thought when they went to the West End it was the best, and when they came to me they did me a favour. They knew each other and talked about what I did or didn't do. It was all too local. I thought, I've got to leave, I've got to. I was dying creatively.

We found premises in the West End in the fifties and did it up on a shoestring. We had an Italian shop fitter and on the drawings they had our family name. When the fellow came to paint the name up over the shop, he assumed we would use it. 'Oh no,' we said, 'it's too Jewish-sounding.' He insisted. 'It's an unforgettable name. It stands out.' And so, walking along the ghetto wall (metaphorically), with fear and trepidation, our name was put up. One of my favourite clients looked at it from across the road with me. 'Wonderful,' she said. 'I'm so proud of you.'

My instinct was absolutely right. I was judged by what I did and slowly I built up a clientele. One day the beauty editor of a new magazine walked in and asked if I would like to do a 'before and after', and I said 'Oh, that'd be lovely, I love doing that.' I appeared in those features more or less regularly; other magazines followed and I became known. I was happy and I worked myself to a standstill. Then at the beginning of the sixties I had my 'break-out' and was out of action for a whole year. The business went down to nothing, half my staff left; it was desperate. The marriage was over and we were stuck with a business together. I wanted to go ahead and do things on my own but he wouldn't go. The shop had his name and I didn't have the *koach* to start again. I had met my second husband by then, but stayed in the business for another seven years. I redid the shop, and when it was done it was wonderful, but it was very difficult starting all over again. I was struggling.

One day a woman came in with very curly hair. The hair was too curly to have it short and it wasn't long enough to get it on rollers. So I started to pull at the hair with a hand-dryer in one hand and a brush in the other, and as I'm working, *something is happening*! One of my regular clients was a fashion editor who always wanted immediate attention. She came up to me while I was working and said, 'Rita, what are you doing?' I said I didn't know – and with that she left. 'Oh, my God,' I said, 'that's the end. I'll never be in her magazine again.' Not at all! Half an hour later she came back with a journalist from the *Evening Standard*, and the next day they did a whole page on blow-waving. I didn't name it, they did. It was in the papers, in the glossies, it was everywhere. The irony of it was that I had just installed 20 new dryers. My ex-husband went mad. The whole salon was badly designed for that new innovation, and yet you never could quite believe your luck, that it would last. But blow-waving hasn't died, has it? It was tough making the conversion from the weekly shampoo and set to a six week to two monthly cut, but I survived – was even one of the trendsetters in the sixties, until, in 1968, I left my business.

When the parents got their reparation money from Germany I moved them from Bethnal Green to Brighton. It was a tiny amount. They had no property, but we made a case – father's illness from Dachau. With the money I bought them a flat in Hove. We budgeted and worked everything out so they could be comfortable. They were very happy. My father had his *shul* round the corner and he *daven*ed every day and he loved it. He was extremely happy and he went more kosher than he'd ever been able to afford in the years since leaving home. It was too difficult; we kept things up but it was a struggle. Then when finally he moved here, he said, 'Now I will be able to live the way my father lived – in the Yiddisher way.' He absolutely reverted, he lived by the book – and drove everybody around him quite mad. I'm sure it contributed towards my mother going senile! Well, she didn't like it, she'd moved away from all that. I see the *chazan* occasionally and he always says the same thing, 'Ah, your father helped me a lot. He did the *daven*ing every day.' I love the idea – never mind about the spiritual, he helped me a lot! And he had friends like the *shochet*. I was married 'out' by that time and lived in the country. I'd come and see my father as usual; one day the *shochet* was there, with a beard and these very keen blue eyes looking at me, and he asked, 'Where do you live?' I can see my father's eyes flicking at me; I knew what the signal was – *Zug nisht*! Don't say! The implication was that if I said 'the country', he would know at once there wasn't a *shul* in the country and that I am almost a goy. I got the signal from my father and said 'Oh, I live near Brighton.' My father sighed with relief.

What I found extraordinary was that in the end I found that my father was the man of ritual, order, all that, and it was my mother who was the spiritual, the poetic one. In a way I got that enquiring nature from her. All my life I thought that she's the *meshiggeneh* one, always delicate in her head and the nerves. I think she was like that because she had a certain poetry in her and it could never be expressed. She was illiterate, the usual eastern European, working-class background; she never found expression. And yet, when I look back in my childhood now, it was she who always said to my father, tempering him, 'Morris, *shoin genig. Zei becoved.'* [Enough, show respect.] She was the spiritual one, the modest one. *'Efsher bistu gerecht'* [Perhaps you are right], she'd always say. Not him; he was too passionate, too quick tempered. And because she found no proper mate to express this with, she got very bitter; it all got turned in. So it was difficult for her, poor lamb, and I see it now much better. I've not loved her always. She wanted a lot; she wanted me to be her Mummy, in a way. The generation that left Poland or Russia, they put on their children a lot of responsibility, unfairly.

Jews are always going; if they didn't make a *parnoseh* here, they had to find it somewhere else. My mother's family were all over the place. In England she had no brothers, no sisters; she had to make alliances with my father's family. It was not easy for her. Somehow she always managed to get it wrong. When they came to London, my mother just put an apron on and started cleaning the house from top to bottom. She thought she could repay them, but it was a humiliation in a way for both of them, a misunderstanding.

To this day, I have to make it right for her with whatever family is left. They were fortunate, they left Poland and came as a whole family, so they were a tiny bit smug. They were in the furniture trade and my mother used to say to my father facetiously, your *'holtzene mishpocheh'* [wooden family]. Isn't it wonderfully ironic and poetic! They never could understand my mother not having anyone. She was the only one, an outsider really. I think she was truly displaced.

My parents were never comfortable in any language but Yiddish, but my father tried. He couldn't say 'difficult'; he'd say 'ferdifficult'. 'Ooh, it's very ferdifficult', deadly serious. Yiddish was the dominant language and they never really learned English. When I used to go up to see them they'd try and speak English and I used to say, 'Daddy, *zebrecht nisht di tsayn. Redt Yiddish.'* [Don't break your teeth. Speak Yiddish.] Actually, it was as much about me wanting to speak my mother tongue as making it easier for them. I do miss not being able to speak it now. Yiddish speakers are few and far between. There's a wonderful story about my father. He was so proud learning to read the English paper, but I wanted to bring him up to a more liberal style, and he read the *Daily Telegraph*. I said it was a terrible newspaper and he shouldn't read it. He said, 'I like it, the newspaper. I like it very much.' So I said, 'Read the *Guardian*.' 'All right,' he said. *'Ikh vel laysen dem Guardian.'* [I will read the *Guardian*.] When I came again, I asked him, 'Well, what do you think of it, the *Guardian*? Isn't it a lovely newspaper?' 'A lovely newspaper? *Anti-Semitin, alle.'* [Anti-Semites, all of them.] He had sussed out the tone. I did love him for that. he was a bit of a pig at times, but very endearing also.

In the early days when I was asked to tell one of my stories, I'd

129

find that after a while a kind of trembling started. The more I trembled, the more I could be pitied, couldn't I? And I thought how strange, I thought all that was gone and it was just a story. I no longer want to be pitied. I don't want to tell those stories *again* and have that feeling of being trapped and threatened. Not any more. I want to say, 'Look, *that* happened in history and you were part of it and you still think like that. Now change it!' Now I want to know what happened in our history and why. It's the least I can do. Everything else is sentimentality and nostalgia, of one kind or another.

I think it is a duty, especially in this century, for Jews to know their history, how and why the Holocaust happened. Never mind about faith. We should not beat our chests, repeating our horror stories. It's masochistic. We must counter anti-Semitism not with pleas and tears but by making them acknowledge that our past is their past too. We must stand with pride and make people acknowledge, not in the wrong way but in a good way; make a bridge, but not let them get away with it. What do they think? Their shit doesn't stink? The liberals and the left need to be reminded of their stake in what is going on in the Middle East. Every time Israel does something wrong I want to crawl under a stone – and rightly so – but where else in the world is it different? It's hard to learn that we belong to the human race; neither chosen nor step-people. I've taken a lot of masochism, a lot of shame. The Christian culture has done that to the Jews, for a very long time. I want to get the record straight. It's like being a woman. That is another record to set straight. It's endless, isn't it? But I've had enough of the shame, I've had it up to here. I shall heal my own soul in my own way and from my own experience. I don't have to embrace the world and be so liberal. I'm not ready for that yet. I would have to live another lifetime.

NOTES

1. Meyer Tzelniker was the best known of the Yiddish actors in England.
2. During one of the interviews, Rita talked about the sexual

abuse she had suffered as a child and the terrible consequences it had for her as an adult. At that point she asked to have the tape-recorder switched off. Over two years later, after the interviews had been edited, she made a courageous decision to have that account included in her life story and reconstructed what she had said.

3. A mental hospital in north London.

4. Cooking and eating utensils used during the eight days of Pesach have to be distinguished from those used during the rest of the year. As they could not afford a special set of utensils, they had to kosher them individually.

5. The bowl of water to wash the hands before the prayers after the meal.

6. On 7 November 1938 a 17-year-old Polish Jewish student shot a diplomat in Paris following the expulsion of his parents from Germany to a no-man's-land on the border with Poland. This precipitated organised 'spontaneous' actions against the Jews in Germany, culminating in the Kristallnacht (so named because of the vast quantities of shattered plate glass that littered the streets) on 10 November 1938. Synagogues and Jewish institutions were burned, Jewish businesses destroyed, thousands of Jews attacked, and 30,000 Jewish men were sent to concentration camps, including Dachau.

7. *Yekkes*, or 'jackets', is the ironic term given to German Jews by East European Jews in the nineteenth century when German Jewish men adopted the practice of wearing jackets instead of the traditional gaberdine coats.

8. A left-wing Zionist youth movement, many of whose members settled on kibbutzim, after a period of *hachshara* (preparation).

9. Dachau was the first of the concentration camps, set up in 1933 to contain the thousands of political opponents of Nazism who were arrested. Mass Jewish arrests began in 1938, and most people were imprisoned in Dachau.

10. On 28 October 1938 Polish Jews were rounded up and transported from Germany back to Poland. Jews who had entered Germany as illegal immigrants had stateless passports and were not deported at that time.

11. A number of different organisations and individuals were

involved in trying to arrange visas. The Central British Fund for German Jewry and the Council for German Jewry were located in Bloomsbury House.

12. The Movement for the Care of Children was set up in late 1938, and in December the first transport of 300 children arrived in Harwich. Nearly 10,000 children, the overwhelming majority of whom were Jewish, were rescued in this way. Most were placed with foster parents, many with non-Jews.

13. Beginning in May 1940, the British government interned over 27,000 'enemy aliens' in camps scattered throughout Britain. 10,000 of these men and women were interned on the Isle of Man. The great majority of those interned were Jewish refugees from Nazism. Most of the rest were Italians who had settled in Britain in the early part of the century. About a quarter of the internees were deported to Australia and Canada.

ELLI ADLER
'I Didn't Know What an
Au Pair Was . . .'

Elli was born in 1925, in Vienna, which had one of the largest Jewish communities in Europe, to Albin and Maria Goldschmied. She is an only child. Her father was an assimilated Jew and her parents were socialists. Vienna was the centre of a vivid intellectual and cultural life in which Jews like Elli's father took a full part, and were often in the vanguard. Jews had been emancipated in 1867. They considered themselves loyal Austrian citizens, yet from the late nineteenth century nationalist and Catholic political parties were emerging with a specific anti-Semitic ideology.

Elli's mother was not Jewish. Elli was aware of tensions within the family and, as she grew older, in the wider society. The position of Jews was deteriorating in the early 1930s, first with the suppression of the Social Democratic Party and later with the assassination of the Austrian Chancellor Dollfuss, in an attempted Nazi putsch in 1934. A passionate and authoritarian nationalist, he had tried to protect Austria from Germany's expansionist aims.

In 1936 a treaty with Germany 'normalised' relations between the two states, and guaranteed Austria's independence. German newspapers and other forms of propaganda for the Third Reich were introduced into Austria. By New Year's Day 1938, two leading Austrian newspapers issued a call for all citizenships conferred on Jews after 1918 to be revoked and for a halt to Jewish immigration to Austria.

Austria was annexed by Germany on 13 March 1938. The invading German troops were met with hysterical joy by the majority of the Austrian population. Elli recalls that the anti-Semitism of many, many Austrians could now be given full rein. The new Nazi regime began systematic persecution of Jews on a scale greater than had till then been practised in Germany itself.

The situation worsened throughout 1938. It culminated in the orchestrated pogrom of Kristallnacht. In Vienna alone, where over 90 per cent of Austria's Jews lived, 42 synagogues were burned. 8,000 Jews were arrested and thousands were sent to the concentration camp at Dachau. Hundreds were murdered or killed themselves that night.

120,000 Austrian Jews were able to emigrate by the outbreak of war, many with the help of Jewish welfare organisations worldwide. A few thousand more managed to escape by the end of 1939. Although Elli's mother was born a Catholic, and Elli baptised for political expediency, this in no way offered her protection against racial definitions of who was Jewish. She was a 'Mischling' – a child of mixed race.

Elli was one of those children who left Austria on a Children's Transport organised by the Quakers – the Society of Friends. Like adults, children had to have sponsors, or someone who would guarantee to keep them in education or employment, fed and housed. Elli came here as an au pair aged 13½.

Bewilderingly, in England Elli was the victim of both anti-Jewish and anti-Austrian discrimination. A young teenager, she struggled through her adolescence in an isolated and largely hostile environment. She began work in the clothing trade, married and by the time she was reunited with her mother in 1946, she was a young woman with a baby. Elli's father had perished in Auschwitz in 1942. Virtually none of the 60,000 or so Jews remaining in Austria after 1939 survived.

I'm an only child. I was born in Vienna on 5 November 1925. My mother, Maria, was apprenticed as a dressmaker when she was about 14; my father, Albin, was a sergeant in the First World War. He was a prisoner of war in Russia, and after the war he travelled to Vladivostok, and from there made his way down to Singapore and back to Europe. He was a journalist by profession, and he worked on a very radical newspaper in Vienna. I grew up in a very politically aware environment; we were always socialists. May Day was a great occasion; it was always a public holiday, flags were put out and there were processions.

My father was Jewish, my mother wasn't. I was aware of tension between my parents. I had no idea what they were about until very much later, when I was about 20. My maternal grandmother sometimes came to stay with us: I didn't like her, I wasn't sure why, but discovered later on that it was because she was very anti-Semitic.

I think my mother was the stronger personality. What I didn't realise was that one of my father's sisters was unmarried and he supported her, which was the cause of disagreement between my parents, because it left my mother short of money. And there were these frictions. I've only really lately come to realise what a very resilient woman my mother was.

There was no religious angle of any sort in my family, except that my maternal grandmother tried to convert me to Catholicism, which I resented very much; I didn't want to know. But in 1934 there was a lot of political tension – it was the year Dollfuss was murdered by the Nazis – and my mother was advised to have me baptised for expediency. So I was baptised at the age of nine, which I found quite a hilarious experience, standing there and having this water poured over my head. It certainly didn't make me religious, it was just simply something that happened. I went to religious instruction once a week, which I also regarded with great scepticism, and I certainly didn't absorb any of it.

In 1934 and after, the tension was incredible; the air was electric. I felt it, but I didn't know what was happening or why. I was just told we had to stay indoors, because there was shooting and all kinds of things going on. I don't think I asked why or anything, and I'm sure I wouldn't have been told if I had asked. 'You don't understand,' was the usual attitude of adults towards children.

I don't even know whether in junior school there were other Jewish children or whether I was aware that they were Jewish. I don't know. It wasn't something that I particularly considered: you know, we were just children and that was it. But I think I did feel myself to be Jewish, without being aware of it somehow.

Then, in 1938, Hitler marched into Austria. I had a very close schoolfriend and literally from one day to the next, this girl wouldn't speak to me. I didn't have a lot of friends, I was a solitary sort of child. I found this quite amazing, very distressing and confusing, and I instantly sided with the Jewish girls in my class – there were only five or six of us – who were 'tolerated' until the end of the school year. Then we had to leave. It was a private school. We also had to vacate our flat at that time, and so we moved to a different district, where I attended the local school, until I left Vienna.

When the Nazis came to Vienna it was really a very terrifying experience. There were waves of plane formations going over Vienna all the time. I don't know whether they were the same planes circling or whether they were different planes following on, but it was very frightening. There were a lot of military vehicles rattling through the town, tanks and such, and I think all designed to intimidate the people on the whole, but there were a lot of people who cheered the Nazis. Whenever I saw anybody in a Nazi uniform I crossed over to the other side of the street, because I felt very afraid, but also I simply didn't want to be in the vicinity of such people.

I saw Jewish shop-owners' windows smashed and looted, and signs painted on the shops that they were Jews, and non-Jews shouldn't go shopping in such places. Other shops had signs up saying, 'Jews not allowed'; on park benches and in all sorts of public places it said Jews weren't allowed. In Austria they had the national emblems painted on the flagstones in the street, and I saw Jews, old people, set to scrubbing these things, which was just terrible. I didn't understand why it was but I just found it terrible, it was very distressing. There was a newspaper brought out by the Germans called *Der Stuermer*, which was just full of hatred.[1] I don't know where they found the photographs which they printed, but it was horrible, it was all terribly anti-Semitic and revolting, displayed at newsvendors in the street.

There was a gathering, a rally, in one of the very large squares in the centre of the town, and while I was still tolerated at the school I had been attending at the time when the Nazis came, the whole school was taken to listen to Hitler speaking at this rally, which was just absolutely horrible. We all had to go, there couldn't be any exception. Then there was a sports stadium in Vienna where we were also all taken as well. It was dreadful, all this shouting and 'Heil, Hitlering' and rubbish. I mean, I didn't take part, but it was all very uncomfortable. The whole atmosphere was charged with a sort of mass hysteria.

It really was something sadistic inflicted on these kids, but I wouldn't like to swear that all the Jewish children went. I know *I* was there and I don't know why; I'm sure it wasn't that I wanted to go. I think we were all quite bewildered, and I don't think I ever discussed it with my Jewish classmates at all. It was all too frightening, and I felt that I couldn't even speak to anybody about anything, because one never knew who was listening in, or spying and reporting what had been said.

If there was latent anti-Semitism there before, it was quite overt after that. There was a Jewish girl in the class who was very unfortunate in herself; she was very awkward, she was not very agile, she was short-sighted, and she was also poor. All the anti-Jewish hatred was directed towards her, because she was the obvious scapegoat, and they engraved or wrote all sorts of things on her desk which I always tried to rub out before she herself came to school, because I felt it was just so terrible. I think my contact with my school friends ceased.

In March 1938, I was 12½. My father was immediately arrested because the newspaper he worked for was very anti-Nazi, and most of the people on the staff were Jewish. Three of the proprietors took all the money and left Austria, and left him and some others in the lurch. He was taken into custody. My mother had just had a hysterectomy operation – I didn't know it at the time but discovered afterwards – and she was in very poor health. She was in a terrible state, and she tried everything to get him released. A week before he was due to be sent to Dachau[2] he was released, but was given a time limit of three months to stay in Vienna before he would be rearrested.

My mother tried to get a visa so that he could go anywhere at all out of Austria, but finally he had to leave without any kind of visa, because the time limit was up. He left with two or three other men, and they went to Belgium in the first instance. We went to see them off and I *knew* when I said goodbye to him that I would never see him again. I just had this feeling; it was terrible. We eventually had a card to say he had arrived safely – wherever it was – and some while later we had another card to say that he had arrived in Paris – after a lot of very difficult journeying, through Belgium and avoiding frontier guards and all sorts of hazards. He stayed in Paris until the Germans got there, when he went to Nice, where he stayed until he was reported to the police by somebody. From there he was deported to Drancy, which was a transition camp, and from there he was sent to Auschwitz. My mother had a notification after the war that he died in 1942, at Auschwitz.

I've never felt resentful that my father left me. I've just felt terribly sad that I wasn't ever able to know him as an adult.

I remember a conversation between my aunt – my mother's sister – and my father. My aunt suggested that my father should leave Austria with us and he said, 'What nonsense, Hitler wouldn't dare to come into Austria.' I think my father was really very naive in that way. In spite of all the things that had happened since 1933 in Germany, my father never thought it could happen to Austria.

I think he felt Austrian rather than Jewish. As I said, he never referred to his religion at all. My mother relinquished her Catholic religion when they got married. There was no religious aspect to our family at all. But my father's family were very resentful of him having married a non-Jewish woman. He never visited his family at all until after Hitler, when they realised what a marvellous person my mother was, and all the things she did and all the dangers she put herself into on their behalf.

My father's brother in America, who had gone to the States just after the First World War, refused to be recognised as Jewish. In fact he married a 'Nazi' woman in America and didn't want to have anything to do with his family at all. My father wrote to him that if he did not get visas for one of his sisters and her family he would tell his brother's wife that her husband was a Jew. So he sent this visa for them to go. It was just for his sister, the husband and one son. And they went to the States. Another sister's husband was on business in London when Hitler marched into Austria, so almost straight away she came to London. The youngest sister came here as a domestic, so they all survived.[3]

After my father left, my mother tried to find work to support us. She made an application to the Journalists Union for money, but nobody would give her any, and because she had the name Goldschmied – which was a Jewish name – nobody would employ her, and so life was very difficult. Then we had to vacate our flat, because it was in my father's name, and we moved to a very small place – my grandmother's flat – where we lived in not very comfortable circumstances until I left Vienna with a Children's Transport.

My mother had heard of the Society of Friends and she made application for me to go to England, but because I was only half Jewish I was put at the bottom of the list rather than at the top. I remember going to the office of the Society of Friends on a number of occasions to be interviewed. Presumably I was vetted to see whether I was eligible to come, which I found somehow very uncomfortable.

We had some friends and their son had already left to come to England. These people wanted to give him some money or something of value and there was no way that they could send it, and so my mother accepted some jewellery for this boy, on my behalf. There was no way that I could take this jewellery openly, but she sewed it into the hem of the dress or skirt I was wearing on the journey.

I knew this and I was very, very apprehensive, because there was a frontier search, luckily not very thorough, and if the jewellery had been found then the whole Children's Transport would have been sent back – which was an unimaginably terrible thing. So I was very glad when we were over the frontier, out of Germany.

When we were at the station, because on previous transports valuables or other things had been passed through the train windows from the people being left behind to the children on the train, the train windows weren't allowed to be opened any more. So we couldn't even say last goodbyes to our parents when we left; it was just through a closed window, which was really distressing.

The journey was a very weird experience. It was nighttime when we embarked. I was put in charge of a three-year-old at Hoek van Holland and I thought how extraordinary that I should be put in charge of this child. I was still a child myself. I put this small child on the top bunk rather than on the bottom one. I was told afterwards how stupid that was. I was 13½.

My mother also applied to come to England, to follow me, but wasn't able to, because war broke out before she was able to leave. I left in July 1939. My mother could actually have come to England, but she discovered subsequently that her mother went to this office and said that she was a poor old woman and they shouldn't let her daughter leave her behind. So they cancelled her place for coming to England. That's why my mother had to stay in Vienna, all during the war. She had the most *terrible* time.

She was a very brave woman. She helped a lot of her Jewish friends, took food and coal and anything she could to help them, at great risk to herself. At one time she worked in a bookshop. Already at that time Jews had to wear a yellow star.[4] She served a man and she indicated that he should cover the yellow star up with a newspaper he was carrying and she sold him whatever book he wanted. They weren't allowed to serve Jews and obviously somebody noticed, and for that she lost her job.

Then she worked in a uniform factory. She had to work terribly hard, twice as hard as anybody else because she had been married to a Jew. She was *always* victimised, all the time. She could have changed her name back to her maiden name, but she didn't want to do that, which was very brave of her, but it didn't serve her very well. She finally got a job in a silver factory where very exquisite silverware was made for the German bosses. But there again she had to do three people's jobs for the wage of one, because she had been married to a Jew. She was always under suspicion of stealing. It was dreadful, a terrible experience.

She had Christian friends. The mother of my first school friend, who lived in the same block of flats, was very kind to her and very helpful. She also had her own school friend, who was marvellous to her. If it hadn't been for their support I don't know if she could have really survived, because her own family was absolutely terrible to her and said, 'You see, if you hadn't married a Jew, all this wouldn't have happened to you,' which was less than helpful.

When I arrived in England it was very strange. My aunt, who was in London, met me at Liverpool Street Station, and we went by Underground to where she lived; she had a flat in Chalk Farm. That was a fantastic experience, going on the Underground, wonderful! I stayed with my aunt for a week, but I had a sponsor in Bath and I was going there as an au pair. A lot of children went just *as* children, without having to be a worker of some sort, and went to school, but because I was already 13½ someone decided that I was old enough to be an au pair. I didn't know what an au pair was anyway.

After a week my aunt took me to Bath, to this woman who was a doctor and lived in a very old house. It was a monastery and it had the date on it, built in 1500 and something. It was a very interesting house but it was incredibly dirty; that was one of the things that struck me first of all. We were given a meal which was so *horrible!* It was roast beef with so much *fat* on it. I was nearly ill, but I thought, 'I have to eat this.' It was just terrible, a horrible sensation. Anyhow, my aunt then left to go back to London and I was abandoned in this place!

The doctor was very kind at first. I was sent to school for a year and a half, basically to improve my English. I understood if people spoke slowly enough. I had learned English at school, but I had also had private lessons in Vienna. I had chosen English rather than French because it seemed easier to me to learn.

The doctor had paying guests, patients rather than guests, old ladies; there were some nurses there who were for the terminally ill. She also looked after a number of children, and she had one girl there who was a year older than myself who was very severely spastic – I had to help look after this girl, read to her or feed her or do minor things. After I'd finished going to school it was my task to look after this spastic girl by myself, which was quite something. This girl – perhaps because she didn't like being the way she was, and other people were running about and she couldn't – was very spiteful. She often told lies about what I had or hadn't done, which I didn't like very much.

The doctor was not Jewish. I think anyone could be a sponsor. People like this doctor thought they were getting a cheap form of labour – which is what I was. She didn't actually have to pay me anything for looking after this girl, which would have been a full-time job and should have been well rewarded. She had all kinds of weird people there. She had kitchen staff and there was one woman, I suppose she would have been about 40, and I couldn't understand why she was there. In her youth she had had a baby and was therefore put in a home for imbeciles or some sort of home of that nature. She was another cheap form of labour, you see; you didn't have to pay her a lot because she'd had this illegitimate baby years ago. She had another girl there who stole most of my underwear. Dreadful, but she had these people out of homes for delinquents or something, because then she wouldn't have to pay them good wages.

I only had contact with my mother through the Red Cross in Sweden, and that took a very long time. I also corresponded with my father, but I somehow didn't appreciate how long correspondence took to arrive so I didn't write as frequently as I might have done. He wrote quite a number of letters to me, and I suppose when you are young you don't think of these things. The same with my mother.

I felt very isolated. There was a boy there in Bath about my own age and we talked quite a lot. As far as I know there was no Jewish community, and I certainly wasn't aware of any. I had no contact really with *anybody* who was like myself. There was a girl there before me, also a refugee, who went somewhere else – she was a little bit older – and she implied that she was glad that she was leaving this doctor's place. I couldn't understand at first why, but then after a while I realised why she was glad to leave. There was one point when I was going to run away because it was so horrible. I had it all planned what I was going to do. Somebody from the Society of Friends came to visit me and asked me if everything was all right and I said, '*Yes*.' Of course, I shouldn't have done. They might have found me somewhere else, but I thought I wasn't really entitled to say, 'No, I don't like it here.' My aunt and I corresponded, but again I felt I wasn't entitled to complain: I was lucky to be in England at all.

I wasn't really aware of what was going on in Europe. There was a war, and that was a terrible thing, that of course I knew, but I had no idea. I did not read the papers.

When I was 16 I had to leave Bath because I was an enemy alien[5] and Bath was a protected city because the Admiralty were moved there during the war. I had always wanted to be a nursery nurse,

d. Ruth Adler

Ruth and her mother, Warsaw, 1919. The
blouse and brooch worn by her mother were
borrowed for the picture.

Ruth's mother (left) with a friend, Warsaw,
1905.

Stepney Jewish School outing to Seaford, 1925. Uniforms had been introduced by the head, Miss Rose.

A portrait of Ruth at 20, taken in 1932 for her identity card, which she needed because her husband was stateless.

Ruth with her younger son in 1936.

e. Rita Altman

Rita (right) with her friend Trudel, who was killed in the holocaust.

Rita and her younger brother Herbert in 1938 or 39, in Germany.

Rita in her twenties, London.

Rita with her mother outside their shoe
shop and cobblers in Germany, 1938.

Pages from Rita's family album. The top caption indicates that the boy and girl seated, and the two adults standing between them all perished in the Holocaust, while the rest, Rita's cousins, were survivors of Auschwitz. Bottom left is Malka, Rita's aunt, a survivor of Auschwitz, and bottom right reads 'Father's sister and her children: All three perished in the Holocaust.'

A page from Rita's family album. Pictured top left are Malka's two children 'snatched from her arms – put to death in gaschamber' in Auschwitz; top right are cousins 'after Liberation in Paris'. Bottom right reads 'Reunion – after Holocaust'.

f. Asphodel

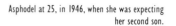

Asphodel at 25, in 1946, when she was expecting
her second son.

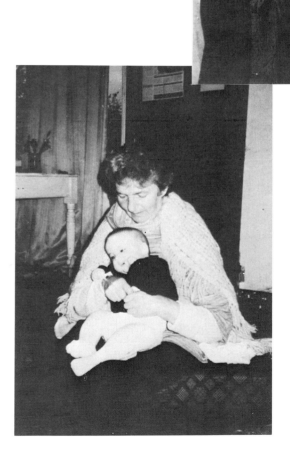

Asphodel on her 65th
birthday, at a women's
spirituality weekend.

Asphodel, 1989.

and a place was found for me to train somewhere in Somerset. So I was sent to the wilds, where there was very overt anti-Semitism. I was referred to as 'that Jewess' and 'you Jewess' and all sorts of things by other nurses. I felt everybody was very anti-Semitic, which I didn't feel quite to the same extent when I was in Bath.

I was there till I was nearly 18. It was really in the depths of the country, between two small towns, and there was no bus service. It was a Georgian mansion which had been a boarding school but which was taken over by Bristol council as a residential nursery. Most of the children who came to the nursery were from Bristol. Either they had been bombed or were from one-parent families. We had 40 children there from age two to five. It was a beautiful place and I appreciated, in a way, that it was visually very beautiful, but I didn't like it because it was totally isolated. One of the nurses had a bicycle and so we could cycle into town when we had time off. The nearest town was four miles. There was a village down a very steep hill, but all the young people had gone off to the army or to do war work. Most of the inhabitants were rather ancient and we had no contact with the outside world really.

One of the nurses, an older woman, was particularly anti-Semitic and she was dreadful, she really was. I was the youngest – I was 16 – and they were all fully trained nurses. There was a couple who were still in their mid-twenties, but the most anti-Semitic one must have been at least 40 or older. I didn't react to it. I couldn't, I was just sort of frozen. I suppose there must have been times when I cried, but I don't remember. It was just totally incomprehensible to me. *Why?* I had escaped victimisation, I thought, and there it was again and I didn't know why at all. After about 18 months I decided I'd had enough there and I wanted to come to London. We could save up our days off and, because there was nowhere to spend time off locally, most people did – we had four days off a month – and went to wherever their homes where. I usually came up to London to stay with my aunt. One day I said to her, 'I don't want to stay there any longer,' so she helped me organise it.

I enjoyed the work up to a point, but it wasn't what I had visualised nursery nurses' work would be like. But as I had started on this career I thought I ought to finish it. So when I came up to London I worked for Paddington Council in a day nursery, and finished my training there.

I was always regarded as an enemy alien and enemy aliens had little grey identity books. Every time I went anywhere at all I had to report to the police to say I was going to such and such a place, and when I arrived I had to report to the police to say I had arrived from so and so, and then the reverse when I went back. It was a terrible chore. Once I came up to London and I hadn't reported within 48 hours to the local police. When I eventually did go, I had a sort of caution that if it happened again dire things would happen to me, so I was very careful not to overstep the mark again. You were an enemy alien if you came from Germany or from Austria, whether you were Jewish or not. That was it. A school friend of mine came with her mother and they were interned, the mother with the child.

I found myself a room. I was very young and innocent, and I found this ghastly room – in quite a nice house, I thought. It was all very dingy because of the blackout and there was this minute room which had a bed and a cupboard in one corner, and in order to shut the door I had to stand on the bed because it was so tiny. It was incredible. There was a gas appliance outside so other people could use it, and I was always putting money in without getting the full benefit of it. It was a very strange arrangement. The landlord was a horrible man and once he made advances to me and I pushed him away, but some time afterwards I discovered that this house was a brothel!

I left very soon after that. God, it was horrible. I had absolutely no idea. I was incredibly naive.

When I was working in the residential nursery I earned enough, because I had board and lodging, and whatever money I was paid was enough for me to pay my fares to and from London and to spend some money on clothes. When I came to London and worked in a day nursery it was very different. I was paid £2 a week. We had all our meals at the nursery, but I had to pay some rent and I had to pay food at the weekend, and I found it didn't cover all that. I probably paid 10s a week rent, bus fare was only three ha'pence a time, but even so, it wasn't quite enough. There was one nurse I always borrowed 5s from on the Thursday before being paid on the Friday, to tide me over.

My aunt and uncle had a flat in Kensington, but they had bought a house in Beaconsfield and had let this flat to a couple whom they knew. There was a room available, so I moved and that was absolute luxury. There was a bathroom and constant hot water; it was wonderful. I stayed there quite a long time, until I met my boyfriend. He lived in West Hampstead, but he moved in with me and this couple didn't like it very much, so then we moved somewhere else. This was almost at the end of the war.

My boyfriend was also a refugee. I met him at Young Austria, which was an organisation set up for Austrian and German refugees in Westbourne Terrace. They had a lot of social activities. There was a restaurant there where you could have a very cheap meal and they organised camping trips and all sorts of things. It was very nice. As far as I know they were all Jewish refugees.

I had to go to Swallow Street for some reason, the main office where all the enemy alien data were kept, and if anything cropped up one had to go there. The police officer there brought out a file the size of which absolutely staggered me! This file was all on me. It was absolutely amazing. He told me about myself, and things that I hadn't a clue about, and apparently this Young Austria was a Communist organisation. It was affiliated to the Communist Party. I didn't know that it was a Communist organisation, but basically I was not only an enemy alien I was a Communist as well! It was incredible. He told me, 'You've been here, and there and . . .' You know, I was staggered, absolutely staggered.

But I only took part in the social activities, I didn't really want anything to do with their political activities. A lot of Young Austrians were very politically involved, and quite a few went back to Austria after the war. Some went back to East Berlin and were active there, but I wasn't really interested in that at all.

I think my father's socialism did influence me politically. I have always felt a sense of justice, and if I saw anyone who was badly treated by a person in authority I felt very angry and resentful. In various jobs I've had I've always stuck my neck out, not only on my own behalf but also on behalf of other people. I've always been socially aware, though I wasn't politically active. Now I'm a member of the Labour Party and I belong to CND, but that's as much as I'm involved politically. I was also a trade union member when I was working, but other than that I'm not an extremely politically active person.

Most of my contemporaries in Young Austria were living with boys without being married, and our attitude to sex was really quite free and easy; we didn't think it was a terrible thing to do. I don't think many of the people in Young Austria got married to each other, they just enjoyed being with each other. I think perhaps I might have been regarded by an older generation as being promiscuous but I didn't feel that, even though I had several boyfriends with whom I went to bed.

I feel that because I left home at an early age I had a much wider aspect of things than I would have done if I had stayed in my own environment. My mother had a very rigid upbringing and I think had she been here, I would probably have been much more controlled and not allowed to do what I felt I wanted to do.

Though my mother was always very reticent about discussing sex as such, she did tell me what to expect about the period, so I knew. But what I wanted to know was how children came to grow in a woman's belly, and she was very reluctant to give me any information at all. All she would tell me was that when two people came very close together, then . . . and I suppose she then left it to my imagination as to how this came about! It didn't tell me a great deal actually, but subsequently I discovered what happened. There were no books available at the time, none at all, I just found out! In Bath there was a nephew of the doctor's who was about my own age, and we discovered things together. We didn't put anything into practice, but we discovered each other. I enlightened him on a number of things, for which I think he was quite grateful!

I took my boyfriend to be introduced to my aunt and uncle and they were absolutely horrified by him. I can see now years later why, but at the time of course, I couldn't appreciate it. One aunt threatened to put me in a nunnery or the equivalent of such a place, just to keep me away from him, which was the most stupid thing to say because it only made me go the other way. We went and applied for a special licence to get married, which again was an utterly ridiculous thing to do. But that's the effect this dictatorial attitude had on me then. I got married in 1945.

We wrote a letter to my mother to say that we would guarantee her keep and her accommodation, because obviously they didn't want people here whom nobody could support, and they weren't *allowed* to support themselves. I was already married and had a seven-month-old baby. She was granted permission to come here in August 1946.

I went to meet her at Victoria Station. This was a *very* strange experience. As a child you have a picture in your mind of what your mother was like when you left her, but when you're grown up it's all different. There was this woman in the middle of August with a fur coat standing on Victoria Station, and she was just like a stranger – which she was. Six years is a very long time. I had been a child and now I was a grown woman. It was a very strange experience.

None of the things which I subsequently discovered had happened to her she could say in her letters, and towards the latter part of the war I had no correspondence from her, so I had absolutely no idea what sort of life she had led until she came. Years and years later she was finally able to talk about it, because it was such a horrendous experience for her.

I worked until two months before my baby was born, in 1946. I started working in a dress factory because I didn't want to be a nursery nurse, I decided. Somebody I knew was working in a factory, and two or three of us went there. Although I was familiar with a sewing machine, I had never been in place like that. I sat down to this machine and put my foot down on the pedal, and it zoomed off in an alarming way! I tried it out two or three times and I thought, 'Well, I'll get a job,' and I found some advertisements and went along and said I was an experienced machinist! I actually managed to stay there two whole days, by which time I managed to acquire some knowledge! There are two types of industrial sewing machines, and the threading up of one machine is very complicated, but I learned how to thread it and actually to handle it, so after two days I was an experienced machinist and I managed to keep the job. Quite funny really!

My first baby I had in hospital. Because it was shortly after the war and there were very few hospital places and none available in my area, I had to go to Bath to have my baby. I was really quite upset, because I didn't know many people anyway, and there would be nobody to come and visit me in hospital. I remember the day before I was due to go to Bath I thought, 'Well, I must clear up,' and I was scrubbing the kitchen floor on my hands and knees, quite mad, and during the night I started going into labour. My husband called an ambulance, and I was taken to Hammersmith Hospital. I never had to go to Bath, which I was very pleased and happy about. At that time you weren't allowed even to put your feet on the ground, out of the bed, and I was in hospital a fortnight. Quite ridiculous.

When I came home I felt slightly depressed, but I didn't know anything about post-natal depression at that time. I just snapped out of it, I suppose. I was not quite 21. Even though I'd been a nursery nurse, I knew the rules by the book; it was quite different. Personal relationships and such things hadn't entered into that kind of education. There I was with this baby and nobody whom I could really ask, except to go to a clinic. But then it was very theoretical – of clinical – in the sense that you just asked the baby's weight and all that kind of thing. Nothing more. I had no one in particular to go to for guidance at all.

I felt very isolated – I had no friends at all. My friends in Young Austria were so involved or committed to their politics and I couldn't commit myself in the same way, so it was a mutual split really. And other friends I didn't really have. I think this was because everybody was against me marrying my boyfriend, the father of the baby. It made me all the more determined to marry him. But subsequently I discovered he *was* undesirable. Eventually I got divorced.

My husband was a Hoffman presser[6] in the East End, where all the rag trade was situated. We were living in North Kensington at that time, in a furnished flat. It was very nasty. My job was in the West End. When my mother came, she stayed with us for a short while, but we only had two rooms. My uncle found somewhere for my mother to live, and then, also through my uncle, she got a job. She was working quite soon after she came, without a work permit at first, but eventually she got one.

In 1947 I had my second daughter, by which time my husband went out in the morning, ostensibly to go to work, and came home in the evening, but at the end of the week there was never any money, so I don't know what he was doing. He had all sorts of excuses for why he didn't have any money, and by then my mother was supporting me. We were given notice to quit from the flat because he hadn't paid the rent, and the children and I moved into my mother's room. Incredible. There we were in this one room. There was a very small room where the children slept, but basically everything went on in one room. The people to whom the flat belonged thought this was getting too much, and a health visitor or inspector came and said that the children and I had to move because it was overcrowded. We had no idea where we were going to go.

I went to what was then called the Workhouse, somewhere in Camden Town, with the two children. It was horrible, absolutely horrible. There was a *huge* dormitory, the children were always crying and it was filthy. It was most depressing. Then my aunt and my mother found a small place for us, one room and a kitchen, that was quite nice, and after 10 days we moved there.

I then managed to get the children into a day nursery, which were still quite plentiful, and I went out to work. I worked as a cutter in an underwear factory. That was all right. I don't know how long I lived in this small flat with the children, but Margaret, one of the women in Young Austria who was married and lived nearby, asked if I would like to look after her children while she and her husband went on holiday and stay in her flat. I agreed because I thought it would be a change of scene. I had a help, but there were four children aged one, two, three and four. That was quite a job! She had a flat, also in North Kensington, on the top floor of a very big house. This woman help and I took the four small children in two prams to Kensington Gardens every day. That was a *shlep* to go up there and back! Margaret's brother came in the evening and helped put the children to bed and bath them.

We became very friendly and Henry eventually became my second husband.

While I was still living in this small flat my first husband came to visit the children. He took them out over the weekend and he treated them to taxi rides and bought them expensive toys, and of course, when he brought them back I had great trouble settling them down. 'I want to ride in a taxi, not go on a bus like ordinary people!' It usually took the whole week, and then it was the weekend again and he came round. We had a great many rows and eventually I told him to get out, I didn't want any more of it. That was basically the end. Ingrid, my elder daughter, was then about four and a half.

Occasionally he gave me some money for the children, but it wasn't really worth all the hassle. I suppose I was very hard up and I took whatever money I could, to help. Finally after he became violent, I divorced him and I made it a stipulation that I didn't want any money from him and I didn't want him to come and see the children and disrupt their lives. So they never saw their father again.

I remarried in 1953. Ingrid was seven and Sylvia was five and a half. It wasn't very easy. The children were at school at that time and I worked, because I felt I had to contribute something to their upkeep. Henry didn't earn a great deal of money and it was very difficult to expect him to provide for somebody else's children.

I have always worked – except when I had the youngest – mostly in the rag trade. We still lived in North Kensington, but when she was born in 1958, the flat was getting a bit cramped and we bought a house in Ealing. My mother put up the money for the deposit. There was a small flat at the top which she occupied and we had the rest of the house. My mother was still working, also in the dressmaking trade. She retired when she was 60.

When the youngest started school I went out part-time. I had a job as a shop assistant for a few years – D. H. Evans, which was all right. I had to give that up because I had phlebitis, a sort of inflammation of the veins. Then I had a job in a laboratory, testing various materials. I remember asking for a wage increase and they offered me thrupence, the old thrupence more an hour, and I was very indignant at that. It was quite a small firm and I said it was an absolute insult. I had an interview with the managing director there, and I said that it would be the same if they offered him 1s an hour, and I couldn't accept thrupence. We also had to sign in and out in a book. For some reason they installed a time clock for clocking in and out. I usually spent the whole day there from when I arrived at nine till I left at three, and they demanded that at lunchtime we should clock out and in. I said, 'There's no point, I stay on the premises,' and they said, Yes, I had to do this. I wanted a logical explanation why and they wouldn't give me one. They gave me an ultimatum. If I didn't clock out and in I would get the sack, and being stubborn, I got the sack! They felt I was a trouble-maker anyway.

I found a job in a laboratory attached to a paint factory which wasn't really very good. It was quality control, but it wasn't as varied and as interesting as the last job. Then they were taken over by a much larger concern and we were either made redundant or offered a job in another factory, making car paints. The working conditions were so appalling, I only stayed there three months, and nearly had a nervous breakdown. It was *dreadful*, quite apart from the awful smell of the place.

I was then off for about three months. By that time I'd had enough of being at home and I eventually got offered a job in a school laboratory. So I said yes, because it would be very suitable because of the school holidays. At this school I worked, I think, four years. It was a very rarefied atmosphere being in a private school, and there were terrible tensions in the staff-room always, and these petty jealousies – 'My subject is more important than your subject,' that kind of thing.

I was there as a lab technician: it was very hierarchical, particu-larly the science department, where I worked. The head of the department was very dictatorial and she often addressed me in front of the children in a way I didn't like at all. It was really because of her that I left. I couldn't tolerate her attitude.

I transferred to the state school system but I was just a number on the payroll. I was just nobody, and nobody really cared whether I came or went. It was very unsatisfactory. And after eight years I resigned, because I got very fed up with the job. I suddenly decided that I wanted to do cooking, and I started cooking. And I've got my own business.

I really sublimated my feelings all along, all the time that I was married, and I always felt that if something went wrong it was my fault, rather than the fault of us both. It took me quite a long time to realise that what I took to be my fault were Henry's projections of his own shortcomings on to me. I was really this conventional housewife, keeping a woman's place and all this kind of rubbish, until the youngest was 17, I think. Yes, when I was 50, I realised that I'd had enough and that I had to assert myself, that I didn't want to be a doormat any more. I packed my bags and walked out. It wasn't quite as simple as that. I had to look for somewhere to live, and Henry couldn't understand why I was leaving, although I tried to explain to him on a number of occasions.

It came to a head over a bath which the neighbours had thrown out into the garden and which I wanted to use as a pond or a flower tub or something, and I asked Henry to negotiate for me to acquire this bath. He didn't for quite a number of weeks, and finally somebody came and took the bath away and I was just hysterical about it. I said, 'That's it, I've just had enough.' He to this day thinks that it was because of this bath that I walked out, which is, of course, quite ridiculous! It was all the things in the whole marriage which accumulated, which we couldn't communicate to each other about, it was just the end of the marriage. I eventually found some accommodation and moved out, and Henry subsequently said that he could understand if I'd gone off with another man, but he couldn't understand that I left him just because of this bath! Quite absurd!

I lived on my own for about two years, and I then met a man, John, whom I subsequently lived with for a couple of years, at his flat. I then bought this house where I now live and he moved in with me, but the relationship then changed, because I think he felt he wasn't in control somehow. After some time his ex-wife dumped his youngest son, who was then 16, on us, which made life very difficult, because he was a very difficult boy. He got involved with the police because he was caught stealing cars and driving them away. He had odd jobs, none of which he could keep. He got involved in fights in pubs, ringing up at midnight or after to come and fetch him or whatever, and after some months I said I couldn't cope with this any more and David would have to leave. I wanted him out in three months time, which rather shocked his father, but I said this was it. The following day, after having told John this, the police came – it was a Sunday morning – and asked if David Smith lived here, so I said, 'Yes,' and I called his father. They wanted to arrest David for receiving stolen goods, and I was very glad that I had said that I wanted him out before all this came up. He was sent to a remand centre, where he was for a month, and one of the conditions for his release was that he would be with his father and his father would supervise and look after him, so that was really a good way for me to end the relationship altogether, because I think it was coming to an end anyway. I've been alone since then and I've really quite enjoyed living on my own without the hassle of living with somebody and having to cook meals at certain times and so on.

Since my daughter told me she was a lesbian I have looked at women in a different way and am aware of women's attitudes and outlooks much more. I wasn't shocked, not at all. I think through her I have become much more of a feminist than I was before. I've always been a socialist and it's easier to become a feminist through having been, or being, a socialist.

My business now is doing something creative, whereas all the jobs I had up to then were just dead end and nothing could come out of them. I feel that cooking is a creative thing to do. I have, I think probably all my life, searched for some outlet where I could find satisfaction.

NOTES

1. An anti-Semitic weekly founded by Julius Streicher, published between 1923 and 1945. Its 'vulgarity' apparently even offended the sensitivities of some Nazi leaders, who tried to suppress it.
2. Dachau, near Munich, was the first concentration camp set up

by the Nazis in 1933, before the first session of the Reichstag (parliament) began after the Nazis came to power. It was to detain communists and other 'agitators'.

3. Jewish refugees found entry visas to America and to the United Kingdom difficult to obtain. Financial guarantees had to be obtained from relatives or sponsors, if the refugee did not have ample means of support. The Nazis increasingly made greater financial demands on Jews trying to leave, which made it harder for them to satisfy entry requirements. For both women and men, a domestic permit was the easiest to obtain. This was an option since the employer offered board and lodging. Coming to train as a nurse was another possibility open to refugees.

4. Amongst the ancient restrictions and prohibitions revived by the Nazis was the yellow distinguishing mark; in the case of the Third Reich, a star emblazoned with the word Jew.

5. The category 'enemy alien' included refugees from Nazi persecution who were also seen as a possible threat to national security.

6. A type of steam press used in the clothing trade.

MAYA NAGY
No Heroes, No Martyrs

Maya was born in a small town in western Hungary in 1919. Her parents were divorced when she was three, and she and her mother went to live with her maternal grandparents.

Hungary has an ancient Jewish community and Maya's family had lived in Hungary for as far back as they could remember. As a child, though, growing up in a small town, Maya never felt that she belonged. She was Jewish, and yet not part of an orthodox community in a town whose Jews were predominantly so. She was also growing up in an increasingly anti-Semitic country. In the year of her birth, pogroms killed 3,000 Jews in Hungary, following the defeat of the brief communist regime in which some Jews had been involved. The new right-wing regime established anti-Semitic legislation, barely 50 years after Jews had first achieved full civic and political equality under the old Austro-Hungarian Empire.

By the time Maya left school, anti-Semitism had intensified under the influence of German National Socialism. Anti-Jewish laws prevented her from going to university and from working. These laws, which also expropriated Jewish property, deprived a quarter of a million Jews of their livelihood.

As allies of the Nazis, Hungary gained territory from the partition of Czechoslovakia and joined Germany in the invasion of Russia in 1941. By the middle of that year, the combination of territorial expansion and more radical 'racial' definitions of who was Jewish – for example, those baptised as Christians – meant that at least 850,000 people in Greater Hungary suffered extreme discrimination.

The failure of the Hungarian government to carry out mass deportations of Jews, and thus to contribute to the 'Final Solution', was one of the reasons why Germany invaded Hungary in 1944. Following the invasion, the most brutal anti-Jewish measures were enacted, the impact of which Maya recalls in her interview – wearing the yellow star, ghettoisation and deportation to concentration camp.

Maya was taken to Auschwitz. She was evacuated from the camp in the months before it was finally liquidated and survived the forced marches that followed. She was one of about 1,000 Jewish women freed into the hands of the Red Cross. 70 per cent (450,000) of the Jewish population of Greater Hungary were murdered or died during the German occupation.

Maya has rebuilt her life twice – once after the war and again when she came to this country in the late fifties as a refugee. Her interview shows that her ability to work lovingly with others, particularly children, survived her own terrible experiences. Her personal philosophy has been not one of acceptance but of striving to come to terms: 'I've learned in this not very easy life that . . . if one has had many bad experiences, one can't just say, "I wish I hadn't had that", because it adds up to "I wish I hadn't had my life." '

My grandfather owned a little manufacturing plant – we called it a factory, but the Hungarians overstate everything! It was part of the house, but it didn't take up a lot of space. It was a very simple affair. One man could do the more physical side of it and my grandfather, and later my mother, did the business part.

My mother's background was not very religious. The main holidays were respected, but my grandfather used to go to the synagogue on Saturdays, I think, more for company and community life than for any religious feeling. But it was a Jewish home, in the sense that there was no question of our having other aspirations.

My father came from a very typical, Jewish Hungarian village background.[1] Farming, a small shop, a small pub. There were a lot of children – I can't remember how many aunts and uncles. They weren't more traditional, religiously, but it was much more of a peasant life. They were just different from everybody else in the village due to their Jewishness. They were the only Jews there. My father became a doctor and one uncle became an engineer, but all the others remained villagers.

156

My parents had got married in 1913 and then came the war, and my father was away in Russia in captivity. I was born in 1919 after he came back, and they were divorced in '22. Divorce *did* happen, but it was an event with social implications and the fate of a divorced woman in a small town wasn't easy. My mother felt very, very unhappy because of it. Although I must have been very small, I actually remember how unhappy she was and how much she suffered because of the Jewish ritual of divorce.[2] I have vague, really fleeting memories about her anxiety and humiliation. You see, because the community was orthodox, and she was not, the whole thing must have been a great imposition on her. That my mother suffered, I *do* remember. If she wanted a Jewish divorce, it had to be performed by the orthodox rabbi; there wasn't another one. She had a normal legal divorce, which was probably very unpleasant too. My own memories of her may be coloured by my own anxiety about what was happening among the adults.

I saw my father very rarely after that. There was hostility between my grandmother and my father. My mother played a passive role, but my grandmother was very militant and hostile in the divorce and forbade my father to see me. When he did see me, they were snatched opportunities and they were very traumatic for me, always.

I went to Jewish elementary school from the age of six to 10. All Jewish children, whatever background they came from, went there. It wasn't the custom to go to a Christian school; even for Jewish children who were extremely assimilated, who tried to mix with the gentiles, there was no question of it. I can remember only two very rich families who just didn't send their children to school at all, but gave them private education at home. I was a very unhappy child and I was anxious at that school. The classes were enormous, 60 or more children. So the whole atmosphere was very unpleasant. I have memories of urine-smelling corridors, and the anxiety about what would happen if I were asked and I didn't know the answer. But I don't think it was a worse school than any other school with large classes during those years. I got all my Jewish education at school. We had lessons from the Bible and Jewish history. I was taught Hebrew, which I found very difficult; we weren't required to understand what we were reading.

The Jewish community was pretty large; enough to fill a large,

157

architecturally beautiful synagogue. Our social life was conducted with the Jews who were similar to us – assimilated Jews, but Jews who did *not* pretend not to be Jews. It was typical of Hungary that, for instance, a manager running a large estate for some aristocratic, rich Jew would very often be Jewish, but *almost* denying his Jewish identity as he was much more a part of this Hungarian gentry life. They certainly dressed more like them – breeches with riding crops and so on. They assimilated in many ways, much more than the town Jews. These were the ones whose children did *not* go to the Jewish elementary school. They lived a sort of double life.

I didn't have any contact with non-Jewish children for the first four years of my school life. But then from 10 to 18 I was 'sent' – I would never have chosen to go there – to a Protestant boys' grammar school, where again there were 50-odd people in a classroom – except that I was the only girl! You see, my mother, having divorced, was not able to settle down again in life. She had bad luck with another marriage: my stepfather, a lovely man, died after about six weeks. Then there were efforts, afterwards, to get married, but it was increasingly difficult.

So she felt very strongly that I should be independent, and not someone who was waiting to be saved from being a divorced woman and so was at the mercy of the kind of marriage she made. She was a suffering person, not a feminist in the modern sense of the word, but maybe deep down that's what it amounts to, because I have memories of my mother almost conditioning me, doing it with such regularity and such force, saying that you must not be at the mercy of a man – which happens to you because of marriage. You must be an independent person. In fact, all she would have liked for herself was to get married to someone again, even for the third time. But because of her own experiences and her own bad luck as a woman in those times, she was quite determined that I get a grammar school education.

There was no girls' grammar school in that small town, and there was no question about boarding school – I don't know whether they existed at all for girls at grammar school level. It was a very cruel thing, which my mother did unwittingly, sending me to that school. It accepted girls only on condition that they were top of the class, so that the teachers need make no effort to educate them. I didn't have to be *top* of the class, but I had to reach a certain standard in *every* subject. So there was no question of me relaxing in those subjects which I found very difficult, like science and mathematics. I was very good naturally at languages and Hungarian literature and other similar subjects, history too. But maths and science, as is so often the case with anxious children, were very, very difficult for me, *excruciating*. How I did it I don't know, because I don't know anything about these subjects, and I probably forgot everything the moment I left school.

By the time we left school there were three girls, and the boys' numbers had diminished somewhat. There were about 50 of school-leaving age. But the really traumatic thing was entering a class of at least 50 boys when I was 10½. Recently one of them, who is now a grandfather in Budapest, visited me here. He said, 'We were all in love with you.' Well, I didn't realise that. I did feel that some were very unkind, very aggressive and hostile. Not physically so – that wouldn't have been tolerated by the teachers. They were very physically aggressive to each other, and quite violent during playtime.

I wasn't the only Jewish child in the class; there were Jewish boys. One was one of those who tried to be as little Jewish as possible. Another was a jovial Jewish boy of the kind of village Jewish, small-shopkeeper background who was much more accepted by the others then the Jewish boys of my type of background, because he was rough and rather vulgar and he allowed himself to be teased and be told that, 'You are just a bloody Jew.' He laughed at it. I think he participated in their sexual adventures and so he was more easily accepted, although never quite one of them.

Hungary was an anti-Semitic country. It was increasingly so as we were growing up. I entered that Protestant grammar school in '31, and, of course, Hitler was already on the scene then. And increasingly the whole school became *very* anti-Semitic, and some of the teachers too. Boys went to Germany on holiday to learn German and they also learned Nazism. It was very, very much on the increase, and it was very strong when I left that school in '38.

For instance, there was a big conflict. There was a school-leaving ceremony which was traditional – this was a very old school,

159

it was 400 years old at the time when I was there. It was a very bad school, but a very elite one. There was a tradition that three leavers walk slowly, arm in arm, singing a song about the old student leaving the *alma mater*. It was rooted in German student ceremonies.[3] The idea was that the three girls – they were all Jewish – should walk arm in arm. The anti-Semitic majority wanted the three Jewish girls to be separated from the rest. One boy, who was my friend, objected to that. He was very different from the others; not in *every* sense, but he wasn't anti-Semitic. And he said, 'No, each girl must be joined by two of us, and lead the whole procession.' It was a nice idea, but he had to fight for it. In the end I became ill. I was relieved that I was home. Anyway, that was the culmination of an anti-Semitic wave in that group.

The teachers were anti-Semitic, but they did not become National Socialists, apart from one member of the staff who later became a member of the extreme fascist party.[4] But there was a change in their behaviour as teachers towards us three Jewish girls. I think there was some toughening in their behaviour towards the Jewish boys, and some remarks made, trying to humiliate them.

I don't know what these teachers were like in the staff room, but in the community they did not stand up against the move towards Nazism which was taking place at the time. There were no heroes of this kind. Later on, when Hungary was already under German occupation and we had to wear the yellow star, this one particular boy, my classmate, came and visited me – which was not on in those days – and asked me when I had last been out for a walk. I said, 'How do you think I would feel going out for a walk with this yellow star burning on my back?' He said, 'Come on!', took my arm and took me out. That's the only memory I have of this kind of courageous behaviour. But my memory of everybody really cooperating with the German occupation is not typical of everybody else's, because it was a very anti-Semitic small town, where everybody knew everybody else and the pressures to conform were very strong. My present husband's memory of the German occupation is different. He survived it, he wasn't deported because he was in Budapest, and there people had more courage to help Jews. Not everybody did so, of course. There were very few – very, very few. But there *were* people, whereas in my home town, where

I experienced the occupation, nobody was saved by a gentile person. Nobody, not one member of that Jewish community was saved in this way.

I don't remember a time when I wasn't aware of there being anti-Semitism and me being Jewish. I can't say that I always felt it as a threat. The threat element came into it when the political situation deteriorated. But rejection, yes. I wished I hadn't been born Jewish. When I was small I had very religious spells. I reacted to my elementary school's religious education by becoming very religious and encouraging my grandfather to be more so, in the way that children want their parents to live up to their ideals. But that was a small spell. After I got into the Protestant school I wished I wasn't Jewish, and I studied the New Testament and felt deep down that I was Christian. During adolescence I had this period of trying spiritually to detach myself from my Jewish background and be more like the other community I – well, I can't even say 'belonged to', because typical of the whole experience of growing up under those circumstances is a sense of *not* belonging.

When I was a young child, I didn't belong, because the majority of children came from religious homes. My mother didn't wear a wig,[5] and their mothers did. Then later on I didn't belong on more than one account. I was a girl in a boys' school, and whatever contact there was immediately became of a very precocious sexual nature, a constant excited flirtation. It was a very unhealthy atmosphere. Then, after a while, with this spell of reading the New Testament and trying to be a Christian, I really rejected the religious education which we did get once a week. I rejected it outright in the first years of my adolescence and later on just ignored it, because by then I was trying much more to be agnostic and started to be influenced by socialist ideas.

After I left school I would have liked to have gone to university, but by then it was not possible for a Jewish girl or boy to go. We were not admitted. So I went to Budapest. I knew I wasn't going to stay at home. I did *all kinds* of things. I went into an office for a while, but I was dismissed soon because of the 'Jewish law', a general label for restrictions on employing Jews and Jews taking certain jobs.[6] It affected me almost immediately. Then afterwards

I did all kinds of courses, whatever I could, and I also gave lessons, and lived a busy life just trying to keep myself in Budapest. I did a course in hospital nursing for children. It had a content of child psychology, which turned me on. That was my first contact with this line. By then, of course, you were also restricted in what courses you could do.

I went back to the small town because I married a young man from there. He was 13 years older than me, and he was the youngest member of my mother's social circle. I married him in 1940, and he was called to do service in a labour camp[7] a few months after we got married. So I never really lived with him for longer than a few weeks, because after that it was very infrequent visits home, or me visiting him in camp. They were Hungarian organisations – the Germans didn't come till '44. All the men who were healthy were taken. In practice, that was almost everybody.

By then I had a job working with children. But I couldn't really bear the small town. Again, I didn't feel that I belonged. I was on friendly terms with the other young women – there were many of my age whose husbands were away in labour camps. But I still never felt at ease, so I ran off as soon as I could to Budapest to be with my real friends.

My husband was not very far away – 50 miles or something like that, until he was sent away to Transylvania, which was already a more serious affair. He was around but the visiting was very limited, especially from the camps; he could come home, maybe every three months or so. It wasn't a continuous marriage at any point. He was in and out – more in than out.

Not for a moment did I think about leaving the country. Isn't that funny? Maybe I was just too limited to think in such terms. People did not try to leave. Not in that small town. The community didn't break up in this way.

The Germans came in on 19 March 1944. I was in Budapest. I went home and in a few days' time we had to wear the yellow star. My husband was away in a work camp. Our flat was occupied. Various people were billeted there, so I had only one little room left. Some of these people were quite nasty. Fascists, a Nazi couple. A Jew wasn't supposed to have so many rooms – we had four or five – and in any case we were soon sent to the ghetto. Each largish town had one and the Jews from the surrounding villages came to it. It didn't go on for very long. Ghettoisation started in June, and I believe that some time in July we were deported.[8]

I had a full-time maid in those days and one of the first rules was that the servants had to leave Jewish employers. So she left, and took some of my things, which she kindly offered to look after, mainly bed linen and things like that. They would have been taken away. She kept them, and later on I found them again. But other things like jewellery, which I gave to someone to look after, were lost. There was always a very good excuse: that the Russians took it;[9] and the Russians did take a lot, an awful lot, so you couldn't check if a particular ring was taken. But so what if my own jewels were missing? Later on, when I came back from the concentration camp, the *whole town* was missing.

It so happened that my mother and grandmother had their own home in the part of town cut off for ghetto purposes. So they did not have to move, and I moved in with them, which was at that moment very good. There was a landlord near by, a wealthy landowner. He suggested that some of the young Jewish women come out of the ghetto to his estate, under paramilitary supervision, and work there. I went because anything was better than being in the ghetto. We just did nothing but strawberry picking. I think we did it 10 hours a day or something like that. It was extremely exhausting; I mean, almost killing. You are just broken, broken absolutely, from this bending. We did it for a month, and suddenly we were taken back, and the deportation procedures started.[10]

I have few memories of this time. There was the frustration of the helplessness. You did not *know* what was going to happen next. There was one woman there – I knew her very well, a close friend – who had already come away from Vienna, away from all that. She committed suicide. We should have known *then* what was going to happen, because she *knew* what the next step would be. There were a few suicides. One childless couple. But not in the ghetto itself; it happened when we were taken out.

The ghetto was terribly tense, because we never knew what the next step would be. People who had been on *bad* terms suddenly became on very good terms. For instance, a friend of my mother who had not spoken to her own brother because she disliked her sister-in-law suddenly spent most of her time with her. Middle-aged men who had not been put in work camp because they were the wrong age, any prominent citizens, were interned. So the 'brains' of the ghetto, in a sense, were taken out. The young men were in work camps and this middle-aged elite of the community was interned. There were really a lot more women than men in the ghetto. Old people, women, children. It was very crowded, of course; several families living in one flat. So there was the tenseness due to the overcrowding. The *whole* Jewish community was there. I had lots and lots of cousins whom I had never met before in my life who were also there, because they lived in various villages around.

What I do remember is the awfulness of the various steps before deportation. From the ghetto we were moved to a factory. That was the first step. A brick-manufacturing plant, because that had a large open space in it – no walls, but sheds, where they kept the bricks. By then, in the brick factory, we already had to sleep on straw sacks. A lot of old people got sick. It was pretty awful.

Before they put us into the waggons, they took us to the open swimming pool. The town had a very nice one. And we spent . . . well, what is a night, what is a day? It didn't matter. Whatever they wanted to do with us didn't finish by the time it was night, so it went on. People just *collapsed* with exhaustion. Already it was part of breaking people, I suppose. The object of *that* exercise was that there were cabins around the swimming pool, and people were sent into the cabins individually and their bodies were examined for jewellery. Women's bodies were examined *inside*. In case you took your jewellery in your body, you see, to the concentration camp. Women searched us. One or two of them were local midwives.

I do remember one thing. Some sort of paramilitary organisation helped with the deportation. One of them was a relative of mine, whose mother was Christian and his father a Jew. A distant cousin, whom we never met, living also in one of the villages. He came up to me in this uniform and said, 'They have now taken everything from you except your wedding ring. But I know that they are going to take that too when you are put on the train, so why don't you give it to me?' I took it off and *threw* it away somewhere, and said to him, 'Go on, go after it. Look for it.'

That sort of thing also happened before I went to the ghetto. We had to leave everything in our flat. A lady came up, the widow of a physician, and said, 'I just came to see how you are. Look, they are taking all these things away from you. Why don't you give them to us?' So I think I picked up some sort of cleaning equipment, a broom or a pan. 'Goodbye!' But not the silver, not the other things. It didn't matter really. I could have given them to her. Probably if this would, heaven help me, happen now, I would say, 'Well, take what you like.' But I couldn't then. I was furious, and I couldn't think so clearly. 'Yes, she is right after all. This is all going to be taken away by the Germans. Why shouldn't she get it?' That would have been too rational!

So then we were taken to the trains and put into trucks. There was this awful trek. I was with my mother and grandmother. We were crowded, so crowded. It was a tragedy. My grandmother, who was a source of food and goodies all her life, took out from somewhere some sort of cold drinking-chocolate. I think it was just plain cocoa, with a little bit of cold water poured over it. Heavenly! Heavenly! I don't know how she managed it. It was in a glass jar. I mean, they had *really* taken away everything from us; we didn't have any luggage. Where she got it from I don't know. Somewhere; what the midwife couldn't take away from her.

I think the journey took about a week. It was terrible because there was no question of lying down. People just leant over each other. There was a good deal of fighting. Sometimes they stopped for hours, just nowhere, and again that was pretty awful, because we didn't know where we were or whether we had arrived or not. That's horrible, that sort of thing. Things *happen* to you, you are *completely* out of control. I didn't know where we were going. I didn't know, when I arrived, where I was. They said all kinds of things to us which were lies. They said we were going to Czechoslovakia, to work in factories. I am quite sure that very little was known by many ranks. The lower you went, I felt, the more genuinely they didn't know where we were going. This didn't mean that the German SS, the top ranks, didn't know what they were involved in. Of course, whatever they said to *us* was a complete lie.

165

I just felt that. It was very carefully done. They did not have to lie – it was for no real reason. They could have said that we were going to Poland to work in a factory, but no, they said, 'We are taking you to Czechoslovakia.'

The *complete* helplessness of it comes back to me ... of things being *done* to you and having absolutely no control over them. And, of course, physical suffering; enormous physical suffering. The tremendous shock of the experience.

After we arrived – there – we were separated. My grandmother, who was old, was taken in one direction and my mother and I were taken in the other. Everybody knows the name of that chap Mengele,[11] who did this job, who separated my grandmother from us, and all the old people. Then we were taken to a building. Part of it was a bath – showers – and part of it was a crematorium they had built there. There they stripped us, completely, took everything away from us. We didn't have much left, but people had a little bundle on their back or in their hands, a basket or handbag, something like that. They stripped us completely and they shaved our hair and gave us the striped clothes we wore in Auschwitz.

For me the last straw was when they took my toothbrush. I just suddenly felt – well, it was a dangerous moment for the loss of self, of identity. Not to possess a toothbrush. That was the first possession I got back when I was liberated! They diminished a person. These toothbrushes taken away – I'm sure they didn't *need* them. It was all part of this process of dehumanisation. I smoked in those days, and I remember I asked for a cigarette. One of the humiliating things there was that the women's showers were supervised by men, inmates – Polish Jews, German Jews – who had got some sort of job. It didn't mean that they were secure to survive, but they had a few more privileges. Anyway, I asked this man for a cigarette, and I was standing there naked. I was young and, I suppose, good-looking, and he looked at me. They were slightly better fed, those people, and he still had in his eyes something ... later on that disappeared completely, because men were with men and the women were with women. That sort of look disappeared – or I didn't notice it any more. He said, 'Get on, that's not what you need here.' He was very decent. All I can remember really is that he looked at me, standing there, up and down, without hair and naked. But – I didn't really need a cigarette any longer.

When we first got off the trains, what happened was mostly being pushed. My grandmother was pushed. She was moving out and someone pushed her in *this* direction and my mother hung on to me and we were pushed in *that* direction. We just waited in crowds, speculating, and saying, 'Where are we? When are we going to meet the others again?' And somebody said, 'Oh, this separation is just for office reasons.' *Somebody* always said something, but never was anything known. We didn't know where we were.

I realised that I was in a concentration camp, but not in a death camp; I didn't even know its name. Mind you, this may not be typical. Probably when the German Jews arrived there, earlier, it wasn't quite so smoothly organised. Then again, I may have been in an extremely shocked state. I didn't stop *thinking* at all, there isn't any question of something happening to my mind, but the emotional shock must have been very great.

Anyway, that's what happened really. And it is complicated when you have your mother with you. The fear and the guilt and . . . she was young, much younger than I am now. She was very pretty, and she held on to my coat. She was allowed to stay with me. She looked much younger than her age. She held on to me, rather than to her own mother, perhaps sensing – well, I don't know. Obviously she was a mother before she was a child. At that moment, when the three of us were separated, she could have been pushed in the *other* direction, in which case she would have been gassed within a few days or hours. I don't know how soon my grandmother was gassed. But my mother clung to me, and she got over *that* part. Sooner or later other women happened to meet inmates who told them something about where we were, but I didn't know what it meant. Maybe at a certain time I knew I was in Auschwitz, but I didn't know that Auschwitz was *Auschwitz*, I didn't know that it was a mass extermination camp. I knew it was terrible, but I didn't know . . .

After we had been stripped, we were sent to these barracks. There were lots of identical ones. That was awful. People were crowded into two tiers, but there were no mattresses; it was just bare wood. I cannot remember going to sleep until it was all over – I must have slept, because you can't survive for almost a whole year without sleeping – but I cannot. It was one of those peculiar things; when I got out, I could not remember ever sleeping. I must have slept only minutes or moments, or so restlessly that I did not have a memory of escaping into sleep. It was one of those awful things, for *me*, but some people slept deeply, and snored. I never have been a very good sleeper. For me it was an additional difficulty; *there*, under the worst possible circumstances, I had a lot of trouble sleeping. Neither my mother nor I could. This piece of wood we lay on was the length of a human being – say, six-foot square: I don't know *how* many people were piled up there, but an awful lot. Thinking back on it, I think, comfortably – if you can talk about comfortably, without rugs and without pillows and without mattresses, just on wood – maybe three people would have been able to lie down. There were *at least* 12 people on top of each other.

During the days, for hours and hours and hours, we had to stand for the roll call – they called it by the German word '*appel*'. It was quite an infernal idea, the way they worked it out. It is very difficult to evoke verbally. Thousands and thousands of women standing in tight rows for five, six, or seven hours, collapsing on top of each other, and being kicked and then beaten until they stood up again. That was terrible. It was one of the means of tormenting people. Every day started in the dark, and we stood there and stood there and stood there in the dark and waited until they had come to the end. I don't really know whether they actually counted us or not.

Some friends of mine from home were also in the barrack, in a different cubicle, and sometimes we got together and we talked about food and how we would make it. For hours and hours we'd say, 'This is how I used to do it, but I wouldn't now, I would do it like this,' and then people invented recipes, and then someone would say, 'There is somebody at the end of the barrack who is a *marvellous* cook.'

Why did women stop having periods, immediately? Malnutrition happened to you over a period of time, but you arrived in Auschwitz on Wednesday and straight away it happened. I think all women

168

stopped; I certainly stopped immediately. I was a healthy young woman. I had been working on the land and had not as good food as before, but you can't be *that* malnourished so soon; it would come much later. There were stories about something they put into the food which stopped it, as part of this dehumanisation.

Two memories I have from that time. On one occasion, fairly early on, a German stepped on my toes – we had no shoes, of course. Well, this can be very painful, and a German boot with a German inside it . . . ! I said 'Ouch!' and then I looked at him and said, *'Entschuldigen Sie,'* Excuse me. I knew the excuse was a reflex. If somebody steps on your toe in the underground, even if you are the one who gets hurt, then you say sorry. That was what I was doing. Just for a moment I forgot where I was. He looked at me and hit me on my face. I had asked him to excuse me! (It must have been very early days there!) He looked at me and said, 'I did that because you have such a stupid face, without any expression.' I remember afterwards thinking *there* about what was behind it. It must have been a tremendous reaction to finding out that this woman, whose hair has been shaved, with no shoes on, still had this reflex from civilisation left in her. That was my theory afterwards. The reason I remember it, and I remember very few things, is because I thought about it. I fixed it in memory by thinking and thinking and thinking about it. 'What happened inside this man? To want to hit me?'

The other thing is just how inhuman some people became. The process went very far in those people who had certain privileges and jobs. One of the barracks was just used as a latrine. One of the most humiliating things was that you couldn't go when you needed. You were sent there when you didn't need to go, and couldn't go when you needed to. Interference, intrusion into the most *personal* things in one's life. On one occasion we were sitting there and I suddenly felt that all the mess was splashing up. One of the men in charge was having fun pushing it so that it came up. In my memory this was one of the most awful things that happened to me there, in those few weeks in Auschwitz.

Then my mother and I left Auschwitz.[12] When the Germans were going to take you somewhere, you were just made to stand in the open beforehand; you never knew if you were going to stay there for five, six, seven or eight hours. I have no memory of the circumstances of the journey, but I know that we always travelled in cattle trucks, so we must have on that occasion too. You must realise that we had no coats or anything, just this one striped robe and no underwear.

We found ourselves in Frankfurt;[13] I was told much later that was where we were. In a way it was better there, because the barracks were smaller. There was even a dentist. This was a workforce rather than bodies kept together for one reason or another, the situation in Auschwitz. A workforce, but of the *most* unproductive work possible. I was told by an inmate that we were building or repairing the airport. Whether this is true or not I could never find out, and I never particularly wanted to afterwards. The job consisted of navvying, lifting very heavy grass bricks all day, and carrying them a long distance. I think that most of the time one carried them in one direction and then one carried them back, because nothing ever got built or repaired, as far as I remember. What I do remember is that – though I can't use the word human, because it was not human – barrack life wasn't quite as devastating; no clothes, no heating, autumn coming on, but I have vague memories of my mother actually trying to roast a potato in an open fire – of there *being* fire, some sort of possibility of sitting around; not on chairs, obviously, but not quite the animal life of the Auschwitz camp.

We went on from there. Again there was no preparation, no being told; that was an important factor in the whole thing, that you never knew what was going to happen next. We were transported to Ravensbrueck,[14] also a very notorious place, and by that time there were a lot of very sick people, mainly with typhus. People were also dying simply of malnutrition too. I caught typhus there. Ravensbrueck is a memory for me for this reason. One woke up every morning – it was already late autumn, we probably spent Christmas there – and there were people lying there dead. A little later, by the time you came back from the lavatory, they were piled up in the middle of the room. Sometimes you saw someone from your own town among the heap, or someone you had befriended there. It was always a guess who was going to be in the heap of dead bodies in the morning. If someone looked very sick during the day, one knew that this person would be among the heap the next morning.

My mother, I don't know how, got a piece of cotton and a needle, and somehow she found little pieces of cloth, probably from sacks, and she put together a patchwork little blazer for me against the cold. Ravensbrueck is near the sea and it was very cold. A very interesting, beautiful landscape there, in a strange way. It was there that I felt, spending hours in this landscape, that it would never be possible to put this experience into any form of art, except through music perhaps, because no words are needed there. I thought that good art is made up of some human experience that is transformed by imagination, but this will not be part of the human experience and no one will be able to imagine that this could happen in the twentieth century. I remember standing around and being aware of beauty under these circumstances.

The Russians were nearing and we were taken on by train. Probably the Germans didn't know where we were going, because by then they were running away from the liberation forces. So there was a very, very long and terrible journey, which is the most awful part of it all. Partly because it was so long, partly because my mother died during this journey, partly because I was more and more ill, and because of complete and utter hunger. It wasn't a question of not getting enough, or no good things; just nothing, absolutely nothing. I remember people eating toothpaste – you know, officers throw these things away. Not a whole toothpaste, that would have been too good, but the end of one. Everybody was a scavenger. I tried to scratch the salt from the side of the truck. I was trying to feed myself with it.

When the train stopped, everybody was so weak that they fell on top of each other. Those that happened to be at the bottom just simply couldn't get up, because the ones on top of them couldn't. This was also a way of dying. This is how my mother died. I saw her thrown out of the wagon when we next stopped somewhere. That was obviously the *worst* thing. And I didn't really know too whether I had been on the top of the heap. It happened at night, and by the time it was morning there was no way of knowing. These are the kind of things which come up if you are in analysis perhaps – fantasies, fears and anxieties – but they happened, you know.

An attitude to death developed – not to my mother's death, but earlier on, when there were these piles of bodies. Somehow one got detached. I looked for faces and registered someone I knew, but one had very strong defences, or I must have had, because I can't ever remember thinking that *I* might be there one day – and that was a very strong defence. It never occurred to me.

On the journey we were stationary for a very long time, because the war was catching up with us by then. There was nothing to eat any more, so we hung around the officers' messes waiting for potato peel and carrot peel, that sort of thing. I can't remember having carrot, but that would have been really marvellous. Do you know a little bit of the Old Testament? The story of the manna? Well, I discovered what manna meant, because I thought that raw potato was the best possible thing in the world; you couldn't eat anything finer and better. I made up my mind that if I got out of there, I would never ever do anything with potato because it was the most beautiful thing eaten raw. It occurred to me later that I tasted so many things into this raw potato, that manna was anything which tasted heavenly, whatever it was. But raw potato *was* heavenly food; it was marvellous; it was beautiful. I never tasted it again! But don't, of course, for a moment imagine that we had a lot of raw potato.

We only moved at night, and we just sensed that we were nearing the end. They wanted to take us somewhere nearer the Western Front, away from the Russians, but eventually we stopped in Hamburg. There was a fairly large camp there by then, and there was actually a barrack for the sick. I happened to find a girl from my town there who was acting as a nurse. She was no more a nurse than I, but she was one of those adventurous and courageous people who fought for their own lives in ways which were useful for them, because they had a little more to eat, and anyway, just to be able to *do* something was better than just to be one of the masses. She always had leftovers of food, because people were so sick that they could not eat, and I asked if she could please give me some. She said quite honestly, 'I haven't that much left over and I want to give it to those whom it still can help.' She was absolutely right, because if I had not been liberated very soon afterwards, then I would have died there in Hamburg. I don't even feel that she was unreasonable, not at all, but it was April, as late as that, when for the first time it occurred to me, 'I'm actually going to die, there's no question about it.' As late as that.

Then, one day there, something happened. The SS disappeared and we were taken over by ordinary German soldiers. I still had enough mind to realise that it must be a good thing. We were taken by these people to Copenhagen, where the Danish Red Cross took us over. Denmark was *still* occupied. The war ended on 7 May, and this was the end of April really. Right at the end of the war.

There was a woman there in Hamburg who was marvellous. Every Central European Jewish family had poor relatives. We lived in a small town and these poor relations lived in Budapest. Throughout my childhood I'd hear, 'Now you have grown out of this we will send it to Aunt – .' One day she turned up. She had lost contact with her own children by then; it was after my mother died and she started to mother me. She fed me; she went round to find food. But the most important thing that she did was when we were marching to Copenhagen; I kept falling, because I was terribly weak by then. Though she had not strength to *lift* me, she kept pushing me forward with her foot, and that saved my life. The terrible thing was that after the war in Budapest, I was unable to carry on the kind of relationship with her which conveyed what I felt about her and what I owed her, because later all her children became very leading communists and history again interfered with these relationships. But deep down there she lives as this woman who pushed me to freedom and survival with this gentle movement of her foot.

I didn't have the dramatic experience of people who were liberated by the British and the Americans. I belonged to the so-called Bernadotte Project.[15] I was lucky enough to get into this consignment, because it meant that the moment we were in the hands of the Red Cross we were carefully monitored, to make sure that we shouldn't start eating immediately. Thousands of people died who were liberated by the Russians and Americans by being *given* food or storming stores. So I didn't have that tremendous feeling, 'Ah! Now I am free.' But I have a story of my own.

I remember the boat trip from Denmark to Sweden. I *knew* where I was, I knew that there was no more Wehrmacht,[16] there were no soldiers any more; even though I was very ill, I knew that something very good was happening. One thing: almost all the women had little bundles; you'd find a piece of cloth and then put something in it and then you could carry it. A little potato peeling maybe; maybe somebody found a needle – the little treasures. I'm sure my mother had one. The typhus was carried by lice – we all were full of them – and, of course, the first thing that the Red Cross did was to throw away these things. Some women were screaming because they didn't understand, and I remember, though I was weak, saying, 'It's all right, you don't need that. Let them take it.' I just somehow persuaded them to throw the bundles away, into the sea, overboard. That's perhaps the only time I remember that I could be of any help to anybody. I don't remember myself being a source of comfort to anybody throughout this period. I was too run down.

Then comes a story which is, to me, worth a great liberation experience. We were taken to a small town in the south of Sweden, very near Denmark. The Swedes are marvellous when it comes to life-saving: they *descend* there, like efficient angels, and then cope with the situation. They used a school as an emergency hospital. First, I was given a toothbrush – that's why it's so important, because it all started off with one. Civilisation, being liberated, started with being given this toothbrush. Then I remember lying on makeshift straw sacks, our beds, and this relative was near by. I remember feeling very bad, and they called the doctor. It is amazing that I managed to hold out until I was in the hands of a doctor. I think this is absolutely miraculous, as if I somehow wouldn't lie down. Obviously, if the war had lasted two months longer, I would have died. There must have been this element of, 'Just a little bit more, just a little bit more, just a little bit more,' because afterwards, I lost consciousness.

A doctor came and examined me. I just remember looking up at him – I was lying, too weak to move – and saying, 'Please tell me what is wrong with me, because I'm on my own and you can't go to my family and inform them. I must know.' This is my great liberation story. I don't know if you have ever read Thomas Mann: *The Magic Mountain*? I was lying there and I told him that he must tell me what is wrong with me, and then I said, 'I don't want to be a Madame Chauchat.' You see, in the book, they all had TB – the magic mountain is a sanatorium. After that girl from my town told me, 'You are too ill to be given anything,' I developed a fantasy that I had this quickly killing form of TB. I told you that that's when I started to be afraid for my life. That was within a week of liberation, and I had never thought of the possibility of my dying until then. The doctor looked at me for a minute and said, 'You have not got TB.' But I had never mentioned TB, I had just fantasised, and in this exchange there was this feeling that I could communicate at the level where I felt at home at last.

In fact, I had typhus, and with that I lost consciousness for a very long time – at least a week, if not longer. I woke up in a hospital for epidemic diseases. The coming-to was also very traumatic. I saw somebody else in another bed and got up and went to the wash basin, over which there was a mirror, and my face was all black. I had very fair hair, beginning to grow, sort of sticking up, around this black face, as if it had shoe polish on it. I think I started to scream, or the woman must have rung the bell, because in a minute nurses came round and put me back on to the bed and told me I must not get up. Typhus makes your heart so weak that I could have died *there*. This black stuff was against scabies, which you get from dirt. I knew that my whole body was full of scars, caused by scratching and rubbing, and they had treated it with an ointment while I was unconscious.

For me, this liberation probably meant life. I don't want more drama than this! In a human sense it's a great memory for me. I had *trust* from the moment when I didn't see anything to fear from the Red Cross. I felt very happy then, to know that I was in good hands. I arrived in Sweden on 1 May, and the war was still on. If it had gone on, say, till the end of May, I wouldn't have lived, probably. I weighed 28 kilograms [61 lbs].

One day in the hospital they asked me whether I knew anybody in Sweden. I said, 'I only know of a person who is a friend of friends.'

A Hungarian living in Sweden. I said his name was Dr D – , because a doctor, I think, was so important for me in those circumstances. In fact, he was an engineer! So they found the name in the Stockholm directory and I wrote to this man from the hospital. He later showed me this letter, and I got the shivers. Because the lines went completely diagonally, from the top corner and down. No straight lines at all. I said the following thing to him:

> Dear Dr D.
> *I am a friend of Anna and Gertie and if two quantities equal a third then they are equal to each other. Please send me a rubber mattress because my back aches very badly.*

You see, there is a mathematical rule that if two quantities are equal with a third, they are equal with each other. If $a = b$ and $c = b$, then a also $= c$. Because I was so thin, lying was very, very painful. So I wrote to this unknown man and he got the letter and sent me everything I wanted. He got hold of a rubber mattress somehow. What you want when you are landed in a hospital after all *that* is – a rubber mattress! I was lying there and I thought if I could have chicken soup and a rubber mattress, these things would be heaven! I also asked him to send me the same books which I had been reading just before we were taken, and I started to build up a little side table next to the bed of my new belongings. That was very important, picking up life by having belongings. He sent me a little silver candle holder, all kinds of small things – a piece of Hungarian embroidery. My new bundle started to take shape.

After hospital, probably about six weeks, they sent me to a convalescent home, and I couldn't stand it any longer. I couldn't stand the mass of people, knowing that I was living in a civilised country where people had rooms of their own and I still had to sleep in a dormitory. I needed the quiet of my own room for sleeping. By that time sleep was such an urgent thing that I could not stand it any longer. And I just ran away.

I went to Stockholm and through my friend I found some very primitive lodgings. That friendship started me off making friends with other people, eventually finding some decent accommodation, and a very rewarding job. It was trying to find relatives scattered

around the world for young displaced persons. We had very important work to do at that time, trying to make these contacts so that
some long-forgotten uncle somewhere in South America would
know that there was an orphaned child from Eastern Europe
searching for him, who would like to join him, or just know that
there was a member of the family alive and concerned somewhere.

After a while my job reached its limits. If people didn't respond
to requests for contact within three or four months, then they
didn't exist – or didn't want to – so the importance of the job
decreased. Increasingly, I was working directly with the refugees,
carrying on very interesting detective work and correspondence,
working with people. I suppose it was a sort of therapeutic element
in my life. Through this work I found out that there were schools
for young displaced persons whose mother tongue was Hungarian,
or who came from parts of Eastern Europe where Hungarian was
also spoken. I wanted to work directly with them.

These were children who were left alone in this world, who were
around puberty when they were taken to concentration camps, and
their family did not survive. They were completely alone, except
for some who knew they were going to relatives abroad later on.
Most of them thought of going back to Hungary, and I know that
quite a few of them did, and made their life and careers there.
Some went to Israel.

I was found a job in a school not too far away and so I did
not have to leave new precious friendships, which were obviously
important to starting a new life. There were 30 adolescents between
15 and 18. Before I arrived this group had been camping out in a
disused Swedish castle somewhere, and they really became the
menace of the whole area, because their behaviour was so hostile
and rebellious and very disturbed. I never saw them at that stage,
but I had heard about it when I was appointed. There were
rumours, too that they were really like savages. People who went
there, visiting lecturers and social workers who were interested in
refugee problems, were quite shocked by the completely rejecting
and aggressively regressed and hostile behaviour of these children.
Then they were moved to this school, where I joined them. I was
expecting difficulties. I had a very hostile reception by approxi-
mately half of them, telling me in no uncertain terms to go back

where I came from, even if it was Hell itself – not just with menacing words but also brandishing all kinds of sticks and other things.

For a few days I think I was alone with the group, apart from the caretakers. It was a very difficult start, but at the same time extremely fascinating. I told them that I was appointed to teach, but of course they weren't interested in anything that I could offer. When I looked around I could see that although these were 15- to 18-year-olds, they were like very young children. Their emotional outbursts were full of testing and provoking. The way they behaved was very disturbing. They wanted it to be and I realised it, and I had to be very calm and controlled.

I knew that they had been through dreadful experiences, dreadful enough for grown-up men, let alone for young adolescents, and I felt that they were terribly suspicious of the *whole* adult world, because, after all, they had been let down by adults *generally*, not just Nazis. They were very young people when they got into these terrible circumstances, and I felt that their suspicion and hostility had generalised on to the whole adult world, including me. They really *were* orphans, literally – and emotionally very much so. Although there was all the threatening and hostility and rejecting, it was quite clear that what they needed was caring, and one just had to get to the point where this was accepted.

I was liberated in May and I began this work in the autumn of 1945. I didn't give a thought to it at the time, but looking back on it, I'm amazed that I could. I think it showed that I was left in one piece after my own experience. You see, the one thing that bothered me all the time was that I hadn't done anything against the Nazis. I just *allowed* them to do things to me and to my family. I did not participate in active resistance, which in Hungary was very, very weak anyway; and I was living in the provinces, which was more difficult than in the capital. But I could have done something against it, in a passive way. For instance, to flee, even if I did not become a resistance fighter, which I'm *completely* unsuitable for. But I just couldn't go underground, somehow. That would have been possible in Budapest – we know people who did it. But I just *allowed* them to trample on me and on my family, and so I felt all the time that no way was I a hero just because I had survived.

That was one of the things that I think I managed to get through to these children. They had no right to live the rest of their lives using as capital: 'I have suffered so much.' I think this was one of the most important things that was somehow conveyed, and I spent quite a lot of time on this. I think that this attitude played an important part in the first breakthrough in their behaviour: 'Look, you are no heroes, no martyrs at all. Something terrible happened to you as a result of terrible things happening in the world, but the heroes are the ones who fought against it. We didn't fight. We're not martyrs. We just happened to be there.' Somehow this got us together.

There was no open discussion of what had happened to them. I think I would do something of this kind nowadays, but I was very young and inexperienced myself then. But I did do something which I think helped, in this direction. You know I was appointed there as a teacher? But, of course, I just had to choose the things which I felt able to teach, rather than a desirable, structured cur- riculum. So I picked things like English and Hungarian language and literature. Poetry played a large part. One could tap uncon- scious processes and discuss, and quite a lot came out about parents, feeling abandoned and so on. I taught a bit of history too. I was very pleased when I managed to set up German lessons – part of this philosophy that we are not here to revenge but to participate in some sort of building-up of a civilised world. Every- body attended them, which was very interesting.

But the thing that I'm trying to comment on was child develop- ment. That was something I could teach. I realised very soon that it worked as a two-tier thing: they participated in it as grown-ups learning something about future roles, but they were also very much involved in what came out about the nature of childhood and feeling in childhood. That was an area where all kinds of things could be – I put this between inverted commas – 'worked through', because we never spoke about the way they had been treated individually. Not that it was taboo. Maybe there was an unspelt-out agreement. I certainly did not initiate any discussion, but I referred to it in certain ways. For instance, nothing happened that is not built into human nature, and only the circumstances were such that can bring out that sort of thing and must not be such again. When you discuss children, their very strong feelings of all kinds, it's possible to talk about what gets stirred up under certain circumstances. I think the therapeutic element in that set-up was that there was a person there who came from the same place, i.e. Hell, but said, 'Come, come', somehow.

There was some sort of normalisation too. They were adolescents, after all, so on sexual, social and moral issues they came in at their own level. But on another level in these child development classes, one could go a bit further. When you discussed mother-child relationships, obviously feelings were jolted about their murdered mothers; all kinds of things came up which I found it difficult to cope with. Looking back on it, I think I just fought my way gradually through this, though, of course, I thought a lot about the double function of these classes. It was also a practical matter, because I had to teach what I could do. But I knew it was important.

I got a lot of support from the Swedish people who were responsible for the establishment, but I did all the actual work. I think I was able to bear it because I was young, and I had this philosophy which I had to work out: the fact that I'd been there and what had happened was not enough; I'd got to make my life – not as if it hadn't *happened*, because it had – but just as a normal person. This experience did not last very long, because the school was closed down when the children reached the age when they gradually went into work. It was a measure of success that they were able to, and also that several of them said that they had found out there what they were really interested in.

The school was closed down some time in the spring of 1946, and I was transferred to another school. It was from there that I went back to Hungary. But, when I think back, because it was the most testing thing, and because I did it on my own, I think that those few months with these children was maybe the most important thing I ever did in my life.

It's very silly, but it never occurred to me not to go back to Hungary, because of important friendships. Also, I was not against what going on there at that time. It looked very promising.[17] I wish I hadn't gone back, but I did, although several of my friends were very, very much against it – rightly so!

Nobody close to me had survived. Some cousins, an aunt, an uncle who was in London – all my other uncles and aunts were killed, and my father and mother and two grandmothers. My first husband had been killed. My aunt stayed in Budapest, an important relationship for me. But by that time friendships meant more to me than family. Returning was an overwhelming experience. I learned very soon that the one thing I must not do is to talk about my experiences, so I went into analysis. I wanted to talk *there*, where it was all right. It was too much for people. I learned that lesson while still in Sweden. It's hard to talk about what early morning roll call was like in the concentration camp, and I shut up, I think, after two attempts – I just looked down and I never talked about it.

Life was on the move, very much, when I went back. Getting married was an important thing, and apart from finding marvellous friends, who gave me a home, I started university, which had not been possible during the Hungarian-Nazi period because I was Jewish. It was the start of a new life. My second husband had been our friend. He wrote to me in Sweden. I didn't go right back to *him*, but I went back to live as a friend. We were all very young and building up second relationships because husbands had disappeared.

It was a period of great disillusionment on the political scene. We all wanted to believe in the new Hungary, but it turned out very soon to be a terrible regime. I had a job which could have been interesting, but everything was so interfered with by politics that I couldn't enjoy it. I went to university part-time, and then I got a job in education. Again, it was interfered with by politics, but it was possible to get away from it. So I enjoyed it there. I'd studied psychology, philosophy and economics part-time while I had a job. It took four years. Of course, running a household was easier, because we all had our main meals out, whether we worked or studied. There was very little to buy anyway. The country was still very poor.

In all that time I went for a very brief visit, just once, to my home town. It was pretty awful. Apart from one or two friends, all the people who constituted my childhood were gone. I had to go back and get a few things. The most valuable had gone. I got back most of my household linen, which was very important in those days, very difficult to replace. I still have some of it in this country, which represents continuity in my life, especially as my life has been so broken up in stages, geographically too.

I knew that either I would not leave Hungary or I would come to England. I have always loved this country – rightly or wrongly. I have always loved the language, and although I had no friends here and I had marvellous friends in Sweden who all wanted me to go there and would have made my life very much easier, I did not want to go back there. I had very fond memories of it, but it's not somewhere where I wanted to live. So I chose the difficult start, but I'm so glad I did, because I feel so much at home here.

The political climate in Hungary was absolutely awful, but in my case I did not *have* to leave the country, because I was too much of a coward to go on the barricades and fight in the Revolution of '56.[18] I was just riding that, with friends. But my personal life was in a crisis then, after the break-up of my second marriage, and other personal problems at that time, and friends persuaded me to take a risk. Here was an opportunity to start a radically new life. After all, it had been a mistake to go back to Hungary after the war, although I wouldn't like not to have had the experiences I had there and the friendships, or to be without the experience of my marriage, which turned out not to last but was a very important relationship for me. I'm glad I had this experience. I've learned in this not very easy life that you now begin to know that once one survives something which is very bad, one is glad to have known the experience. I mean, I don't want to go as far as to say I'm glad I've been to a concentration camp – that would be a bit too much! – but if one has had many bad experiences, one can't just say, 'I wish I hadn't had that', because it adds up to, 'I wish I hadn't had my life.'

It was very difficult to get out. On the first attempt I was arrested immediately a few yards from the frontier and taken back to Buda-pest, interrogated – very unpleasant, extremely unpleasant. On the second attempt, the man who was paid by me to get me across the frontier lost his way, so we found ourselves in a very, very dangerous corner of Czechoslovakia, Austria and Hungary – very dangerous and they were watching like hawks. He wanted to leave me there in the hands of some organised group, to get across the frontier. I just begged on my knees for him to get me across.

I found myself 50 miles from a small town, in a Red Cross Reception Centre, where refugees were given some help. I got away from there next morning and got on to a bus and went to the town, where I knew that friends of mine had already arrived and were staying with relatives. I arrived there in the early hours of the morning and I stood outside a café until they opened. I asked them to let me wash and have breakfast. I think I had some things which I sold them. I washed and afterwards I sat down and ordered an Austrian breakfast. Then a newspaper arrived, and I felt I was in a civilised world because it was a free newspaper I was holding in my hand. So I felt already very much liberated. But it was a difficult start.

First of all I went to Vienna, so that I could arrange my entry to Britain. Several hundred of us queued up at the British Embassy. Then I was taken here in England to some sort of reception camp, and I couldn't tolerate it any longer; no more camps for me. I just totally couldn't bear it. So after a day or two I managed to escape. I had the address of an uncle in London whom I thought might be of some help. It wasn't easy. But I got out, and stayed one or two days with him, which wasn't pleasant. Then I was rescued by a friend of a friend. I went to live in a provincial town and I stayed there for two years.

I only want to say about my life here that it was very difficult, but even then, I knew that everything was always getting better, never worse. I was taken in by a friend who had no spare room or bed, so I shared the bed of her six-year-old son. But next day we had a camp bed, so although I shared the room, I had my bed. The next thing was I went to a hostel, which was pretty awful because I'm not comfortable in places like that. Everything that is very correct in life is difficult for me. But from the hostel I managed to find one small room with a terrible landlady, but much better than the hostel. And the next lodging which I found from there –

after several months, admittedly – was again a step forward, and so on. But looking back on it, it was terrible. No bath. To live in a provincial town on your own, in digs, in the late 1950s. There was nothing you could do as a lonely person. I was on my own and it was very hard to be there. I came as often as I could to London. But the shared bed became a camp bed, the camp bed turned into a hostel, the hostel into digs, the digs into a small self-contained something, and everything gradually became better – back to my kind of world.

In those years in Hungary after the war, if I had been asked by a foreigner what I was, I would have said Hungarian. Maybe I would have added Hungarian Jewish. But now I can say that having been Jewish is a much more important thing than having been Hungarian in Central Europe, in these historical times.

I think my very strong Jewish identity developed in 1967, during the Six Day War. Suddenly I felt, if Israel loses the war, it's not worth living. And it came on me quite suddenly that I'm much more Jewish than Hungarian, that my Hungarian identity is accidental. I am basically Central European Jewish. I could have been Polish, I could have been Czech. It just so happened that I was born in Hungary, and I'm quite glad, because I love Hungarian literature and art and music, but it is secondary to the fact that I am first and foremost Central European Jewish. The Jewishness is the more important. It has never diminished. It was a great revelation, the great onslaught of a strong sense of Jewish identity, and it's still with me. I can't say it's increasing, because it came so strongly that it can't increase.

I still wouldn't like to live in Israel, I like to live where I am. I'm more contented than I've ever been since I've been here, and that's it. I'm very Jewish. And it comes out quite suddenly. I remember when I was interviewed by one of the specialists over a recent illness and he took my particulars, he said, 'I'd forgotten to ask you what your religion is?' I said it was Jewish, and he said, 'Well, it doesn't really matter,' and I said, 'Yes. It does matter to me.'

NOTES

1. About half the Jews of Hungary lived in small communities, many of fewer than 1,000 Jews. In rural areas Jews were often craftsmen, small shopkeepers or publicans, as well as estate managers or distributors of agricultural produce.

2. A *get*, or divorce, under Jewish law can only be initiated by a husband. It must be given by the husband of his own free will, unless it is imposed on him by the rabbinic court, and accepted by his wife of her own free will. Part of the ceremony involves the wife's acceptance of the *get*, which is delivered to her.

3. In Germany and Austria there was a long tradition of deeply anti-Semitic student fraternities, which presumably had its influence in elite education throughout the Austro-Hungarian Empire.

4. The Arrow Cross, the Hungarian fascist party.

5. The *sheitel* customarily worn by Orthodox Ashkenazi women.

6. A *numerus clausus*, restricting Jews entering higher education to 5 per cent, had been enacted in 1920, and though 'liberalised', it was never abolished. In 1938 and 1939, the first two Jewish Laws were enacted, which imposed paralysing restrictions on the Jews economically and politically. The Second Law, for example, allowed only 5 per cent of Jews to engage in economic activity.

7. In May 1940, special labour units were set up for Jews, who were enlisted but excluded from army service.

8. Ghettoisation, the concentration of the Jewish population of a town or area into an overcrowded, confined place, was one of the steps on the way to deportation, and was the fate of much of East European Jewry. (Huge numbers of Russian and Polish Jews were shot by the Einsatzgruppen, special units who followed the invading German army and whose purpose was to kill Jews before ghettos could be established.)

9. During the liberation of Hungary by the Russians.

10. Once the Germans had invaded Hungary, the deportation of the Jews to the death camps of Poland happened very quickly. In less than four months 437,000 were sent to Auschwitz.

The deportation of the Budapest community began in June. A combination of circumstances halted deportations in July, but after the government fell, the Hungarian fascists came to power in 1944. A period of intense terror began. 98,000 Budapest Jews died on forced marches and because of random terror attacks, starvation, disease and suicide.

11. Mengele was the doctor who performed the selections which took place when a transport of Jews arrived at the camp. Strong men and women were selected for forced labour while the young and elderly, and women with children, were gassed immediately. Mengele also performed many barbaric 'experiments' on inmates.

12. Because of the Allied advance, it was decided to evacuate the camps and to destroy the gas chambers and crematoria in order to conceal the evidence of genocide. At the beginning and end of 1944, groups of Jews were evacuated from Auschwitz to forced labour elsewhere, in preparation for the liquidation of the camp. Maya must have been among them. The camp was liquidated in January 1945.

13. A town on the border with Poland.

14. The only concentration camp set up specifically for women. Women were transported to Ravensbrueck from other camps from summer 1944 onwards.

15. Through the agency of Count Bernadotte, a Swedish statesman and vice-chairman of the Swedish Red Cross, and representatives of the World Jewish Congress in Sweden, several thousand women, including at least 1,000 Jews, were liberated from Ravensbrueck and other camps near by. Maya was one of them.

16. The German regular forces, as distinct from the SS.

17. Maya returned to a country in the process of becoming a Soviet satellite. The Hungarian communists assumed complete power in the country after rigged elections in 1947. In the last free election, in 1945, the CP had polled only 17 per cent of the vote. In Eastern Europe, political, religious and cultural freedoms were eroded away from the late 1940s on.

18. There was a popular, anti-Soviet uprising in Hungary in 1956. The uprising was quickly quashed by Soviet troops.

Communist rule was restored, but 160,000 refugees left Hungary during the uprising.

ASPHODEL
A Pinhole in the Darkness

Asphodel was born in 1921, the youngest of seven children, and one of only two who survived. Her parents were both immigrants from Poland who met and married in England, but died while Asphodel was very young. They lived in Portsmouth, where there was a small Jewish community. Her mother, like so many Jewish women of her time, was the economic mainstay of the family. Her father's expectations around economic responsibility conflicted with those of his English-born second wife, with tragic consequences.

Asphodel's delight and pleasure in education stand out in contrast with her otherwise painful and isolated childhood. After leaving home in her teens, her relationship to her Jewishness was put in abeyance until the 1980s, when both political events and the nature of her studies brought it to the fore again.

In contrast with most women of her generation, Asphodel lived her adult life as an independent woman and a single mother. In making the choice to be independent and self-reliant, Asphodel was clearly motivated by personal politics which were recognisably feminist.

She joined the Communist Party in her teens and remained a member until 1956. She was one of the relatively large number of Jewish people who joined the Party in the thirties and forties because they saw it as the organisation at the forefront of the fight against fascism. The Party also provided her with a political framework for her beliefs in women's rights to independence. She later joined the Labour Party and was a councillor during the sixties. Always a feminist, the emergence of the Women's Liberation Movement opened up new possibilities for her, and for many years now Asphodel has given her wholehearted commitment to women and to feminism.

At 65 Asphodel recalls the stages of her life up to and including old age. For most women it is a time for conserving strength, but for her it entails a full and active life as a feminist, with continuing research and study, teaching and writing, and always a warm and loving commitment to and support for women. The events she relates are full of ironies and devastating contrasts. The struggles and difficulties stand in contrast to the generosity and friendship of other women, and to her own determination, optimism and resilience. Her account stands as a powerful testimony to her strength and vitality in countering the obstacles that beset her, and in taking on challenges both personal and political.

I'm 65 and I'm happy now to be with my own age group in the Older Jewish Women's Group. In the years when I was working in London in the feminist movement, I felt the lack of women of my age strongly. It seemed as if you couldn't be a real feminist if you were older. The thing about age is that it's not bad, and the thing about the menopause is that it releases your energy. I've got a place to live, I've got energy, I have my health and strength, and I think that younger women should know that there's a wonderful time coming when they're 50. I started as a Jewish woman, and now I'm on the ending stream of my life. However long it lasts, I'm finishing it as a Jewish woman, but as a feminist Jewish woman, as a non-observant Jewish woman and as one who believes I can reclaim the past of our Jewish women, our foremothers.

I changed my name to Asphodel in my fifties, when I experienced an age crisis. I realised that while I saw myself as a person, I was seen by some others only as a mother figure. They saw my age and not my self. When I thought I was relating to them as a person, in fact they were relating to me just as 'older', a sort of stereotype in which my own self had disappeared. One particular incident upset me terribly; it was like a bomb in my heart. After a lot of tears and grief I remembered the myth of Demeter and Persephone, where Persephone is raped and taken to the underworld. When her mother eventually brings her back, she and her mother are identical. Some myths say she's wearing a wreath of asphodels.

An asphodel is a small, quite undistinguished, lily-like flower that grows in profusion in the Mediterranean. It grows on the graves of the dead in the Elysian Fields. No matter what the weather, an asphodel is there, so it's the symbol of immortality, of revival and regeneration. And I thought, 'That's my name.' At that moment I changed. I left Pauline behind and as Asphodel I was renewed. I could be older, but I could get strength in being old; I could celebrate my age. It made a huge difference to me.

I was born on 25 May 1921 in the London Hospital, Mile End, the seventh baby. My brother Charles was 16 years older than me, the other five all died either at birth or immediately after. My poor mother had me when she was 40. I was the last and I survived. I've always thought I was a survivor because of this. My mother died when I was five and she took her own life, and my father died when I was 11 and he took his own life, so this a very difficult time to talk about.

We lived in the Jewish community in Portsmouth. My parents were both immigrants from Warsaw. My mother had come on her own when she was 19; her family stayed in Warsaw and I understand they all perished. I did hear there was a girl of my age who looked like me. I often thought about that. My father had come with his family and they had met here in the East End. As I remember my father, his English was very bad, even much later.

My brother told me something about the life in Portsmouth. My father (like many immigrants) expected a woman to do everything, including make the money. He expected to sit and *daven*, go out with his mates and pretend to be learned but really, as far as I can make out, just do nothing in particular. He expected to be what they call a *gantzer macher*, but he didn't expect to take responsibility of any kind. In the *shul* there was a big chandelier with a little label hanging from it saying it was presented by my father. My mother started a little shop. She came as an immigrant with no money but she was a woman and she got on with it. She started selling bits and pieces and apparently it did well. She was very good at handicrafts and sold her own work. During all that time my mother was having her pregnancies, going to term and losing the baby, running the shop, making the goods, seeing to everything and doing all the housework.

Apparently, just before I was 18 months old, my mother got some sort of paralysis. I was sent away from this Yiddish-speaking home to a Christian boarding nursery school called St Anne's in Cheltenham. As far as I know, they never visited me. Why did they send me away? That is the big mystery. If they could afford to send me away, and if she was ill and couldn't look after me, she could have afforded to have had somebody in the house to look after me. Why should a Jewish family send their child to a Christian, English, alien environment? When I was five they transferred me to a Jewish boarding school in Brighton. One of my earliest recollections is the headmistress calling me to her study and telling me my mother had gone to heaven. I remember looking out of a little window with a white curtain to see if she was there, flying up to heaven.

In 1928, when I must have been seven, I was brought 'home'. I had settled down in the boarding school; I was perfectly institutionalised and did well at the school. However, my father had remarried and I had a new 'mother'. I know it was 1928 because I remember going into Woolworth's, presumably with my step-mother or with her mother, and here was this fairyland of lights and in these fairy lights it said 'Christmas 1928'. I'd never seen anything so wonderful.

It was terrible being yanked away from this school. I was 'the best girl in the school' because I was so good, studied so well and spoke so nicely, having been well trained to do these very things. The other girls used to worry and cry about their parents; I didn't worry and cry about mine. I remember being very happy at boarding school. I liked learning Hebrew because I felt it was something to do with being part of something, that I wasn't just an isolated nothing. I must have got quite a strong sense of being Jewish from that school because when I came home, I was quite fully aware of what being Jewish meant and how important Hebrew was.

I always remember going home and this woman putting her arms round me. She clasped me to her bosom and I thought she was going to suffocate me. I thought she was a kind of witch, because nobody had ever done this to me before. I was a tremendous reader; by the age of seven I'd read everything in the school library, especially fairy stories, which are often full of evil and difficulties. I thought this was the witch in the wood and she was going to kill me, like Hansel and Gretel. I always remember that feeling of panic. So this was not a very good start to our relationship, because it was my stepmother who wanted to love this poor little orphan girl. I didn't say anything to anybody and I was shaking with fright. That was a very bad start – and it continued. I wouldn't talk to my stepmother, because I had this idea in my mind that if I didn't communicate she could have no power over me. Of course, my stepmother was very hurt and after a time she didn't talk to me either. My father withdrew from the whole situation to *daven*ing. I put my sanity down to the fact that one had to go to school. If I hadn't gone to school, I think I would have retreated into some sort of autism.

My stepmother was a daughter of an immigrant. They were Yiddish-speaking also, but she was born in Bradford and she'd worked in a mill. When she met my father, he appeared to be well off, though even then he must have been in debt. Presumably my poor stepmother thought he didn't need to work and she would be the wife of a well-off man. My stepmother had a baby when I was nine. There was no money. There were mounting debts. They sold everything in the house.

By that time I was literally reading everything. At home there wasn't much to read except the Jewish encyclopedias. I used to read about demonology, angelology, spiritualism and all sorts of things. I graduated from fairy stories to the Jewish encyclopedia and it was all the same story. I had this inner life and I got into the whole business of God and the hereafter, immortality and the devil. I also read about the goddesses, about Isis and Astarte and Ashteroth, the goddesses of the ancient Near East. They were very much more to my liking than God. I used to go to *shul* and hear about God. I was in the gallery. There were the women talking; there were the men downstairs with their *tallises* on, doing everything, like carrying the law around. I always used to think with the scrolls of the law, that they were dressing and undressing them. They looked like girls in their skirts. I used to think it was very naughty for these men to take these girls' dresses off.

In the meantime I was going to school and this was the saving of me, because I was divinely happy there. I went to an ordinary elementary school in Portsmouth. I used to be the best girl of the school. I was teacher's pet without knowing that was bad. As far as I was concerned, there was this wonderful teacher whom I adored and who looked after me. Our teacher was an elderly woman, rather severe, yet very loving at the same time. She always kept her distance, was always very polite to me and had lots of talks with me. The one thing that I ever remember my father saying was at the end of term when I got a brilliant report and he said I was a good girl and that learning was a good thing. It was a very Jewish remark.

So my life was bound up with reading and school. This was my place. It was an old-fashioned elementary school, a big red Victorian building with an asphalt playground. When you came to school you took your outer things off and you put your nice white pinny on. You took it home at the weekend and you were supposed to bring it back clean. We were told over and over again, 'There's no shame in a thing being darned or patched but there is shame in a thing having a hole in it.' Although I'm not much good at anything else in the sewing line, I'm pretty good at darning and patching. I didn't do games because Jewish girls don't show their legs; my father apparently wrote a letter and said I wasn't to do games because it was unmaidenly. As a result of that I not only didn't do games but, living by the sea, I never learned to swim, and I never learned to cycle and I never learned to dance. None of those things can I do to this very day.

We did English grammar and poetry and composition. There was a lot of spelling and grammar; I used to find grammar very interesting. We had to share books. We had twin desks that lift up and an inkwell on the right-hand side and pens and nibs and ink – you always got ink all over your face. What I liked best was the poetry. We had a green, soft-leather poetry book and we had to learn the poems and recite them. I used to write poems too. Poetry for me was another world, a beautiful world, an allowable world. You were allowed to sit and read poetry and you were allowed to say it out loud. Then in arithmetic we used to do times tables. Every day there was half an hour of times tables. We remembered by chanting. That's how you learned. You didn't understand very much but you learned facts very well. When you were called upon for facts, as you were in examinations, you had no difficulty whatever in recalling them because they'd been drummed into you day after day. I would think that a third of the school day was spent chanting something or other. It was nice. You felt part of the school, part of the society, because you were chanting – at least, I did, because I didn't really talk to anybody.

In 1932 I was 11 and in those days we had what was called 'the scholarship'. You stayed at a state elementary school till you were 14 or else you got the 'scholarship' and went to grammar school. There wasn't much doubt that I would get it and I thought I would please my father by doing well. So I took the scholarship and had to go in one morning to find out the results. They told me I was second in the whole of Portsmouth, the first girl. We were let out early. My teacher was very pleased with me. I rushed off home to tell the good news. When I got home, there was a strange atmosphere in the house. There was a policeman and the *rebbetzin* and various people. I couldn't make out what was happening, so I asked the policeman. He was quite a young man and he looked terribly embarrassed. He said I should go upstairs. There was my stepmother in the bedroom, distraught. She threw her arms around me and said, 'Oh, Pauline, we've only got each other now.' My father had committed suicide that morning, so he never knew.

After the tragedy of my father's death, the family moved to London where my stepmother's sister, my Aunt Rachel, and her husband and their three boys were. I think Aunt Rachel was very supportive to her sister. Her husband was a good Jewish man, who saw he had to do something for this widow and orphans. First of all we lived over a shop in Stroud Green Road, in a big room all together, and it was pretty hard. My stepmother had no money whatsoever; my father had died because he was in debt. The Jewish Board of Guardians and various Jewish welfare organisations helped, as did her family. She was a good seamstress and she took in dressmaking. Her mother helped in some way towards this enterprise.

Her brother-in-law made it possible for her to get a flat in Muswell Hill. It was the downstairs of a house. It had a garden, a front room, a back room, a kitchen and a scullery. The back room the other three slept in; I slept in the front room, which was the parlour. They never sat in it because they sat in the kitchen. I used to sit at the desk and do my homework. It was a sort of haven for me. Often after school I used to go to the public library, and get loads of books and read them, in the summer at any rate, in Alexandra Palace gardens or Priory Park. In the winter I'd read them in the library. I used to sit around and daydream, think about what was going on in the world. I'd get home about eight and have lentil soup, which my stepmother would have made. We had lentil soup every day, except Saturdays, when we had chicken and a *shtickel kugel*. My stepmother would light the candles on Friday night and we had fried fish if we could afford it. She lived on very little; I remember her saying that if she got £2 10s in a week, she was well off. She had my stepgrandmother, herself, my sister and me, all on this £2 10s. We had no money. Shoes were a problem always; I used to feel it was a terrible thing to have these big feet continually growing.

It had eventually come out that I had passed the scholarship and I went to High School, which I loved deeply. I was there in the thirties and the headmistress was a radical liberal educationalist who really believed in education for women. At my school, which was a straightforward grammar school, we had a very broad education and, provided we were prepared to work, we could do almost anything we liked. You could ask to go to a museum and some museum trip would be arranged. One of the teachers would invite two or three of us to her home once a month. She would have chats about the world and show us photographs. It was part of the education. I felt it was very enriching.

I didn't go into religious assembly because I was Jewish. This gave me a certain cachet. I must have been a horrid girl really. But I do remember the headmistress calling me in to listen to a talk she was giving at assembly, in which she was telling the girls not to be anti-Semitic. This was in the thirties. She gave several long speeches about the marvellous heritage of the Jews and that they were to respect the Jews. As a result I think I got a certain standing as a representative of this wonderful people who did all these great things.

Friendships were very important. I was very solitary at school until I was about 14, and then I suddenly made friends with two girls. One was a Jewish girl who was a great influence on me and this was an approved relationship. The other girl, Lilian, was the daughter of an Irish woman who was parted from her husband and she and my stepmother didn't like that relationship at all. We had an emotional, loving relationship which my stepmother very much didn't like. And although it never actually got physical, it was getting towards it. We wrote loving poems, almost love poems but not quite. I think we were both hovering on the brink and not quite knowing how to get into it or over it. We got very emotional with each other and it was very exciting and very lovely, but at the same time Lilian was more emotional than I could cope with. It was all very well when we were doing poetry but when it actually came into life, it was too frightening and I withdrew. Then Lilian used to get into tremendous tempers. I rejected her because I couldn't take the tantrums.

I got free school clothes and shoes, being an orphan in terrible circumstances. This was important because they were very expensive. When I was 14 I took the Junior County Scholarship, which gave me 10s a week extra, which was almost a wage. So I always felt from the age of 14 that I earned my living. That was why I was able to stay on at school. When I was 16 the Junior County Scholarship came to an end. I had taken a preliminary exam for Oxford, which I had passed, but a girl had to be 18 to go. There was nothing I could do, so I left home and I started work.

At the library I'd read up very carefully what the law was about leaving home. I'd found out that at 16 you could leave home and, provided you led a god-fearing life and didn't get into trouble, they couldn't send you back. I had only two things that I ever thought belonged to me. One was a brown, cardboard suitcase which had come with me from boarding school, the other was a red, paisley-patterned eiderdown, which had also come home with me. I couldn't pack my red eiderdown – I've always regretted it – but I packed my case with what very few things I had.

I also knew that it was dangerous being destitute, because they'd send you back. Once I'd started living in London, my brother saw me once a month. Charles was a bachelor and lived in a room near the British Museum. He used to take me to the pictures and have tea in Lyons Corner House and give me half-a-crown pocket money. So I had half a crown and I got on the bus and went to Victoria Station. I knew if you had a case and you went to a railway station you wouldn't attract attention.

Eventually somebody who appeared to be a railway policewoman came up and asked me whether I was waiting for someone. I said I'd run away from home. We were terribly polite to each other. I think it must be very different today. She asked me to accompany her to the station-master's office, where she gave me a cup of tea and a biscuit. She asked me what my plans were, and I said I didn't know. She asked if I would object to going to a girls' hostel, and I said I'd be delighted. Arrangements were made and some other woman accompanied me in a car – I don't think I'd ever been in a car – to a hostel at 49 Cleveland Street, at the back of Middlesex Hospital: the Emerson Bainbridge Hostel for Young Women and Girls in London. It was next door to the Emerson Bainbridge Hostel for Fallen Women, so they got me to the right one first. In those days they were very worried about what was called the White Slave Traffic and I'm quite sure that that was the reason that the policewoman came up to me.

The matron didn't ask me any questions. I was shown to a dormitory and I was as happy as can be. It was 15s a week for breakfast and dinner at night and lunch on Sundays. First thing in the morning the matron sent one of the older girls out with me to a job agency and I got a job on the spot. From the next morning I started work and earned 30s a week. Take-home pay was 26s 2½d and I paid her 15s of it. The only thing that was really troublesome about that was that I never had money for shoes.

I'd only eaten kosher food until then and the first thing that happened to me was I was given bacon for breakfast. That was my first big test. I looked at this piece of bacon and I put it to my mouth and waited for the ceiling to fall. It didn't fall, so I ate it. That was the big moment. If something had happened when I put that bacon to my mouth (a rumble of thunder, for example), if God knew that I was on my own in a strange land and all these things were happening, then I'd have gone home.

197

There were about 10 women in the dormitory. It was rather like a hospital ward, with curtains round the bed, one bathroom to every floor. There must have been about 30 girls – we called them girls, you know – in the hostel. They were almost entirely young women who'd come up from the country to get jobs. The hostel was very like any institution. There was a common room with a piano and quite a number of the girls played or sang. There were some books, newspapers and magazines. A lot of the girls sewed or knitted or did handiwork of some kind. I read, of course. There was quite a lot of activity. You'd come home from work, sit down and have your dinner. Then you'd go into the sitting room and there was a wireless and sometimes the girls would dance to Henry Hall and his orchestra. It was very pleasant. If you went out you had to be back by ten thirty. You had to pay, you had to be in on time, you had to clean the bath after yourself (I got into trouble once because I didn't), you had to keep your bit of the dormitory tidy; that's all you had to do. Once I was in the hostel, it was as if I was five years old.

I had a job, I had somewhere to live and some money. I was at peace, I was happy at last. Since I've been in the Women's Movement I've heard so much from women of bad sexual experiences when they were young. When I was young I had no bad sexual experiences whatever. I knew nothing about sex, for all my reading. I was very prudish and very frightened of sexuality. Until I was 18, I didn't have any sexual encounters and I wasn't interested. Consequently during that time, when a lot of girls were going with boys and worrying about it, I didn't. As they say, although I wouldn't say it now, in those days innocence was my armour. I was so innocent that I didn't understand anything. Walking through Soho, men used to make remarks to me and I didn't know what they were talking about. I think it was so obvious, they went away. The two years from 16 to 18 were very happy years. I didn't have any worries that I can remember.

I was very happy with the young women in the hostel and I loved them dearly. The sister of one of the women in the hostel was training to be a nurse. We used to go about a lot together and I was very fond of her. Then she got engaged, so that was the end of that, because she couldn't see me, she was busy. It's always a man comes in between. I loved the women much more than the men, but somehow it was taken for granted by all the women that the men had to come first. Even if you'd much prefer to just have the evening with a woman or to go away with a woman, if a man wanted you to go and you were with that man, then you went. So all of our friendships were frittered away.

I got a job as a junior filing clerk in the International Broadcasting Authority at the very beginning of commercial radio. It was only for about six weeks but I really loved it. And then the letter came through from the London County Council saying I'd passed the exam. Because of the background that I'd been brought up in of insecurity and a slump, everybody took it for granted that I would have to leave IBA, where I was divinely happy and doing well, and go to the LCC because it was a safe job for life, with a pension. There was never any question about it. I left and went to the LCC, which really was dead boring and I hated. Now the Greater London Council is no longer here and commercial broadcasting is the biggest thing on earth. If I'd stayed in commercial broadcasting I have no doubt at all I would have had a completely different, much happier life.

I was in the Parks Department of the LCC and was made Personal Assistant to the Chief Officer, purely because I was a pretty girl. I had no shorthand and typing and very few skills and knew nothing whatever about the LCC or parks. We were offered a shorthand-typing course and I refused it on the grounds that if I did shorthand typing I'd become a secretary. Being a secretary was a good job but I saw the way the secretaries were nothing more than nursemaids to these men. It was a Labour council under Herbert Morrison and the Chairman of the LCC Parks Department was Mrs Hugh Dalton. She took to me and I liked her. Mrs Hugh Dalton must have been in her forties and I saw her as a model. She was a strong, determined woman who got her way and there was this ineffectual boss who shivered when she came in the room. She lived near Victoria and I used to run backwards and forwards, carrying papers and having little chats with her. She was a great influence on me. Although I found out later that women don't get the jobs because they're women, when

I was a girl I knew nothing. I was an open book, a sponge which soaked up everything. I went into the world every day and the world imprinted itself on me. And as far as I could see, here was Mrs Hugh Dalton and this was the kind of woman I was going to be.

One of the chief clerks was a nice man, also on a job for life. He had been in the First World War. One day we all had to go into Battersea Park for the afternoon; there must have been about 40 or 50 youngsters. He had a lot of gas masks and he was giving us gas-mask training; how to put them on and how to put them off and what to do if a greenish-yellowish cloud (chlorine gas) comes towards you. We thought this was a tremendous lark and went prancing around with these silly gas masks on, until I noticed he was crying. This middle-aged guy, who'd been in the First World War, who was training us to survive in the next; he couldn't bear it. That was 1938, 'Peace in Our Time'.

Then, at that time, I became interested in politics. I used to go to Trafalgar Square, where there were rallies for Spain. I remember not knowing what to think. Then I realised that the fascists were anti-Jewish, so I decided I'd have nothing to do with them and went to the other lot. That's how it goes. I joined the Communist Party purely on the Jewish ticket, as you might say. The communists seemed to be the fighters against fascism and therefore I would join them.

In the post room at the LCC I met Stanley. He was not Jewish; he was very mild mannered, not particularly good-looking and a pacifist. He became a conscientious objector during the war. He introduced me to *Peace News* and for a time I became a pacifist. I used to say, rather uncomfortably, what would happen if the Nazis came, but at that point I was able to put that on one side. Stanley hadn't had any girlfriends. He was much older than me; he was 26 and I was now 17½. We got to know each other and got very fond of each other. We went to a pacifist community in Essex somewhere and stayed there for weekends. There wasn't the pressure that there is now; you didn't have to sleep together. It was a big thing if you did and was acknowledged to be so.

When we felt we wanted to sleep together it came out that

Stanley hadn't slept with anybody either. I had never seen a man's naked body and I didn't know what men looked like. I was dead scared. In the British Museum, I always looked away because pure young daughters of Israel didn't look at men's naked bodies. So I read Hannah Stone, *Modern Marriage and Birth Control*, and we talked about birth control. What the books told you was that women could and should have orgasms and that it was the job of the man to see that women did. And so right from the very beginning, we found that I could have orgasms. Stanley was extremely gentle and friendly and loving and sympathetic, and it was very successful for both of us. I have the kindest, most loving recollection of it all. Stanley had moved from home and had got a room in a rooming house; I had moved from the hostel and had got a room in the same house. One Saturday afternoon we were lying on the bed and the sun was pouring in and we'd had a lovely time. I remember looking out through the big windows and saying, 'Stanley, there's lots of silver planes coming over.' And the bombs started dropping. That was 1940.

I walked out on Stanley. There were several things. First of all, I fell in love with a Communist called Harry, and secondly Stanley was pacifist, the 'Phoney War' was over, the fight was on, and we used to have all these quarrels. I don't think Harry fell for me at all, but I was available and I was full of ideas about how I didn't believe in marriage. He was Jewish and a communist and he'd been in the Soviet Union – so he was a kind of projected fantasy figure. It was highly unsatisfactory; Stanley at least was a real person.

It was the Party line to fight fascism, so I joined the ATS. There was a nice woman there called Sergeant-Major Rider and I got a job as her assistant because I came in as a clerical worker from the LCC and there was a lot of administrative work to be done. I got on extremely well with her and she found me very useful. I'd been with Sergeant-Major Rider for six months, doing extremely well, and then the dread day came when we had to take intelligence tests. I couldn't do them – I thought it was something complicated involving mythological symbols. And so I couldn't stay in this job which was banded for a woman of intelligence, which I obviously didn't have, and I had to be downgraded. I decided the only way out was to have a baby. I told Harry and he shuddered, but I assured him that I would never expect him to keep it and I would be independent. I wouldn't say that now. So I went ahead and had a baby and got out of the ATS. And here endeth my youth.

When I had Jim I was 21. I had no relations, no money and I didn't believe in being kept by a man. Truly life became very difficult. It was made better by friendship. When I was pregnant, in October 1942, I was selling *Daily Worker*s outside the Kilburn Co-op. A woman who must have been a little more than 10 years older than me stopped and bought a *Daily Worker* and had a chat and invited me to her home – and this was Dorothy, who is still my closest friend and is now approaching 80. It was Dorothy who introduced me to feminism. She had left her husband and two sons somewhere up in the Midlands and had come down to London to do war work as an independent woman.

When Jim was born, Dorothy brought me some flowering forsythia. I always think of Dorothy when I see forsythia. Of course, Jim's father wasn't there and nobody else came to see me. But Dorothy came, and what I'd have done without her I do not know. The trouble with the facts of life that I read up with Stanley was we only got as far as orgasm. I truly didn't know how babies were born. I didn't know whether it was an operation, or if they just popped out, or came through the navel. I'd never given it a moment's thought. I knew you had pain, so when the baby started to be born and I had pains, that was all right. I got to hospital with these pains and they gave me castor oil and that wasn't at all all right. I still didn't know what was going to happen. When it did happen it was terrible. There was this horrible anti-Semitic midwife who kept saying, 'Bear down'. Now, this didn't mean anything to me. She shrieked at me, 'If you don't bear down, you dirty Jew, your baby will be dead, and a good thing too.' I just cried and, of course, tensed up. Luckily a medical student walked in and said to me, in a nice quiet voice, 'What's the trouble?' I said, 'I don't know what "bear down" means.' He said, 'Push' – and so I pushed. And Jim was born.

The question is, what did I live on? After they threw me out of the ATS I got a job in a bookshop, for a time. Then I got a job in a Trotskyist lampshade factory. I didn't believe a word they said, although unfortunately they were talking the truth about salt mines and all the rest, but they were quite nice and I made lampshades for a pittance, but enough to live on. For a few months Harry came and went, but he paid the rent. The only thing you can do and take the child with you is cleaning. There was a woman I cleaned for in Hampstead who was a communist. Betty seemed very far away from me. She was bourgeois and well off, even though she was a communist. She had quite a big sitting room and started a home factory. We made little bits for wireless sets for Cossors. She organised a crèche in her home; Cossors paid for the nursery nurse to look after the children and we could breastfeed. There was a British Restaurant up the road, so we could have lunch cheaply. That was really very nice indeed, and suited me and Jim.

I was living in a half-ruined house in Hampstead, one half had been bombed and boarded off and the other half was liveable in. This house figured largely in time to come, because I went back to it and Tommy was born there later.

All was well for a bit, but then London started being bombed again and Betty said she couldn't run the home factory any more. The Anna Freud Nursery was organising an evacuation of children to Scotland because of the bombing and Betty's child was going. They said Jim had to go and I'm sorry to say that I allowed it, for a time at least, because it seemed the thing to do. Then the bombing didn't seem to be so bad, and I went up and got him. I got some cleaning, but you don't earn a great deal, and I lived on porridge and carrots and an occasional egg for the baby. It was terribly difficult. Then I saw an ad in the paper which said the Women's Land Army was looking for women as cooks in their hostel. I immediately wrote away and told a lot of lies about how I was a good cook, and had an interview. I confessed that I'd got the baby – but by this time my 'husband' was in the army. I bought a Woolworth's wedding ring and I was now respectable. I got a job as a cook in the Land Army with Jim in Kent, and that was a fantastic experience.

There were 40 Land Army women and a warden and me. I was cooking for them all and looking after Jim, who was then about a year old, and using an Aga cooker, which I'd never used before.

However, I got on immensely well with the women; they were wonderful. I used to get up at ten to five in the morning, and worked about an 80 hour week, cooking and washing up. I learned to cook as I went. Except that it was incredibly hard work, it was very good. The Land Army women all played with Jim and made a fuss of him and I got on tremendously well with them. That went on for a year and all would have been well if it hadn't been bombed. I remember being under the old wooden kitchen table with all the girls crowding over Jim, while the house came down. We burrowed our way out. Afterwards they were dispersed and I was told the Land Army had taken a decision some time before not to employ women with children.

Jim's now two and it's early 1945. I went back to the good old Trotskyist lampshade factory at King's Cross and Jim went to Parkhill Road Nursery, which was fine, until 8 May 1945. When the war ended the matron of the nursery said, 'Now the war's over, the nursery closes. You can all stay home. The jobs are for the men.' Now, that was the end of a long period of discomfort and distress, but the beginning of a worse one. Then I was in real trouble. Because there was no nursery, I couldn't go to the lampshade factory. The cleaning jobs were snapped up before you could look round. I didn't have any work. Something was wrong with the drains in the house I was living in. I went to a woman doctor and said I was feeling ill and she said, 'I suppose you're pregnant. Unless you admit it, I can't do anything for you.' As I was dragging myself out of the room I said to her, 'Well, doctor, just before I go, can you tell me what to do about having blood in the urine, because it's worrying me?' She diagnosed infective hepatitis. Jim got ill too and it really was very difficult.

Just about this time some Party friend of Harry's turned up – Harry, who had taken not the slightest bit of interest from that day to this in the child. His friend had come at a terrible time when everything was filthy and he was shocked. He said that a Party member couldn't live in this way and the baby must be adopted. He put it to the District Committee and there were several meetings. It would be done through the Party. They would find the right person and then I could rehabilitate myself. And so ill was I, and so ill was Jim, that I agreed. It only occurred to me 35 years later that all those Party members who came to district committees and made speeches could actually have given a tiny bit of help to somebody who had no money and who was ill and who was literally starving. But I remember saying it wasn't fair and they said, 'Comrade, you must consider what is in the best interests of the working class.' And it occurred to me at the time – well, surely I'm part of the working class. They said as I was known to be a communist, I mustn't live in a situation which the British working class would find distasteful; I must be respectable and therefore the baby must be adopted. Somehow it was too much for me and I allowed it to happen. And there was a twist in it; Harry wished to take more responsibility. The father of the child didn't produce £5 or any little thing like that, but he'd found this splendid Party couple who would take the child and were excellent in every way. And so that's what happened. I went off the Party for ever at that time, although I didn't leave officially till 1956.

Why does one stay in the Party? Because I really had no family, my heart and soul were in the Party, and in this I was with my generation. It wasn't just something you did, something you joined or didn't join; it was your whole life. We really thought the future was in our hands and we had to fight and struggle for socialism. And the betrayal of *that* is something else. In 1956, when we realised this was all a huge con, all this blood and sweat and toil and tears literally was for nothing, or for worse, it was terrible.

When Jim was 16 I wrote to his adoptive mother and said could he have the choice of seeing me and I'd like to know him. She wrote back and said he was just taking his O levels and it would be a bad idea and she'd write again. Well, she never did. And then two years later I got a letter from Oxford from Jim. It's like a Victorian novel. He said that he had been moving a desk and a letter had been caught in a drawer – my letter, which of course he never knew about. So he came to see me and we renewed relationships. I'd last seen Jim when he was two and a half and he was now 19.

After Jim's adoption the Party thought that they had a responsibility to me and they found me a job in the Friends of Democratic Poland. I worked there for a couple of years. They produced a paper called *New Poland* and I learned a little bit of journalism. At the end of the war there was the squatters' movement, in which I was very involved. It was a spontaneous working-class take-over; the Party decided we would support it. One of the activists was Sidney, who was on the *Daily Worker* and who'd been sent down there to report what was happening, and he became Tommy's father.

Sidney got sent to Scotland by the *Daily Worker* and I went up to Glasgow with him. By that time I was using a Dutch cap. There ought to be a plaque on the site, 36 Spencer Street, where City University now is, of that birth control clinic where we all went. The men would queue up outside and boo every woman who went in. That was one of the very few places you could go without being married. It was run by one of those wonderful women doctors who ran birth control clinics in the thirties and forties. It was the winter of 1946–7, one of the coldest winters of the century, and the water all froze. I couldn't rinse out the Dutch cap because there wasn't any water, and so I got pregnant. Sidney couldn't stand it. He got immensely dreadful and said, 'You're ugly, you're horrible, you make me sick to look at you.' Sidney wanted me to have an abortion. He knew a nice Jewish doctor in the Party who did abortions and he made an appointment for me to see him. First he was pleasant and friendly but very matter of fact and brisk, and then instead of just looking at me as a pregnancy, he looked at me as a person. He came across from the other side of the big desk, sat by me, took my hand and said, 'You don't want this abortion, do you?' All the memories of Jim and losing Jim came up at that time, and I said, 'No, but what can I do?' and I started crying. He held my hand and said, 'You're a strong woman. I'll do it if you want me to but if you don't want me to, I won't.' I said I didn't. Many women have no choice; society took away a woman's possibility of life, if she didn't have an abortion. If the world was different, we wouldn't have to have abortions.

I left and came back to London. A friend, Jean, had my old room in the house and when I came back I shared it with her. We really loved each other very deeply. I'm sure today we'd have had a lesbian relationship, but then we didn't. Then she moved out because I was pregnant and I had to have the room. I've always been terribly lucky in my women friends. Tommy was born in that room. This time I didn't go to hospital. I had a midwife at home and it was lovely. I had a good birth; she sat and read detective stories between the pains, and they had a party in the room next door. Sidney turned up and was sorry and he was quite supportive for a time. And then the Party said we had to get married, because now we had a baby we had to be respectable. So then I got married when the child was six weeks old.

We found a little flat in the Caledonian Road. I breastfed for nine months and was working part-time for *New Poland*. Then, after I weaned him, I put him in a nursery which had been restarted in Hornsey. I always used to say I'd done a day's work by the time I got to work, and coming home I had to go from work up to Hornsey, back again, do the shopping somehow or other, and then make supper and do what cleaning was done – and have a Party meeting in the room.

When Tommy was two, I decided that I couldn't stand Sidney a minute longer. I had £40 saved up. I got a copy of *Dalton's Weekly*, saw a cottage advertised and took it. I went to live in the country and started anew with Tommy. Eventually I found a woman to have Tommy during the day. Mrs Rivers had a little boy the same age, and in fact Johnny Rivers is still Tommy's best friend. It was a real second home for Tommy. I'd only worked on *New Poland*, but I presented myself at the local printer's as a journalist. He was a bit suspicious of me at first but it worked. I wrote a guide book to Hastings and then he introduced me to Mr Powers, who wanted an editor for a little paper about Alsatian dogs. It wasn't full-time and I got various other jobs, and also did book reviews and little stories for the *Evening Argus*.

Mr Powers also had a trade paper. He put a lot of money into synthetic fibres and he wanted a paper to push them. He asked if I would like to work full-time on the paper for £10 a week, and so I started my work career in earnest. I got in very early indeed on the synthetic fibre world. In the end, I was a real textile authority in the trade press. From 1950 to 1980, work was the one thing in my life which was constant, as distinct from love and sex and children and home and family, none of which was constant. And I own this house because I was able eventually to pay off the mortgage, as an independent woman, without the help of a man.

I was living as an unmarried woman with a child and it was possible for me to work. I was not part of that push back into the home that so many women experienced.

When I got Mr Powers' job, I had to go back to London to do it full-time. The problem immediately started of what to do when Tommy came home from school. I started employing an older woman and she never came on time, and the same happened with another woman. This became absolutely disastrous because I could see this job was going to be my life force. The problem was from four to half-past six and, of course, holidays. I noticed that a Green Line bus stopped outside the door near Victoria Station just as I got to work at nine thirty in the morning. One Saturday we got on the bus going the other way, to see where it went. It took 55 minutes and went to Wrotham in Kent. We got off in the middle of the village, and lo and behold there was a village school. So at one end was the school and at the other end was my office. Well, if that wasn't a sign from heaven, what was? We stood there looking around and along comes a policeman. I said, 'I'm looking for somewhere to live with Tommy.' 'Oh,' he said, 'Well you couldn't do better than Mrs Bridges!'

He showed us how to get to Mrs Bridges', which was a mile along the Pilgrim's Way. There we met this woman who told us to go away. Poor Tommy, who was just five, had had a long ride and then a long walk in the sun, and then this apparently bad-tempered woman shouting at us, so he started crying. She picked him up and said, 'Oh, poor little thing! Fancy dragging him along here. I'm sure you would like a drink of milk, wouldn't you, darling!' So good old Tommy got us in. He did me proud and behaved exactly as he should have behaved. It turned out that poor Mrs Bridges (whom I still see, at the age of 92) had lost her own son some years before, of leukaemia. She had gone deaf as a result of the shock and had been a recluse ever since and Mr Lang, the policeman, saw in me and Tommy some rescue for Mrs Bridges. There were three rooms upstairs empty, but you had to get water from the well and there was a WC without water. I paid her 30s a week rent and another 25s for looking after Tommy and giving him his tea in the evening.

In the morning I took Tommy into the village and left him at school and got on the bus. Mr Lang saw him across the main road out of school every day and on to the Pilgrim's Way. I used to follow on a couple of hours later, picking up his balaclava, his gloves, his bits and pieces as I went. And then when I got there I had to do the washing and cleaning up, carry the water and empty the slops. It was a long day, but putting Tommy to bed was a nice time. He'd had his tea and I'd read to him, or later on he'd read to me. We'd listen to *Dick Barton, Special Agent*, together. Although it was a very hard life, the fact that the Bridges were there meant that no matter what happened I could get to work. The problems associated with going to work and having a child are so terrible; they are all to do with being in two places at the same time. During the holidays Tommy used to go to the Rivers' a lot. This was why I was able to get on with my work and get established, because if it wasn't Mrs Bridges, it was Mrs Rivers.

It wasn't at all a bad time. This life established me in my work and it established Tommy as a country lad and he got looked after. The old boy, Mr Bridges, liked him and so Tommy would go tramping around the hills with him. I had this off the record relationship with a married man called Frank, which was sometimes very exhilarating and wonderful, mostly it was pain and suffering. Occasionally a woman friend would come down to see me at a weekend, but I had no social life really, except at work to a certain extent. Furthermore, I was a 'loose woman' – in the village there were some women who wouldn't have Tommy in the house. He didn't have a happy time because of that and became a rebel.

I was going to move to a little house which had water and electricity and in that week that I was moving, I realised I was pregnant and I told Frank. This is a man I'd been with for years and he'd always supported me over my decision not to have an abortion 10 years earlier. And then, when it was his responsibility, the first thing he said was, 'Of course, you must have an abortion.' This time, I couldn't see any way out of it at all. Not only wouldn't Frank support financially, he wouldn't support emotionally, and so I was really desperate. Abortion was still illegal, so what was I to do? I realised what I had to do. I moved furniture all week – I knew it was the twelfth week and a dangerous time in a pregnancy – and I also moved the baby.

We got to the bungalow and as the removers went, I had a haemorrhage on the kitchen floor. Frank just stood there looking. I quickly put some newspaper over it, and thought, 'I'm having a haemorrhage; maybe I'll die.' There was no telephone in the house, I knew nobody, the removers had gone, it was Friday – and then I heard his car go. He'd left me, knowing what was happening. I managed to *shlep* around to get towels and put pillows under my feet and lay on a mattress bleeding. I was frightened of bleeding, so I lay. I didn't make a cup of tea, I didn't go to the loo, I didn't do anything for 24 hours, because I was frightened of dying. And nobody came, of course, because nobody knew I was there. After the first 24 hours the bleeding got less and I was able to change my clothes and put on some sanitary towels, still doing very little. On the Monday morning, the milkman called. I gave him some money and he rang my friend Mary, who dropped everything and came and looked after me. She was marvellous – washed everything, did everything. Who do you go to in trouble? You go to women. Never mind male lovers.

While I was still at the bungalow in 1956 I left the Party, and within a matter of months I joined the Labour Party. It was my first experience of real English politics as distinct from the Communist Party. When Tommy was 11 I moved to Rochester to be near the grammar school, and in 1964 was elected as a Labour councillor. Three years later they sacked me because I was too radical. I came to London, where I got a much better job, which meant going into the City, going to conferences, going to shows. In this particular world I became a *mentsh*, someone who was recognised.

I was always driven by my independence and – we didn't call it 'feminist' in those days – my feminist feelings. I suddenly noticed in the newspapers that women were getting together and agitating. I realised that something wonderful was happening. This wasn't the Labour Party, it wasn't the CP, it was women. I was then approaching 50. I noticed the meetings and I wanted to go, but I was frightened because I thought I was too old. Then I met a younger woman who invited me to a Women's Liberation Movement meeting and said, 'You can learn from us, and we can learn

210

from you.' It was such a good thing to say that I went – and never looked back!

It was wonderful. Nothing will shake me, but that sisterhood is powerful. Of course there are differences and of course those differences must be celebrated, but basically the oppression is of women. For me, the Women's Movement is the present and the future and it's the only way. My pleasure and my privilege and my joy has been just to to talk with women. As one woman said, it's like a pinhole in the darkness. If any of my experience can just be a pinhole of light for some woman to look through and perhaps get a little bit of strength, then that's it, for me. Women give me their strength and I give them mine.

But I've also experienced a lot of ageism where they (as I understand it now) feel threatened by an older woman. In the early 1970s at a woman's conference there was a workshop on motherhood which I went to. There were half a dozen or so younger women in the room and when I sat down, two women got up and said, 'If that woman's going to be here,' looking at me, 'then we're going.' The woman who had convened the group looked a bit startled and said, 'Why?' and they said, 'Well, we want to talk about our mothers and we can't with her.' So I went. To them motherhood meant bellyaching about their mothers and they couldn't in fact talk with a woman of 52 there. Although I say I've encountered cruelty, I've also encountered great friendship and great support, which very much outweighs the other.

I had been a militant atheist for some years. I felt that the idea of God in heaven and God's servants, the priests of whatever religion, put people down, and as my feminist consciousness became raised, I saw more and more how they put women down. I began to ask myself why society put women down under the blessing, literally, of God and the priests. And then I saw an ad in the *London Women's Liberation Newsletter* saying a matriarchy study group was about to form to look into the origins of women's oppression. I immediately joined. Here I was introduced to study and research on goddesses who were either equally powerful or more powerful, who were goddesses in their own right in the ancient world and in pre-industrial societies. Alongside these goddesses were priestesses and alongside the priestesses were ordinary women, in these cultures, who took part. Sometimes they did it equally with the men and sometimes they were the leaders. And this had been totally forgotten; not only forgotten, totally overruled, totally occluded, and great efforts had been made to trivialise it.

This group was a transformer for me, because the women in it were keen on study. They were academically oriented. They were also much younger than me. I was the only one without a degree and the only one who'd left school at 16. And I was the only Jewish woman there. I used to read the Jewish encyclopedia and I was familiar with goddesses such as Isis and Ashtoreth. Somehow this all came back to me in a new way and I returned in a sense to the Jewish encyclopedia, to the goddesses of my childhood. I began to understand the whole roots of our oppression. Strong women like mothers-in-law and stepmothers, the older women, became the devils, and the young women, damsels, who were willing to be slaves to men, became the heroines. I learned all this through studying the roots of our women's past.

We produced an issue of *Shrew*, the Women's Liberation paper, called *Goddess Shrew* in 1976. It was a sell-out; it was incredible. It got a notice in the *Guardian* with my address on it and we had 500 letters from women in about two weeks. But at the same time we also got assailed by the academics, who said there's no evidence and these women are just daydreaming. This upset the academic women in my group. I said, I'm sure we haven't dreamed it up, I know that it's there. I thought, when I retire maybe I'll be able to find some way of finding out.

I retired before I needed to, but the job was getting too much for me. But what was I going to do when I retired? One of the young women in the group was a student at London University and she told me the place was littered with leaflets about mature students. I had got matric in 1937 and that matric got me into university in 1980. I joined a famous theology department with a famous divinity degree which was Christian-oriented. I decided that was the ground I wanted to be on. I believe that Judaism and Christianity have overturned previous religions. I wanted to find out about my *own* culture that I was brought up in, in this country, with a Jewish background and a Christian culture to live in.

Being a Jew hadn't been at the top of my consciousness. For 40

212

years after I'd left home I knew that I was a Jew, but I didn't bother about it. And then going to college meant that I had to think about it. I'd left school 40 years before in an atmosphere of anti-Semitism; I'd come back to school and here was anti-Semitism. What was so incredibly painful was not that the tutors were anti-Semitic as such, or not overtly so; it was the content. I understood for the first time where anti-Semitism came from and I was studying it with all the highest academic talent at my command to help me, and that became almost unbearable. I was studying it among young people, some of them no more than 18 or 19, who were going to become vicars and teachers, and they were being taught anti-Semitism. I learned that I had to no longer 'pass' and not bother about being Jewish. I had to stand up and be counted; I had to object; I had to point out. One tutor actually said, 'You've made me tear up 20 years of notes.' I believe I got one of the textbooks withdrawn because it was so anti-Semitic. So I really did a lot of political work of that kind at college.

At that time I had been getting very uneasy in the Women's Movement. I had been feeling that there were anti-Jewish feelings. And this brings up the whole vexed and difficult subject of Palestine and Israel. My feeling about Israel is that Israel must exist, and that anyone who's lived through the Holocaust knows that Israel must exist. At the same time the Palestinian Arabs have a right to their territory and some arrangement should be made. Neither should be dispossessed of their territory.

I found that I wasn't able, as a Jewish woman, just to say that in the Women's Movement and be listened to. I found that there was an emotional uprush of anti-Semitism. They took up the line of 'Israel must be destroyed', and I couldn't bear it. At college, where I might expect it from the Christian hierarchy, and in the Women's Movement, my sisters – the same thing, a different angle but the same thing. And so my Jewishness was high on the agenda; it became almost top of the agenda in a very short time. I got involved in various Jewish groups: a Jewish Radical Group and, for the last couple of years, the Older Jewish Women's Group.

Matriarchy links up in the end with Judaism. Matriarchy's a very loose word. I'm talking about women's power in the past and how it helps us gain power at the present. I give slide shows and lectures on women of the past as symbols of our power. I always say, the reason for doing this is not only to reclaim women who have been lost and bulldozed out of history, but to reinspire ourselves for today's struggle. What I found in getting the academic tools to discover the material that is lying there in libraries and that nobody ever looks at, was that women were much more powerful in the past and particularly in religion. I found they were powerful not only in other religions, but the Jewish religion. I found that just as in the other religions there were female aspects of god, so there were in the Jewish religion. Even up to a very late date, the destruction of the second temple, there were groups of Jews where the women were as powerful as men.

My belief is that what destroyed it was the Romans. In AD 70 the Romans destroyed the Jews and just a few remained and they happened to be the Pharisees, who went to Yavneh and set up their school. The Sadducees and the Essenes are known about, but there were others as well. Some of the others certainly worshipped a consort of Yahweh, as well as Yahweh, with priestesses, as a sect of the Jewish religion, but they were wiped out by the Romans. All the Jews in Jerusalem were wiped out except the ones who have founded the Jewish religion as we know it today. They were very anti-woman and so, from then onwards, we get the religion which is thought to be traditional Judaism. But my matriarchal researches tell me that it's only traditional back to AD 70, which isn't all that amount of time, in our culture.

As a result of the degree I wanted to do more. So now I'm registered as a graduate student, doing research on the figure of *Chochma*, 'Wisdom', who is a very difficult figure. Even the rabbis say she's difficult, because she comes out as a person in her own right. In Proverbs 8 it talks about how Wisdom was there from the beginning, and was daily his delight. In the Book of Wisdom of Solomon in the Apocrypha, Chapter 7, there's a long panegyric about the qualities of Wisdom: how beautiful she is, how she taught humankind everything, how she stretches mightily from one end of the world to the other and she orders all things well. 'I, Wisdom, formed the first father of the world.' Where do we have a 'she' elsewhere? I got very excited about this. I'm now trying to put together more information about the figure of Wisdom. Was she a turning-point? Was she the last time in the Jewish tradition where we had a female aspect of deity coming right out into the open? How she was part of the world, as well as being the creator or being with the creator?

I was an atheist for a long time and came into matriarchy research for purely political reasons without any idea of spirituality or religion, which I was much against. But in researching the goddesses and our foresisters, the spiritual opened for me where it had never opened before, and I found that I began to feel things that I'd never felt. They made sacred places in the shape of the Great Mother; the stone circles are in the shape of a woman's body and you enter it by the vagina. When you go to such a place, you can't just stay political, in the sense of out-there political or academic; your heart or your stomach or something moves and the emotions are there and you really begin to feel. The female aspect of God is in all of us. She was put down as we were put down. In raising her we raise ourselves, and in raising ourselves we raise her. And this is my religion. We can regain our spiritual side as women, and I fight for this. But I let women know that I'm Jewish and that I'm particularly interested in rediscovering the female side of the Jewish deity.

My attitude to men is that they must change. They must recognise their oppressive position and actions towards us women and change them. This is absolutely necessary. I see some of them are beginning to try to do this and I welcome it. And some of them in my family and in my life I love, despite the pain. But my first feeling is for all women.

AFTERWORD

I recently met my half-sister Rosemary again after 49 years. She had emigrated as a young woman to New York, and after a short time my stepmother had followed her and they both settled there. Our reunion came about by chance through meeting someone who knew her when I happened to look in at a Jewish book fair, and who wrote to her about me. She sent me a marvellously warm and loving letter, and after a couple of months I managed to get myself to New York and meet her. It was quite wonderful. She welcomed me without reservations and told me all about the family history. My stepmother had lived happily in Brooklyn, had worked till she was over 70, saw her daughter married and her grandchildren born and grow up. She died in her eighties. It turns out that the family did try and search for me during and after the war, unsuccessfully. In particular Rosemary, when she became adult, wanted to find me. My stepmother, however, never really forgave me and cut me out of a family photo. But Rosemary and her husband and children immediately made me feel part of the family and now we correspond regularly and I hope we shall meet as regularly as possible.

MIRIAM METZ
It is a Tree of Life

Miriam Metz was born during the Second World War in a small town to which her mother had been evacuated from London. Though of a younger generation than the other women, her account of growing up in the East End in the forties and fifties is reminiscent of accounts of life there in earlier periods. Her experience was of an East End vibrant with Jewish life, especially in the markets and synagogues, in the face of a communal mythology that says the Jewish East End ceased to exist after the war. Being the daughter of Yiddish-speaking refugees was unusual at that time and marked her off from other Jewish children whose families had settled in the East End decades earlier.

There were many contrasting influences in Miriam's early life. In her early childhood there was the Yiddish-speaking immigrant family, the gentile school, the traditional cheder. *Later she contrasts the richness of traditional Jewish life with the Jewish clubs with their generations of anglicisation, and at school, the polite anti-Semitism of English literature. Her politics were formed within the context of East End class solidarity and a growing awareness of racism, and alongside that, the pressures to assimilate and transcend her background as she moved through the grammar school and on to university. In her early adult life she experienced pressures towards a femininity which assumed the centrality of heterosexuality, in conflict with her awareness of her own lesbianism. She reflects on these different influences in a positive way, without regret or resentment, emphasising the ways in which her life has been enriched by those experiences.*

Central to Miriam's life now are her lesbian feminism and her Jewishness. She was aware of her lesbian impulses from childhood, and, like

217

many girls growing up in the fifties and sixties, she felt mystified and isolated by the negative messages she received about her sexuality. The climate of sexual liberalism of the late sixties started to shift that isolation. But it was not until the seventies that feminism provided a framework for understanding those experiences and the possibility of finding in women and in being a woman great sources of strength. But the Women's Liberation Movement still left a large part of her life untouched and unaccounted for. In the eighties Jewish women have become more confident in redefining their Jewishness and their feminism in relation to one another.

As a teenager Miriam rejected religious practice, but in her thirties she began to appreciate what she had lost in cutting herself off from this dimension of her Jewishness. Not only has she come to perceive her childhood as enriched by Judaism and Yiddishkeit, but she has now, in her own way, come to be a deeply religious Jew, experiencing in Judaism a great source of joy.

I was brought up in Stepney in the East End of London, though I was actually born outside London because, in common with a lot of East Enders, my family was evacuated during the war. At the time I lived in Stepney, just after the war up till the early sixties, it was still very much a Yiddish-speaking area. At least half of the people in the street I lived in were people whose language was Yiddish, who'd come from the pogroms in Russia at the turn of the century. That elderly population was very much a presence in the street and my perceptions of them certainly were very important to me. Then there were Jewish people who were maybe second or third generation, who had a very particular East End working-class Jewish style. And then the non-Jewish population was a very mixed population, including Scottish and Maltese and some West Indians. Very few of the people I remember growing up with were actually East Enders going back for hundreds of years. It was a very mixed area, but I perceived it as half Jewish – but somehow a larger half, if I can put it that way.

I had a consciousness as a child of certain sorts of difference; we were first-generation immigrants and there were relatively few children of immigrants of my age. So in one sense we were younger than the other Yiddish speakers around us, but in another sense we were older than, say, the Jewish children I went to school with, who, almost without exception, were third generation born here. To come from a Yiddish-speaking family already marked you out, as it were, as being of a past generation. At that time it was becoming a minority culture, though if you looked at the Jewish population in the East End, it was quite clear that it was Yiddish and *Yiddishkeit* which held them together.

We went to *shul* always on festivals. We observed *Shabbes* by having candles and *kiddush*, but not by abstaining from travel and going to *shul*, though my father used to go. In respect of Jewish practice, what I now realise is that my parents' whole lives were informed by all the sorts of principles that are set out in the Talmud and the religious writings which one thinks of as being studied only by learned scholars. In a conscious way, I associated Jewishness, through my parents, with things like lighting the candles at *Shabbes*, like have the *kiddush* on Friday night, having all those lovely foods like *challah*, having the Seder, all the preparations for that. My Jewish consciousness was quite formed, in fact, by the practice of cooking special meals for all the Jewish rituals and the important part that children play in them. But at the same time there were all sorts of values which, now that I know more about Judaism, partly through having studied it, but also partly through being older and having experienced a Jewish way of life and a non-Jewish way of life, I now realise were as much part of Jewishness as anything. For example, my parents' attitudes to animals were very insistently kind and protective, putting the animals first, a particular love and affection for animals. And principles about not speaking evil about other people, particularly about having compassion; a Yiddish word, *rachmones*, was very much a word I grew up with and my parents would always try and instil in me a sense of feeling compassion for somebody who was hard up, or being ready to share in somebody's misfortunes. I think that was terribly important. And another side of Jewishness which also came through my parents is an ironic wit in describing the world outside, other Jewish people or the gentile world.

I find it very difficult to cope with the fact that the East End I grew up in is being demolished, or no longer exists. But I'm very much formed by a consciousness of the tremendous vitality of the Jewish East End, the loveliness of the markets, the ways in which people talked, the humour. I was very much aware of it as a child. I suppose my earliest contacts with the wider world as a child were going to the markets and talking to the Jewish stallholders. The Jewish bakeries, the fish shops, the chicken shop – those were lovely. We were surrounded by such very large numbers of Jewish people. If you went to Hessel Street (the main market my family used) or Petticoat Lane, it was always athrong with Jewish people.

And then there was this sheer wealth of synagogues. The way in which a consciousness of the number of synagogues would have been very explicit to me as a child was that that at Simchas Torah you could do a 'synagogue crawl'. You could go to all these different synagogues and get bags of sweets and fruit, which I duly did. There was a sense of literally congregations and congregations of Jews who came together – although their degrees of observance were different, everybody would have celebrated the festivals. The synagogues were full of people at those times. Everybody participated very warmly – I particularly remember this in the Ne'ila service, which comes at the end of all those long periods of prayer on Yom Kippur. The fervour of it has gone now.

Then there's another side of the East End, which I associate with my father and some of the other members of my family, which is a particular modesty. I met through him so many people who were very poor. My father was a member of the Workers' Circle and went there once a week, sometimes with us children – I suppose that was his main contribution to childcare, to take the children out on a Sunday morning and give my mother a rest. Then there were little shoemakers and the like, working in single rooms, who used to greet each other like lost souls – not saying that much to each other, just these particularly warm forms of greeting, and particularly warm forms of welcome to me. They exchanged news of what it was to be an outsider; they were refugees in a world which was already looking in different directions. That particular humorous modesty is what I think of as Jewishness. That particular version of the East End was not associated in my mind with that materialism which is part of our society at large now. I do very much miss that. But I feel myself incredibly lucky to have grown up in that environment, incredibly lucky to have been part of that culture.

The experiences I had as a child also presented to me political dangers which many people thought had ceased to exist. I grew up knowing about Nazism through my parents' stories. That history was made very clear. But also as a child in the East End, I was constantly receiving signals that fascism wasn't dead, which, if you read the newspaper or heard the radio, one was led to believe it was. For instance, near one of the markets we used to use, Watney Street, which was a gentile market, there was a particularly big bomb site and I remember seeing – I suppose I was about six or seven – painted on a wall, 'Slump – or Mosley', with the British Union of Fascists flash. Now, I don't think I was really old enough to comprehend quite what fascism meant and to see its relationship to Nazism – obviously nothing as sophisticated as that – but I did know that the fascists attacked Jews. I'd been brought up knowing about that and I'd known that there were still fascist attacks going on in the East End in the late forties. I was obviously very struck and alarmed by that 'Slump – or Mosley' as a child. At that time, I must say, nobody perceived the idea of a future of unemployment, but that notion of Mosley standing there waiting in the wings as an alternative . . . I also quite regularly went with my family up to Club Row, which was a mixture of pet market and cheap goods market, and somewhere near the end there was a pitch where fascists used to stand, Hyde Park style. And I used to go with my family to look occasionally, almost in this sense of fear and horror but also wanting to see what it was. So there was the sense of that still being around.

My parents' political standpoint changed over my childhood. I have obviously only limited memories of the forties, being born half-way through them, but I do remember a very strong pro-Labour feeling in my household. There was very much that sense of, one follows Labour because it stands for social justice and Conservatism is somehow part of an utterly different world, in the same way that living in Golders Green was somewhere beyond the moon. But it wasn't just my parents. I was very conscious as a child of a great deal of solidarity around supporting socialism, being for Labour. Of course, everybody was for Labour! How could it be otherwise? How could anybody feel differently? I also had a sense of Conservatism being something really very wicked and remote, but also definitely not in our favour.

As the fifties wore on, I became more aware that my father had certainly had very strong communist sympathies, although I don't think he would have ever voted communist. He made remarks about the wrongness of the Queen having a coronation, virtually the only person that I heard saying that. He'd say, 'Who is this gentile lady in a golden coach?' in a rather ironic way, and he refused to watch it on television. I think he, in a romantic way, was communistic, whereas the other adults in my family became more materialistic as time went on. The Macmillan era's ideology was being sold – and they bought it. But I think that's only a part of my political upbringing, because I think I began to acquire a political consciousness as much through my experience of being at school as in the home, and that's interesting too.

There was tremendously strong class solidarity at secondary school, which was a working-class girls' grammar school. I remember that the one thing that all the girls in the school hated was anything that patronised the working class. There was also a sentimentality you could get in a traditional girls' school. When the old headmistress left, she made a speech and everybody was weeping their sentimental tears. And then she said, 'Of course, I've always thought the East End girls were wonderful.' And the mood in the hall turned ugly; there was a collective growl. There was this sense of her having said something patronising.

When there were general elections there was an incredible strength of feeling about the Labour Party. I can remember it very strongly around the 1955 election. We had mock elections at the school and I remember the school captain, a white Christian girl, making this speech saying that if you vote Labour, they will bring in comprehensive schools and we'll all be herded together. And the howl of outrage and passion from all the girls in the school! Collectively, we all wanted comprehensive education, and we were for Labour. That was it!

There was this passionately strong Labour feeling, yet I can't remember anybody having any specific demands. Labour was really a class thing, a great collective thing, feeling affection and loyalty for Labour. Communism was people from the outside; it was teachers and intellectuals coming into the East End trying to get people to be communist. I remember that as a rather widespread feeling. There was this Jewish teacher at primary school who wore a red tie and was a communist. We kids in this primary school thought, ha! ha! another of these characters trying to turn us into something else.

At about 14, I remember thinking of myself as a Tory. I don't know how it happened. It was obviously just a phase I went through. At the same time there was a select group of girls, most of whom were Jewish, in the year above me, who were the acolytes of two teachers, one of whom was a communist. This group of elite girls were obviously 'proper' theoretical socialists; they weren't gut Labour Party like everyone else. Somehow I got drawn into this group, and I remember this teacher turning round to me and saying, 'You know, you may call yourself a Tory, but every single thing you say is actually coming out with the Party line.' And I thought – Oh! Then I was approached by one of these girls to join the Communist Party, and I thought, bloody hell, I'm being got at. I felt quite freaked out by it. It would have been like I later felt about being asked to apply for Oxford and Cambridge, which I refused to do. It would have been a decisive act of cutting yourself off from the collective – although I was very alienated from the collective, and they saw me as an oddball. But there was that sense of it being a real betrayal to 'go over'.

When I was in my teens I went to France for several months, and that made a political connection with what I was aware of in terms of racism about black people. That was a live issue, because there were things like the Notting Hill riots at the time I was at school – 1958. By then there were a few black girls in the school, but lots of us were Jewish or Greek Cypriot, immigrants or daughters or granddaughters of immigrants. Nobody ever had any doubt that that was the same thing, that we felt solidarity and support for black people, that they, like our families and us, experienced racism.

When I went to France, I remember being struck by suddenly realising all about the Algerian immigrants. I was wandering about Paris by myself, and constantly getting picked up by these young

Algerians. And I suddenly sussed out why they were trying to pick me up: because nobody else would talk to them, the desperation for some sort of sexual outlet.

I saw that what happened to black people in our country was not simply a question of 'white people are prejudiced against black people', which is probably how, in my own inarticulate way, I would have thought about it till then, but I saw it was part of a system. I worked out for myself that there was this system whereby countries which had had colonies brought these people into their country and then dumped them – used them and treated them like dirt. I would have realised that anyway, but my perception suddenly went click! You realise you're looking at a whole class of things.

A couple of years later I went to Israel for six months and came slap up against Israeli politics – not in the way it would be seen now, but the total variety of different Zionist groupings and different parties. I saw this poster which said in Hebrew, 'Both sides of the Jordan'; it was a map of the Land of Israel with a hand holding a gun. My cousin said, 'Those are the Israeli fascists. They're called Herut and there's this person called Menahem Begin . . .' That was in 1962. I remember having explained to me by my family there the absolute horror of what that stood for, how terrible it was, what evil politics it was.

The next thing I realised came from suddenly saying to my cousin, 'Where do the Arabs live in Tel Aviv?' And she said, 'They're not allowed to live in Tel Aviv.' There was a radical shift in my life. From that time onwards, I would have defined myself as an anti-Zionist, until the time of the anti-Semitic reactions following the Israeli invasion of the Lebanon, at which time I turned right back.

My school life is really quite rigidly separated into three different schools. Although the bit of the East End I grew up in was full of Jewish people, it wasn't full of Jewish children, so there were only a very few Jewish children in the primary school I went to. That was my first introduction to a gentile environment controlled by gentiles, which hadn't that much room for me as a Jew. I think the headmaster of the school was a very good and conscientious man who wanted to be welcoming towards Jewish children and obviously

224

seemed to be very fond of us as individuals. But we had to say the Lord's Prayer every day and all the teachers were gentile, except for the one Jewish teacher, who was a communist, not an observant Jew. That whole world seemed very alien to me. The poetry we read was stuff about lambs skipping in the spring; it just meant nothing to me.

I was good at school, in the sense that I was academically successful, but I was very isolated, because I was surrounded by very tough and very lively – and I'm sure they were absolutely lovely – East End, mainly dockers', kids. I stood out like a sore thumb. I had no way of explaining that great cultural difference; I just saw myself as a failure who was bullied or persecuted – which I was. The toilets couldn't be locked and the kids would come and look at and mock anyone using them. For me that was an absolute nightmare. I also couldn't bear to use the toilet at home because there were spiders and I was terrified. A large part of my life was fear of going to the toilet and I learned virtually never to go. I didn't form friendships to speak of at my primary school. I was very lonely and isolated, terribly unhappy. I was totally unable to deal with the discipline of the school. I didn't know what I was supposed to be doing and it was never properly explained to me. There were 50 sums in a book and I did them all on the one slate and took it to the teacher, who was furious, because she couldn't read them. Everything I did was wrong. The teacher would say that it was time to go out and I would say, 'I don't want to go.' And she would say, 'You cheeky monkey'. I would get into such trouble, giving innocent answers reflecting my true state of feeling. I was absolutely miserable in many ways, except I was obviously good at writing and I enjoyed doing that.

There was some Jewish education at that school in that a rabbi came once a week to teach us, so I did partly learn to read Hebrew there. I was taught it in this very old-fashioned manner of seeing the *alef* and the *bais* and so on and saying, oh, ah, eh; boh, bah, beh; goh, gah, geh. You sounded these nonsense syllables and learned by repetition – totally contrary to any modern theories of reading, but I learned to read Hebrew perfectly easily that way. The rabbi used to tell us stories and I remember him doing an absolutely wonderful telling of the story of Esther. He was perceived of as a very ancient and stuffy character and yet he obviously did do a successful job.

Until about the age of eight, alongside the primary school, I was sent to what I must count as another school, and that was the *cheder*. It was a real old-fashioned *cheder*; none of this idea of you learn Hebrew as a modern language. This was really there to teach kids to read from the prayer book. It was a room crammed with desks and crammed with children – mainly boys; also a group of girls, who sat towards one corner. The character who ran it walked about with a cane and the kids sat at desks and chanted. It taught me to read Hebrew from the prayer book at a fantastic speed – which I can no longer do. What do you learn this skill for? Well, you're learning it so that you can participate in prayer. There is a prizing of being able to read prayer fast, which doesn't mean that you're disrespectful of it, but it's like running towards something, an idea which I find very exciting. That was such a different world from ordinary school, one which you went to afterwards and which was very much despised. I now see it as being part of the tradition which is only alive now among the Chassidic and very orthodox communities and I'm glad to have been part of it.

And then I went to secondary school, a girls' grammar school, and a third of the girls in the school were Jewish. That was actually very influential, in that for the first time I was part of a large Jewish community of my own age, which I hadn't been in my family life and in my experience of the Jewish East End *shuls*. I knew very few other children. I knew one or two kids in our street but they weren't what I would call friends. I had a few cousins living in distant suburbs of London – only a few, because most of my family didn't survive the Holocaust – but my family didn't have a car and travel was a big number. So I only saw these fabled cousins two or three times a year. So when I went to the secondary school, there was this community of girls of my own age. Again, that was not easy or so happy an experience, although I wasn't really unhappy, as I had been in my primary school.

These girls were all wonderfully lively, vivacious, 'English Jews', which meant that by and large they were third generation. So they were very much working-class English Jews in their way of thinking and speaking. They all seemed to have huge families and spend every single weekend going to a Barmitzvah or a wedding. A lot of their social life revolved around the Jewish clubs, the Brady Club or Oxford and St George's, which I subsequently went to for a time, but they went to those clubs because their parents had been there and it was utterly part of their lives. Their families, their mates, their cousins, all went to these clubs as well. They were very much centred on things like sport, things that I had no interest in. I would have loved to play table tennis, but I absolutely wasn't into any physical prowess. I now see that not just simply as a product of me having been a clumsy child but because I came from a Jewish tradition that did not think physical prowess is important. In the mainstream Jewish tradition, what is important is learning and good deeds and all the rest of it. I remember a lot of those girls as being incredibly agile and wiry, good at sport and swimming, because that was the mode of those clubs. The boys were into football, but it wasn't quite the obsession it is today. And what those girls were into – that was certainly East End precociousness, although now everybody is into that precociousness – was dancing and boys. Of course, the fact that I was a year younger made the gap even more glaring.

I don't think of those girls as being restricted. On Rosh Hashona and Yom Kippur they would all congregate, go down from wherever their families were to the Tower of London and wander about – which I began doing from quite early in my secondary school career. So they obviously were all allowed to wander off together, and so was I. I think people were much less alarmed then about the dangers to girls than they are now. Surprising really, but that's how it seemed to have operated.

When I was at the secondary school, I liked reading and I enjoyed being at home. I was very protected from housework at home. I liked family life most, although by then there were already various difficulties in my family. I liked hearing family stories, stories of my forebears or the family's experiences in Europe. We only had a television first when I was 12 or 13; I became an addictive television viewer and I loved it, watched ITV endlessly. I don't think I was a very happy kid really. I used to like walking the two miles home from school, a very circuitous route which took me around Hanbury Street and all the traditional East End and

227

around Whitechapel and up and down. But I felt very lonely in the holidays because I didn't have regular friends that I went out with.

The school was like grammar schools of the time – very hidebound, very narrow culturally. It didn't let us draw on our own culture. It did something which I suppose is counted as fairly radical: when you were in the second year you had to write a local history essay, but what local history was interpreted as meaning was either the Tower of London or the Whitechapel Bell Foundry, where they made the Liberty Bell, or Chaucer's Stepney or something like that. It was never remotely signalled to us that what we could be doing was actually looking at the Jewish East End, or our own family histories. I became a very fluent writer and was known to be 'good at writing', but I was never particularly invited to relate to my own experience. Some of those essay titles came up in such a way that I wrote elements of my own experience in a fiction that I thought would be acceptable to the school. For example, it was all right to write about your experiences in the East End if you somehow presented yourself as a detached observer but that sense of genuinely writing from the heart – no. I think they would have liked it if we had, but they never directly signalled to us that that was what was looked for, and it was much more in the format of 'a day in the life of a penny'.

I remember as a tiny tot wanting to be a film star, without any idea of what a film star was. I remember also saying I wanted to be a machinist. Lots of the girls were daughters of machinists and they said they were going to be machinists and I said, 'Oh, right, I'll be a machinist too.' I remember family pressure on me to be a shorthand typist or a copy typist, because I was told they earned good money, but I didn't have any particular feelings about it. I never thought that I would go to university, till I'd done my O levels. I grew up in a culture where maybe a boy would do that. Although I'd been very successful at my primary school, I had a period of illness in my secondary school, and had then fallen behind. So although I was good at writing, I'd never been seen as one of the star performers. Anyway, I got quite good O levels and went into the sixth form and gradually I got into taking A levels. I seem to remember making those choices by myself, still having that idea that I might end up as a shorthand typist. My parents didn't stand in my way and they certainly didn't do anything like steer me into the secretarial sixth, which was seen as a separate world. I almost blundered into A levels, not with any firm intentions. Also, I didn't have any alternative and it's a way of delaying a decision. I knew I didn't want to do anything like being a nurse.

Then, once I got into the sixth form I was, if you like, sponsored by a particular English teacher who gave me personal coaching, and I became very committed to doing English and history and French. In the end I did very well at all of them though I couldn't go straight to university because I was still under-age. By then I'd got into English enough to want to do Eng. Lit., but I think there was a horrendous price to be paid. It's only in later years that I realised what the implications were. What was Eng. Lit.? It was a complete acceptance of a certain form of mental assimilation. The poetry you were reading was stuff like Donne's poetry, which is all Christian. You were translating Chaucer. We had these English teachers who said such terrible *chutzpahdik* things to us, like Chaucer wasn't anti-Semitic – if you actually read these texts, of course they were anti-Semitic! T. S. Eliot was one of our A level texts and T. S. Eliot has written the most directly anti-Semitic poems. We had to read and study these poems and we had a teacher at that time – not the teacher who'd sponsored me – who would say things to us like, 'Well, of course, only a committed Christian could really understand Eliot's poetry.' Tough luck on the rest of us, I suppose. That was said by her without any thought. And then, when we read through some of these poems, she said they were not anti-Semitic; he'd written them with a small 'j' so he didn't mean Jews as a whole. Now, that's utter rubbish! I remember at the time thinking, I don't believe that, but all the same becoming very 'good' at Eliot and writing 'brilliant' essays on him. Even when I went to university for the interview they asked me to tell them all about *The Waste Land*. There's a nice opening question for a 17-year-old girl! So with this tremendous verve and commitment I went into this great long explanation of what *The Waste Land* was all about and how wonderful Eliot's poetry was. I had been taught to love all this stuff that actually had a place for me in it as a villain and I wasn't even conscious of it. Of course,

I didn't identify with the evil Jews. I don't know that I did utterly think that that was my culture, but I suppose I did on some level.

The English school system's most attractive form of education was one which didn't even recognise its own anti-Semitism and taught you to do likewise, but it also had no way of making science available to you or interesting to you. The continental European education such as some members of my family had had led them to end up as scientists. Female members of my family – before the Nazis stopped them – had wanted to do things like engineering and didn't think that was anything strange. History I loved very much, and what I loved most was social history. But again, it was very much learning to write and think like Jane Austen. To be fair to the people in school, that was before people had really invented history from below as a school history topic, and it was certainly long before sociology or social studies was taught in grammar schools.

At the time I was at school, feminism was thought of as something which had died out – one thought of feminism as the suffragettes, and they died out after the vote was granted after the First World War. In so far as women's rights were concerned, one thought of votes for women as what it was all about. On the other hand, I was used to this sense of women having the power roles in the school. A lot of the women who taught in the grammar school were single women and I think a fair number of them were lesbians. There were women at the school who lectured us on the importance of being independent and not thinking about marriage, but, of course, we all laughed at it. We saw these women as failures and dried-up old sticks who were obsessed with sex and who were just lecturing us. There were various nasty jokes around the school – 'Oh, she's a lesbian', and 'lesbie friends', and all those sorts of things. I was always very uncomfortable about all that, because I knew I had those impulses myself. From the age of nine onwards I was passionately in love with one woman after another, usually older girls at school, so I could never really join in those things and always had a dread around them. Again I associated that as another level of my own difference – the long experience of a series of being in love with other girls and never being able to speak about it because they never seemed remotely to perceive it or respond to it, and just being rather despairing about that.

So as I grew up in school, feminism would have had no message because it was seen as of the past, not to do with what I wanted. My own desires were certainly not to be shared with anybody and I was desperately thinking, is it going to be a phase? And will the world suddenly go pop and I'll fall for a man or a boy? And thinking that I ought to be talking about boyfriends. If I was in the situation of meeting boys, which increasingly through going off with girls of my own age I was, I felt completely uninterested in them and could sense they felt completely uninterested in me. I didn't know what to do about it, but it wasn't there for me.

I was at university before 'the feminist era', in the early and middle sixties. Most of being at university I did enjoy, but there was this tremendous pressure to be very heterosexual and to be into all these horrendous parties. You went to parties to get drunk and to get off with somebody. It was absolutely hateful. And that was the high era of beehives and backcombing, sticking-out dresses and 6-inch high heels. I was quite into dressing but I hated make-up, I hated parties and I didn't feel I had the right to say so. I remember these really quite kindly friends who tried to take me in hand, actually sitting and making me up one day and trying to turn me into this creature who could succeed at these parties. Now, in a sense, I was quite able to use boys or men for some quick thrill, but on that basis I wouldn't want to see them again. Certainly there just was no possibility there of relationships, whereas I had these intense friendships with women at college. I loved lots of them dearly and there would always be one particular one of them who I was in love with and who would seem to want to spend all her time with me but somehow always had a boyfriend in the background. That feeling seemed to be completely unreciprocated so that I found very depressing.

Like, I think, most lesbians, I went and looked up the only material which was available, which was all that sex book literature which said lesbians wore suits and hung out in these clubs and committed suicide. Obviously I was terrified of that and just thought of myself as a 'normal person' who had those sorts of loves and feelings. And there was this very frustrating experience, when

I was at university, that I was very successful at being friendly with male students – particularly the most glamorous and interesting and exciting ones seemed to love being my friend – but I would never be the one who got invited to the ball. It was a very embittering experience. I couldn't understand it as I do now. Feminism in that way wasn't around then and all the women who later came out as feminists had had experiences like mine. That whole sequence of my experiences of trying to relate to men I now recognise as how men exploit women; they use women for support and intellectual interest and turn to somebody else for sex, and have that complete inability to fuse the two. Whereas in my relationships with women and my friendships, there was always that possibility of a sexual and loving overtone and I would never have wanted to turn away; it was always that they were the ones who turned away.

There were one or two women I now feel exploited me as the men did, particularly one older woman. She was a woman in her thirties who then seemed very old to me as an 18-year-old, and who constantly used me as this confidante and support. I never talked about my life because I couldn't have actually confided to her that I was in love with all these other women and could have felt that for her as well. In fact, she talked to me about another student who'd been in love with her but she wasn't 'like that'! So in other words, from the start of this friendship which she initiated, which she sponsored, which she continued, I had this very firm message: don't get any ideas about 'that'! And there would be these various exploitative men about whom she would then expect me to give her support. There was lots of that. I think by the time that I entered my first lesbian relationship, which came several years after I was out of college, I began to perceive its exploitativeness and feel angry. But there were other friends who ended up heterosexual and who I'd had that warmth and friendship with, but who I don't now feel anger towards because I feel they were very much exploited as well.

Once I went to university, I found myself entirely in gentile circles. There were one or two other Jewish students, but I thought of myself as having grown up and put all that behind me. Now I was free to be just an 'ordinary person'. I thought that I had gained access to a much wider range of choice, although in fact I rejected out of hand all sorts of things which I now see as treasures of our culture, like the practice of doing the Seder. I didn't think that I'd given up anything to become part of this gentile milieu. I just saw it as entering into new freedoms. This secular gentile world I now see as all pleasure without obligation. It's part of a very cruel world, because as long as you can run the race and do well, you're okay. If you can't, then tough luck.

The politics that really shifted me most and immediately after university were gay politics, liberation politics and Third World politics. The last year I was at university, I walked into this hall, and they said there's a teach-in on Vietnam. It was the first teach-in in this country. There was this revelation – politics is people of my age, talking passionately with people who were fighting liberation struggles! That sense of American youth rising up to challenge their professors . . . It was just stunning. It went on all night.

Then there was the whole thing of gay politics and the dialectics of liberation. That was obviously what enabled me eventually to come out. I fell in love with a woman who left her marriage and brought her child with her. We instantly found ourselves in a lesbian custody case, before such things existed. It was 1968. I really believed in liberation politics. I believed that you only had to say – the whole problem was that I'd never said I was gay. And it wasn't like that, because her husband instantly started sending solicitor's letters, so we had to go totally underground, totally closet. It was terrible. I think I was very much a feminist to challenge somebody into coming and setting up a lesbian household when people didn't do things like that, and being very defiant about it, thinking that was fantastic.

We lived together and were happy for quite a long time, and that was absolutely wonderful. We set up house and all the rest of it. We did, I suppose, act just like a heterosexual couple, except we were women. But from that point onwards I didn't say, here is the new world of lesbianism, here is the new world of feminism, because even then that was in the sixties. But I remember being quite conscious that the time had come when I could do things like refusing to go to parties, and I didn't have to conform, and that if one only recognised what one was and lived by it, then one could have a lot happier life. I think that's rather informed my life since, that sense of I'm not going to look over my shoulder and say, they're doing this and they've got that, so why aren't I doing it? I've certainly recognised that, for me, that's no way to operate. But that you've got to actually try and do, not exactly whatever makes you happy, because that's not at all my way of thinking, but you've got to try and live with what works for you and the people you want to associate your life with.

In my first lesbian relationship my lover was terribly keen on Christmas, and I took to this like anything. I really got into the celebration of Christmas, fondly believing that the way that we did it was not Christian. This was a purely neutral thing to do, to celebrate Christmas in a secular way. What I think about it now is that it all became part of this secularised Christian lifestyle. We had Sunday lunch, which was never seen as a Christian ritual. And my family and my experience were totally marginalised. I virtually never talked about being Jewish. I just became this neutral person. But somehow this neutral person was somebody who happened to go into churches on Easter. It wouldn't be to go to a service, just to see what the flowers were like, hear the music. So it was as if her culture was the normal, natural, wider choice-giving culture and mine was part of an obsolete past.

I also encountered anti-Semitism. For example, my first lover's father was directly and openly anti-Semitic. He liked to be able to needle people. He didn't feel he'd got the measure of somebody until he'd found whatever it was that would really upset them. And it took him a long time to find that with me it was anti-Semitism. Every time I'd go down there, he'd start making anti-Semitic remarks. In the end, I stopped going down there. The next time she went by herself with her daughter, her mother said to her, 'Has Miriam stopped coming because of your father's anti-Semitic remarks?' And she said 'Yes.' And that's all was said about it. She knew what it was, but she never challenged him on it. Certainly, while I was there, all those times, she never said anything. And I just put up with it as well, until one day I said, 'I'm sorry, I can't go.'

My early experiences of the women's movement were of its anti-lesbianism, its very particular notion of childcare, which didn't include any notion of lesbians having children or being involved in child-raising. I remember at the time the gay liberation movement – the gay men's movement actually – as being much more supportive. I remember the women's movement as saying, but we're not lesbians and you mustn't think that!

Then I had a period, which I now regard myself as having moved beyond, where I was very much influenced by Marxism and Marxist theories. I haven't moved beyond them in the sense that I don't believe in that analysis – I do think that that's a wonderful form of analysis of how society and economies operate and the whole idea of ideological consequences of material structures and all those sorts of things. That Marxist and socialist consciousness is still very much with me.

Since those days every sort of contact I've had with any sort of Marxist grouping, including Marxist feminist groupings, although I still would in some ways see myself as using Marxist feminist perspectives, has been a real horror. Not in terms of intellectualism, but in terms of how they manipulate and coerce you. It's really horrible.

Every experience I've had also makes me feel more and more anti-men, and especially the experience of working in a place where I see how much they use women, make them work, denigrate them, crunch them up and throw them out.

It was after that that I really came to feminism, which then had had a tremendous impact on my life, gave me a joy in making my life woman-centred and being able to celebrate that and be proud of that. Being able to look to women, and find that women can be autonomous and have so much to give, to give each other and to give the world. That all sounds very high falutin', but it's rather important in my life, although I think I'm not very much of the banners marching down the street type, because I think that's a mode of operation that women inherited from male socialist traditions. The lesbian actions that I really admire, like abseiling down into the House of Lords, for other reasons I wouldn't be that much into, but yes, it's there as a very strong mental presence.

But I must say there have been some sad experiences of working with gentile women in the women's movement. There's that sense of real instinctive embarrassment on their part about Jewishness – you can't really *believe* in all that, can you? Or again, the quite casual anti-Semitism. For example, I was in a collective and one of the women in it lived in Stamford Hill, where a lot of Chassidic families live. In commenting on her neighbours, she said, 'I can't bear it. They're so oppressive to their women.' And I thought, what the hell does she know about their lives? Her instant conviction; she was an instant expert. I actually tried to talk to one of those women once about how I thought the Chassidic tradition of maleness was very contrary to macho maleness, that their ideas about masculinity were totally different, and that there was actually something to be said for that, that you couldn't read their lives according to how we read family lives within this gentile Christian culture. And I remember this woman saying, 'Oh yes, that's very interesting.' But she wouldn't actually have altered her way of thinking because of it.

I've gradually over the years realised how absolutely cool and undisturbed they felt by their centrality. It wouldn't occur to them to feel otherwise than that their universe was the natural one, and anything else was abnormal. And, of course, what's true of women's groups is even more so in the male-dominated world we work and live in. I now feel that, just as lesbianism is marginalised and within heterosexual groups, so Judaism and Jewish tradition are marginalised within a gentile feminist context. Either they ignore it completely, or they go into an embarrassed flutter around it, but either way they can't really handle it – the way that we, or people from, say, the Islamic communities, have been used to fitting in with and taking on board all that bitter cultural baggage, learning it and knowing how to talk about it.

I just accepted that it was my role to enthusiastically enter into that culture and deny my own. If anything, my own could function as the source of some good jokes and that was about it. And there wouldn't be any way of reading the Jewish religion other than by analogy with the Christian religion. They wouldn't be able to see it as a way of life. It was just a mystery.

The other major series of decisions and changes in my life were the return to Judaism. It's something like the last 14 years of my life that I've gradually been returning to Judaism. It started off in my Marxist period, becoming involved in the oral history movement; I was very interested in oral history, and I thought, what about the oral history of my own family and my own people? I interviewed members of my family, very moving interviews, and began reading books about the *shtetl* and so on. Of course, as I read them, I more and more began to appreciate that what I'd rejected in the form of the Jewish religion, which I'd done since I was 12, was actually this very enriching way of life. As it says in the Torah, *Etz chaim hi lemachazikim bo* – It is a tree of life to those who take hold of it. I really believe that. And particularly in the last seven years, I have come to feel very deeply committed and almost in love with the Torah, with Jewish teachings as a way of life and a way of shaping your life. Now, I can't say I live in a religiously orthodox manner such as would be recognised by the mainstream orthodox and ultra-orthodox groups in this country, but I aspire to an increasingly close following of Jewish practice. In my own experience, every Jewish practice I observe, every Jewish ethical guideline that I follow, my life is enriched by it and it is a better way to live.

It runs very contrary to the whole sixties' ideal, which, of course, very much shaped me at university, that you can throw off all these old outmoded political and religious structures, you make your own morality. It's that fantastic arrogance of the sixties' generation, that they were going to throw out everything from the last 5,000 years. There's this concept of making your own morality as you go along – and then you see the consequences of that in terms of the destruction people wrought on each other's lives. I see the Jewish tradition as something totally opposite that says people need to live their lives within a structure. This reverence for a structure which is thousands of years old is not because that's the age tag on it, but because it's been able to adapt to different circumstances. People in different ages have found it a genuine and enriching way of life, not only for the individual, but one which actually ensures that people give to and make interdependencies, not only among other Jews but with all other people. There are obligations towards charity; obligation towards co-operation; obligation towards animals. In the Jewish *brochas*, you give thanks, you give praise, you celebrate. There's an awful lot of celebration in Jewish ritual. You involve children in them, you involve old people in them. They're absolutely wonderful things – and the language is wonderful.

I've thought in recent years how when I went with my parents to *shul*, like all kids in *shul*, I got bored. And what did I do? I flipped through the *machzor*. Now I read the *machzor* with passionate pleasure because there are these most beautiful passages, the strength and the daring of the language. There are wonderful passages which begin with great superlatives of celebration: 'Though our mouths were full of song like the sea, our tongues of exaltation as the fulness of its waves, and our lips of praise as the plains of the firmament; though our eyes gave light as the sun and the moon; though our hands were as outspread as the eagles of heaven, and our feet were as swift as hinds, yet should we be unable to thank thee.' There are these quite stunning passages, all very much about a celebration of a relationship to God, a celebration of a knowledge of ways to live, and I find them wonderful.

It's a very unconventional approach to practice and it's certainly not one which I'm advocating as an ideal, because I think I ought to do better than I'm doing. But the way I read Judaism is almost like standing on its head all the conventions about Judaism, especially those which have been talked abut by gentile feminists. I see Judaism as first of all a religion and a tradition which have always taken a very strong lead from 'the people'. There's great attention paid to the wishes of the people, with the rabbis following the congregations, not leading them, in the sense of altering the rules or reinterpreting the rules to respond to the needs and desires of the people. Take the tradition, for example, of separating women and men in the synagogue, which comes from the demands of women in the time of the Temple that they have a women's space. That women's space in the Temple was called *ezras nashim*, which means 'help for women' – it literally means women's aid. I love that tradition in Judaism which separates men and women, because I am a radical feminist and a separatist and so therefore Jewish practice which separates women and men, I think absolutely wonderful! There are feminists who read that as saying, that's an oppression of women. There is so much evidence in the history of *halachic* practice that women have succeeded in changing the law by pressure that I just don't believe that it's a correct interpretation of either women or Judaism to say these things happen because women were oppressed. I'm not trying to deny that they were oppressed but I don't think that the *halachah* is there as a simple projection of the particular forms of oppression which Jewish women experience. But I rather think that Judaism is full of recognition of the need for women's separate space, recognition of the innate violence of men, and therefore there are a whole load of obligations on men that they should constantly be praying, that they should cover themselves with symbols which tell them not to sin, like the *tallis* and the *tsitsis* and so on. It's almost as if Judaism is saying, yes, men are violent, they need restraining, and they have to fill up their lives with *mitzvahs*. Jewish tradition is absolutely against anything like pornography and out-of-control sexuality. And I more than appreciate it, I feel utterly at home with that.

Also there are stories in the Bible which really inspire me, having made a decision to have a child. The story that really inspired me, not to have a child – because I made that decision myself – but about it being consonant with traditions of Jewish law, is the story of a woman called Tamar. Her father-in-law was the patriarch Judah – Judah of the 12 tribes – and her husband died and she hadn't a son. Now, in traditional Jewish law, it is the obligation of the family to find a widow either a husband from among the brothers or a husband anyway, so that she won't be left alone and unsupported and without children, if she hasn't had any. Her father-in-law didn't do anything about it, so what did she do? It's rather an appalling story in some ways. She dressed up as a prostitute and lay in his way. When he came along, she said, I won't take money, just give me the stick you're holding. She duly got pregnant and when people saw she was pregnant they ran to him as a judge and said, look, your daughter-in-law's illegally pregnant, we should stone her to death. So he said, 'How can we find out who the man is? Let her be taken.' When they came to take her, she found his stick and said to take it to Judah – and then he realised what had happened. The upshot of this story was that she was justified because he had refused to make arrangements so that she could have a child. In other words, what lies behind that story is that women are entitled to have children, and they are entitled to resort to unconventional means to achieve it. Now obviously, what it doesn't mean is that Jewish women are supposed to go out and screw their fathers-in-law. The whole tradition of Jewish law, which I love, is that it is never a simple question of the literal meaning of the words. There is an obligation to study and to study and to study, and to learn what generations of people have said about it, which I think is consonant with the most sophisticated literary theory. When you study the history of how the rabbis interpreted Jewish law, you can see how often they are learning from the people, not imposing on the people.

I first became involved in relating to Jewish women around the Jewish feminist movement. It was very exciting to relate to other Jewish women around the common issues of fighting anti-Semitism in the women's movement, particularly the things that happened around *Spare Rib*.[1] You can sense the happiness of that time in this group photo I have of the first Jewish Lesbian Conference. You can see the smiles on everybody's faces, that sense of it being a very vibrant occasion. I think that Jewish women, having for years been silenced, and seeing themselves as being part of the gentile world without even really realising it, were suddenly coming together, and it released a lot of energy and a lot of positive feeling. Subsequently, I think differences have come out much more. At the last Jewish Lesbian Conference, there were far more splits between women than in the first one.

I feel that feminism at its present stage has not got the benefit of thousands of years of experienced ritual, and I don't think it ever could have. There are those among feminists who say women will create a new culture which drops away all those other cultures. I think most of the women saying that are gentiles who see themselves as having no culture, whereas what they have is a secularised Christian culture. They are secularised Christians but they won't acknowledge that, they can't see it. They may not celebrate Christmas but they have an anti-Christmas, a period of holiday, and they still regard Sunday as a separate day, not as any old day of the week. That notion of having one universal feminist culture I see as ultimately racist because it fails to recognise where different women are coming from – black women, Third World women, and so on. But also, it would be a horrendous thing to destroy all the cultures of the world, to make one new culture. For me, I know Jewish culture is what's made me. I'm incredibly moved by the things in Jewish ritual and Jewish experience; they move me to tears. Now it may be that I'm an inadequate feminist, but there isn't anything in 'feminist culture' that has that impact on me. I think it's because it is the product of the small – in historical time – movements of women, sub-cultures of women, that have made it and it hasn't had that testing of time, it hasn't had that cultural institutionalisation. And even if it did have that, I wouldn't want to give up what I have. I couldn't. It would be like trying to have my eye colour changed; it would be more than trying to have my eye colour changed.

I think that contemporary feminism has no real way of coping with death and bereavement. When I had immediate family bereavements, I can't describe to you how moving it was for me, coming across the Jewish burial society system of caring for the dead, which means that the bodies of your loved ones are not buried by a commercial firm of impersonal operatives but that, on the contrary, the synagogue maintains a group of its own congregants, people who knew the deceased, who wash them and lay them out as an act of love and of compassion towards them. I had the experience of meeting Jewish people in the street when I had bereavements, and being received by them with warmth and love, while women who were quite close friends of mine just couldn't cope with it. And again, living through the Jewish rituals of saying *kaddish* every day, observing the days of mourning, these set-down rituals – I found the experience the only thing which really did help me and did more than help me. It made bereavement, although a very sad experience, one which enriched my life. I've become more of a human being, a whole person.

And I feel enriched by the experience of prayer, the experience of being together with a community who I know don't share my own ideals. On the other hand, feminism is very good at bringing women together around a certain set of shared beliefs. I'm not trying to make them compete against each other. I think the two are terribly important parts of my life, but that ultimately Judaism operates on a different level, a deeper level for me, and it's more fundamental to me in terms of my own experience and my own needs. I think those feelings are very important.

I also feel an underlying sense of sadness around my knowledge, both at first-hand and through the lives of my family and of other women, of the injustices of our particular time in history. The recent move effectively to make anything called the promotion of lesbianism illegal, I find that appalling. I find public manifestations of anti-Semitism, anti-lesbianism deeply depressing. On the other hand, you get older and you have a longer time perspective. I have the historical knowledge that even in periods of greatest depression, there are resistances, there are positive things. There is that biblical saying, man does not live by bread alone. Well, woman does not live by struggle alone. If you have a rich culture, if you have a positive perspective on your life as a woman, then no matter how awful your life is, it is worthwhile. There are possibilities of passing that on to somebody else. There are possibilities of participating in a culture. Certainly, if you look at the lives of the Jews in the Holocaust, there's so much evidence of the amazing courage and bravery of people at that time. Obviously I don't for a moment want to underestimate the horror or use that as some obscene justification of those experiences, but I'm saying, how do you live with oppression? You say, we don't live by oppression alone or by adopting fighting against oppression as a reason for living – but if our underlying ethics, our underlying religion, our underlying politics and way of life are a sufficiently genuine reflection of what human beings can be, then no oppression can conquer that.

Looking back through the generations at what my mother's mother would have wanted for her, what my mother would have wanted for me – no generation is in any way remotely able to predict what the next generation needs or wants. But I do feel absolutely passionately that I want my daughter to grow up with my love of Judaism. I will try and live and work very hard to make that so for her, and that's a wonderful possibility. It is a great object in one's life, to try and bring up a Jewish child. Not just a Jewish child ethnically, but to have that joy in Judaism, and for that to be a centre of the stories she hears, the food she eats, the experiences she has.

I had one lovely experience of that early on, which is directly a Jewish identification experience. I do candles with her on Friday nights and one Friday night, it was very late, so near the start of *Shabbes* that I hadn't had time to lay out the table with the white cloth and *challah* and everything nicely laid out like it should be. I really wanted to make sure I lit the candles before *Shabbes* actually came in, so I rushed to the candle sticks and put the candles in and lit them, saying the *brocha*. And she looked at me, she was just two, and said, '*Challah?*' She was already telling me that she knew that I really ought to have the *challah* laid out. She seems to love the *Shabbes* thing and she shouts out, *omen!* It's really lovely!

Obviously it's only one part of my personal politics, but it's one of the things I feel most passionately about. Of course, I do want her to grow up as a strong and independent woman, but I think she will. One feels pretty sure that children don't change massively unless they have some unspeakably traumatic experience. There's a sense of the seeds of her character already being there and she seems a happy and jolly child. When I was pregnant, I used to think, if she just smiles sometimes, I'll be very happy – and she seems to have a lovely sense of humour and to enjoy laughing. *Naches?* Oy, do I have *naches* from my daughter!

AFTERWORD

'Hmmm. It doesn't show you in the best possible light,' said a friend after she read the edited version. I suppose that's true – and as it should be. Seeing your own interview in print is to have the same reaction as you have to snapshots or tape recordings of yourself. Is that what I really said? Is that what I come across like? In the case of this interview, my reaction is more complex. It was edited from one main interview recording, plus extracts of some other related taped interviews. Together, the recordings were made over a period of three years.

I find myself wishing I'd had time and space to talk at much greater length about my politics, and particularly about my politics around Zionism and anti-Zionism. I simply say in the interview that I became an anti-Zionist after learning about discrimination against Arabs in Israel, and that I turned right back after experiencing the wave of (particularly) left-wing anti-Semitism, presented as anti-Zionism, which greeted the Israeli invasion of the Lebanon in 1982.

This reaction also manifested itself particularly acrimoniously in

243

the women's movement in Britain, and being in the midst of that made me think through my previously smugly held attitudes. Why had I adopted the view that Israel would be best replaced by something called a secular democratic state, when my own experience of coming to understand the corrosion of assimilating to Christian 'secular' society had convinced me that there was no genuinely secular society? Why did I feel it was politically legitimate to call for the dissolution of the Jewish State of Israel, when no similar calls were made for the dissolution of the United Kingdom (Established Church, etc.), of the USA (International Imperialist Enterprises Inc.?), of Iran, Eire, etc.?

But I'll have to resist the temptation to use this Afterword to get into a debate that itself deserves a book. I can't help being conscious, though, of the nagging voices which, like so many Jewish feminists who were around at the time of that debate, I have internalised. 'Aha!' say these voices. 'you see! Pure culturalism. How can you talk about your identity when you don't speak out about the oppression of Palestinians in Israel', etc., etc. The urge to seek approval as a 'good'/'acceptable' Jew to 'secular' socialists dies hard.

I hope women who read this book will be able to share some of the joy and richness that Jewish women have gained from their heritage. I hope too that they will want to read further, and learn more about Jewish life, Jewish traditions, Jewish politics. Whether you see yourself as secular or whether you have a very different spiritual or religious commitment, I think that two traditions which have helped to sustain Jews through the centuries, namely study and the obligation to take responsibility for a personal commitment to study, are the best foundation we have for learning how to make a better world for the future.

NOTE

1. In September 1982, just before the Israeli invasion of the Lebanon, *Spare Rib* published an article by three anti-Zionist women, arguing that every feminist should self-consciously define herself as anti-Zionist. Many women, including anti-

Zionist and non-Zionist Jewish women, felt that the article contained major distortions and factual errors, and that it appeared to be making anti-Zionism a precondition for feminism. Over forty letters were written, protesting about these aspects of the article. *Spare Rib* refused to publish any of them. A number of Jewish feminist groups then began organising protests, and attempting to negotiate with *Spare Rib* for some of the letters to be published. When these efforts failed, they urged women to refuse to publish any articles in the magazine, unless they carried a statement objecting to the policy. *Spare Rib* subsequently refused to publish articles with such statements. There have since been no articles in the magazine by Jewish feminist groups, although a number of articles by individual Jewish anti-Zionists have been published.

Glossary

There are different spellings of transliterated Yiddish words. We have generally used the standard Yiddish transliteration of the YIVO (Institute for Jewish Research), except where there are more widely accepted spellings for commonly used words, such as *smetana* rather than *smetene*, or *cheder* rather than *kheder*.

We have given Hebrew words in the Ashkenazi pronunciation used by the women in this book, which differs from the Sephardi pronunciation adopted for modern secular Hebrew in Israel.

(Y) denotes Yiddish, (H) denotes Hebrew.

alef	first letter of alphabet
Ashkenazi	Most European Jews today are Ashkenazi. Their religious, cultural and linguistic traditions date back 1,000 years. Ashkenazi Jews originally settled in Germany, from where there was a large migration eastwards in the seventeenth century.
bais	second letter of alphabet
baleboste	a housewife (usually one who is houseproud and
(baleboosta)	a good manager) (Y)
bentshing	blessings after a meal (Y)
bezoigen	freshly changed (Y)
brocha	blessing (H)
broiges	falling out, being annoyed (Y)
bubeh	grandmother (Y)
challah	plaited or circular loaf eaten on *Shabbes* and *yomtov* (H)

Chassid	member of a Chassidic sect (Y)
Chassidism	popular religious movement founded in the late eighteenth century, centred around Chassidic rabbis and their dynasties (Y)
chazan	cantor, who leads the service in the synagogue (H)
cheder	religious classes (Y)
chochem	wise guy (Y)
chutzpah	cheek, gall (Y)
cohen	member of priestly tribe (H)
daven	pray (Y)
diaspora	Jewish communities outside Israel. Jews were dispersed into exile after the destruction of the second temple (from the Greek, meaning dispersal).
Erev Shabbes	Sabbath eve (Friday night) (H)
frum, frumkeit	orthodox, observant; religious observance (Y)
ganzer macher	a 'big shot', an organiser, with a hint of self-importance (Y)
get	divorce (according to Jewish law) (H)
goy	gentile (Y)
hachshara	preparation (for kibbutz) – training undertaken on a farm (H)
Hagodah	book read at Pesach Seder (H)
halachah	rabbinical law (H)
heim, der heim	home, 'the old country' (Y)
hora	a circle dance, popular in Israel
kaddish	prayers for the dead (H)
kiddush	blessings said over the wine and *challah* (H)
kittel	white robe forming part of the male's burial shroud, worn by pious Jews on Yom Kippur and Seder night (Y)
koach	strength (Y)
kosher	according to Jewish dietary laws (H)
kugel	pudding (Y)
lokshen	noodles (Y)
machzor	prayer-book for religious festivals
matsos, matsot	unleavened bread eaten during Passover (H)

mentsh	person, good person (Y)
meshiggeneh, *meshuggeneh*	crazy (Y)
mishebeyrekh	a telling-off (Y)
Mizrachi	Jews from the Arab and other Middle Eastern countries, and India (H)
mitzvah	religious obligation, good deed (H)
naches	particular pride and pleasure derived from one's children (Y)
nadn	dowry (H)
nebbech, *nebbish*	poor thing; what a pity! (Y)
Ostjuden	Jews from Eastern Europe (German)
parnoseh	a living (Y)
peiyes, payes	side-locks worn by very orthodox men (Y)
Pesach	Passover (H)
pesachdik	kosher for Pesach (Y)
pogrom	organised, violent attack on Jewish communities (Russian)
Purim	joyous festival celebrating Esther saving the Jews of the Ancient Persian Empire from death (H)
rachmones	compassion (Y)
rebbe	rabbi (Y)
rebbetzin	rabbi's wife (Y)
Rosh Hashonah	New Year – the beginning of the 10-day period of prayer and atonement which ends with Yom Kippur (H)
Seder	Pesach service and meal (H)
Sephardi	Sephardi Jews lived in Spain and Portugal in the Middle Ages. After their expulsion in the late fifteenth century, most migrated east and south to Mediterranean, North African and Asian lands. Some Sephardi Jews migrated north to Holland, where they also retained distinctive traditions.
Shabbes	Sabbath (Y)

sheitel	wig – customarily worn within the orthodox Ashkenazi community by married women, who are obliged to cover their heads (Y)
sheygets	gentile man (H)
shidduch	arranged marriage (H)
shiester, shuster	cobbler (Y)
shikse	gentile woman (Y)
shissel	bowl (Y)
shlep	drag, haul (Y)
shochet	ritual slaughterer (H)
shtetl	small Jewish town in Eastern Europe (Y)
shtickel	a bit (of a) (Y)
shtiebel	small house of prayer (Y)
shul	synagogue (Y)
Simchas Torah	festival celebrating the end and beginning of the annual cycle of the reading of the law (H)
smetana	similar to soured cream (Y)
soifer	scribe (H)
tallis	prayer shawl (H)
Talmud	rabbinical commentaries on the Torah (H)
tante	aunt (Y)
Torah	first five books of the Bible (H)
tsatske	treasure (Y)
tsitsis	fringed ritual under-garment worn by orthodox men (H)
yekkes	disparaging name given to German Jews by East European Jews (literally, 'jackets') (Y)
yeshiva	institute for advanced religious study for male students (H)
Yom Kippur	Day of Atonement – a day of fasting and prayer; the most solemn day in the Jewish year (H)
yomtov	religious festival (Y)
zeide, zayde	grandfather (Y)

Further Reading

JEWISH HISTORY, ANTHROPOLOGY AND FOLKLORE

Baron, Salo W., *The Russian Jew under Tsars and Soviets*, Macmillan USA, 1976.
  Scholarly and detailed portrait of Russian Jewish life and history.

Baum, Charlotte, Hyman, Paula, and Michel, Sonya, *The Jewish Woman in America*, Dial Press, 1975.
  Strong feminist account of the history of the Jewish American woman which also looks critically at how she is represented in contemporary American writing, and her present position in American society.

Burman, Rickie, 'The Jewish Woman as Breadwinner: The Changing Value of Women's Work in a Manchester Immigrant Community', *Oral History*, Autumn 1982.
  Contrasts the position of Jewish women in relation to economic life in Eastern Europe and in early-twentieth-century immigrant life in Manchester; draws substantially on oral history sources.

Cohn, Norman, *Warrant for Genocide*, Eyre & Spottiswoode, 1967.
  A thoroughly researched account of the origins and dissemination of the notorious anti-Semitic forgery *The Protocols of the Elders of Zion*, which was and still is used by all major anti-Semitic groups to justify their actions.

Dawidowicz, Lucy, *The War Against the Jews*, Weidenfeld and Nicolson, 1975; Penguin, 1979.

Meticulous and detailed history of the Holocaust and Jewish responses to Nazi persecution. Includes a summary of the fate of the Jewish population in each country occupied by the Nazis.

Dobroszycki, Lucjan, and Kirshenblatt-Gimblett, Barbara, *Image Before My Eyes*, Schocken, 1977.

A moving visual history of Polish Jewry from the late nineteenth century to the start of the Second World War, drawn from the YIVO (Institute for Jewish Research) photographic archives. Includes both religious and secular Jewish communities, socialist and Zionist movements. Highly recommended.

Fishman, Joshua, *Never Say Die: 1,000 Years of Yiddish in Jewish Life and Letters*, Mouton, 1981.

A large and very readable compilation of key articles and examples on, in and about Yiddish life and culture. Includes excellent examples of contemporary cartoons and emphemera in Yiddish from the nineteenth and early twentieth centuries; most of the text is bilingual or in English.

Fishman, William, *East End Jewish Radicals*, Duckworth, 1975.

Classic account of the Jewish radical tradition and activism among the immigrant generation in the East End of London; very scant references to women, and none to Jewish women's participation in the radical suffragette movement of the time.

Gartner, Lloyd, *The Jewish Immigrant in England, 1870–1914*, Simon Publications, 1973.

Classic account of the history of mass Jewish immigration to England from Eastern Europe; almost exclusively male-oriented.

Geipel, John, *Mame Loshn: The Making of Yiddish*, Journeyman Press, 1982.

An accessible popular history of the development and derivation of the Yiddish language, the 'mother tongue'.

Gilbert, Martin, *Atlas of the Holocaust*, Michael Joseph, 1982
— *Jewish History Atlas*, Weidenfeld and Nicolson, 1976.
— *The Jews of Arab Lands: Their History in Maps*, Board of Deputies of British Jews, 1976.

251

— *The Arab-Israeli Conflict: Its History in Maps*, Weidenfeld and Nicolson, 1981.

Gilbert's atlases represent outstandingly accessible ways of learning about the broad sweep of Jewish history. They are excellently researched and particularly helpful on the history of Jews in Britain, in Europe, and in the Middle East.

— *The Holocaust*, Guild Publishing, 1986.

A monumental history of the Nazi destruction of European Jewry, substantially drawn from survivor and eyewitness accounts, from the immediate post-war period to the present day. Includes many accounts by women and about the fate of women. Contains much particularly harrowing material.

Gillman, Peter and Leni, *Collar the Lot!*, Quartet, 1980.

A history of the British internment of 'enemy aliens', mainly Jewish refugees from Nazi Germany, in the early days of the Second World War, demonstrating the way in which popular hysteria about refugees as potential fifth columnists was whipped up by the xenophobic British press.

Henry, Sandra, and Taitz, Emily, *Written Out of History: Our Jewish Foremothers*, Biblio Press, 1983.

Composed largely of brief extracts from historical source material, introduced and commented on by the authors. Includes the lives of Jewish women in biblical and Talmudic periods, and in Sephardi and Ashkenazi communities over the thousand years up to the nineteenth century. Much evidence on the way in which individual Jewish women were able to play powerful and influential roles; relatively little on the collective life of ordinary women.

Kurzweil, Arthur, *From Generation to Generation*, Schocken, 1982.

An outstanding and very accessible guide to researching Jewish family and community history. Pays careful attention to how to include and research foremothers' history. Includes invaluable practical information on sources and resources.

Marrus, Michael, *The Unwanted: European Refugees in the Twentieth Century*, Oxford University Press, 1985.

A well-researched academic historical analysis of the policies of different countries towards European refugees, including attention to Jewish refugees seeking refuge during and after the First World War, and from Nazi persecution before the Second World War. Also analyses the treatment of the displaced persons seeking homes following the Second World War.

Ringelheim, Joan, 'Women and the Holocaust: A Reconsideration of Research', *Signs*, Vol. 10, No. 4, 1985.

An excellent article developed from the author's oral history research with Jewish women Holocaust survivors; has an extensive and sophisticated analysis of the significance of the testimonies and issues of what constitutes a feminist approach to history.

Rosenberg, David, *Facing Up to Antisemitism: How Jews in Britain Countered the Threats of the 1930s*, JCARP Publications, 1985.

Excellent account of Jewish responses to British fascism.

Roskies, Diane and David, *The Shtetl Book*, Ktav, 1979.

An anthology of stories, pictures, anecdotes and historical material devised for educational use, to give a picture of life in the *shtetls* of Eastern Europe. Includes particularly good examples of authentic contemporary written testimonies of life in the *shtetl*, and some attention to women's occupations and lives.

Rubin, Ruth, *Voices of a People*, McGraw Hill, 1973.

A moving and very readable history of Yiddish popular song. Includes children's songs, romantic songs and political songs.

Schwartz, Howard, *Elijah's Violin*, Harper Colophon, 1988.
— *Miriam's Tambourine*, Oxford University Press, 1988.

Two outstanding anthologies of traditional Jewish folktales, including some from Talmudic times to the eighteenth century and tales from the Jews of European and Arab countries; particularly interesting in what they reveal about the roles in which women appeared in Jewish folklore – as prophetesses, magicians, rescuers and adventurers, as well as in more traditional roles.

Stillman, Norman, *The Jews of Arab Lands. A History & Source Book*, Jewish Publication Society of America, 1979.

Covers the period from the rise of Islam to the late nineteenth century and includes little-known contemporary source material on the lives of the Jews and their relationships with their Islamic neighbours. Sources selected are entirely male, and hence the view of women is very limited.

Vishniac, Roman, *A Vanished World*, Penguin, 1987.

Photographs of Jewish life in the urban ghettos and rural areas of inter-war Poland and other Eastern European countries, often taken with a concealed camera by a man obsessed with recording what he rightly feared would shortly be destroyed.

White, Jerry, *Rothschild Buildings: Life in an East End Tenement Block, 1887–1920*, History Workshop Series, Routledge & Kegan Paul, 1980.

Account of the life of immigrant Jews in a 'model dwelling' in the East End, based on oral history interviews. Includes fascinating accounts by women of their working and personal lives.

Zborowski, Mark, and Hertzog, Elizabeth, *Life is with People*, Schocken, 1962.

An account of life in the Eastern European *shtetls*, based on interviews with immigrants from that society, now destroyed by the Holocaust. Written by anthropologists, it has a curiously timeless, ahistorical quality about it, while it is written about a group of people who, in the period remembered, were undergoing tremendous stress and upheaval and who were frequently attempting to remember events many years earlier.

ORAL HISTORIES OF JEWS

Hart, Lorraine, Libovich, Sue, *et al.* (eds.), *Jewish East End Education Pack*, Tower Hamlet Environment Trust, 1988.

Intended mainly for schools, this pack draws substantially from the Jewish Women in London archives to provide a vivid view of Jewish East Enders' experiences of immigration. It includes sections on home life, work, education, culture, politics and anti-Semitism. There are suggestions for follow-up activities; mainly suitable for the 9–16 age range.

Kramer, Sydelle, and Masur, Jenny (eds.), *Jewish Grandmothers*, Beacon Press, 1976.

Oral history interviews with Ashkenazi women, all born in Eastern Europe.

Vegh, Claudine, trans. Ros Schwartz, *I Didn't Say Goodbye*, Caliban, 1984.

Written by a psychiatrist, herself the daughter of Holocaust victims, it is based on a series of interviews with other French Jews during whose childhood their parents were deported to extermination camps.

FEMINIST ANTHOLOGIES

Beck, Evelyn Torton (ed.), *Nice Jewish Girls, a Lesbian Anthology*, Persephone Press, 1982.

An outstanding anthology of writings and pictures, including poetry, fiction and non-fiction essays by American Jewish lesbians. Includes accounts by women from Sephardi and Ashkenazi backgrounds, daughters and granddaughters of turn-of-century immigrants and Holocaust survivors, and accounts of resistance to anti-Semitism in contemporary America and in the women's movement.

Bulkin, Elly, Pratt, Minnie Bruce, and Smith, Barbara, *Yours in Struggle: Three Feminist Perspectives on Anti-Semitism and Racism*, Long Haul Press, 1984.

Three essays, one by an Afro-American woman, one by a white Christian Southerner and one by an Ashkenazi Jew. Written partly in response to the divisions that arose in the US women's movement over feminists' responses to the Israeli invasion of the Lebanon in 1982, and partly in relation to struggles in the movement over racism.

Kaye/Kantrowitz, Melanie, and Klepfisz, Irena (eds.), *The Tribe of Dina: A Jewish Women's Anthology*, Sinister Wisdom, 29/30, 1986.

Wide-ranging anthology of poetry and prose by Jewish feminists, with a strong lesbian content. Contains translations from Yiddish, contributions from Sephardi and Mizrachi women and interviews with Israeli feminists; reclaiming Jewish culture and history as secular Jews.

WOMEN AND JUDAISM

Biale, Rachel, *Women and Jewish Law*, Schocken, 1984.

A very clear analysis of the complex and often surprising position of women in Jewish religious law (*halachic* law). Based on very thorough research of *halachic* sources and commentaries, it demonstrates the inadequacy of simplistic condemnations of Jewish religious law.

Greenberg, Blu, *On Women and Judaism*, The Jewish Publication Society of America, 1981.

Written from within a mainstream Orthodox Jewish perspective, this represents an attempt to project a strongly positive vision of the opportunities for women living as Orthodox Jews.

Heschel, Susannah (ed.), *On Being a Jewish Feminist: A Reader*, Schocken, 1983.

About the relationship between feminists and the Jewish religion. It includes a range of autobiographical accounts by feminists, mainly from the US, and including one by a British woman. Also gives insights into the progress Jewish feminists in the US have made in entering and influencing mainstream non-Orthodox Jewish religious and community life.

Koltun, Elizabeth (ed.), *The Jewish Woman*, Schocken, 1976.

An influential and very readable early Jewish feminist anthology (but one which includes several contributions by men). Includes material on history and Jewish law and religious practices. Excludes mention of lesbians.

Schneider, Susan Weidman, *Jewish and Female*, Simon and Schuster, 1985.

Lavishly produced and illustrated guide and sourcebook for Jewish women in the US. Strongly oriented towards participation in mainstream Jewish religious and community life. Also contains a very extended contact list of every type of Jewish organization, including those for lesbian women, single women, etc.

WOMEN'S STUDIES

Elwell, Ellen, and Levenson, Edward, *The Jewish Women's Studies Guide*, Biblio Press, 1982.
Drawn mainly from bibliographies assembled for specific courses in US universities and adult education programmes. Includes material on religion, history, literature, etc.

BIOGRAPHY, AUTOBIOGRAPHY, DIARIES AND LETTERS

Bauman, Janina, *Winter in the Morning: A Young Girl's Life in the Warsaw Ghetto*, Virago, 1986.
An autobiography, based on diaries kept at the time, of life in the Warsaw ghetto and then in hiding in 'Aryan' Warsaw.

Chagall, Bella, *Burning Lights*, Shocken Books, 1946.
A touching and evocative memoir of Bella Chagall's childhood in a Chassidic family in Vitebsk, Russia.

Chernin, Kim, *In My Mother's House*, Virago, 1985.
Writing as the feminist daughter of a renowned American communist activist, Kim Chernin interweaves her mother's rich life story and her own, and gives a contemporary account of their relationship.

Clare, George, *Last Waltz in Vienna: The Destruction of a Family, 1842–1942*, Pan Books, 1982.
An autobiography combining the history of the author's family with that of Austrian Jewry, and of Austria itself.

Hart, Kitty, *Return to Auschwitz*, Granada, 1983.
A moving account of life in Auschwitz and after by a survivor now resident in Britain.

Gershon, Karen (ed.), *We Came as Children*, Papermac, 1989.
The story of the children's transports edited from written accounts of a few hundred of the thousands of children who came to Britain as

refugees in the winter and spring of 1938–39. Individual voices are combined to produce this collective autobiography.

Jacobs, Joe, *Out of the Ghetto: My Youth in the East End, Communism and Fascism, 1913–1939*, J. Simon, 1978.
An account by a committed communist of struggles against the rise of fascism in the East End between the wars.

Jewish Women's History Group, *You'd Prefer Me Not To Mention It*, self-published pamphlet, London, 1983.
Autobiographical essays by daughters of Jewish immigrants and refugees on growing up Jewish in Britain.

Koehn, Ilse, *Mischling, Second Degree: My Childhood in Nazi Germany*, Puffin Plus, 1981.
An account of a childhood in Nazi Germany written by a woman of mixed Jewish/Gentile origin – a 'Mischling', or child of mixed race.

Kovaly, Heda Margolius, *Prague Farewell*, Gollancz, 1988.
A memoir not only of the Holocaust but of a life lived in Czechoslovakia after the war, during the Stalin purges. The author's husband was one of 12 Jews hanged after the Slansky Trials.

The Memoirs of Gluckel of Hameln, trans. Marvin Lowenthal, Shocken Books, 1977.
A fascinating diary, originally written in Yiddish. Gluckel was a German Jewish widow who began writing it in 1690 and completed it in 1719. A devout woman, a mother of 14, she was involved in business affairs, becoming a trader and running a factory. Gives a unique picture of seventeenth-century Jewish life in Germany.

Rosen, Ruth, and Davidson, Sue (eds.), *The Mamie Papers*, Virago, 1979.
Fascinating letters written by Mamie Pinzer, a Jewish woman and prostitute, to Fanny Quincy Howe, a wealthy Bostonian, between 1910 and 1922. Highly recommended.

Sassoon, Agnes, *Agnes: How My Spirit Survived*, Lawrence Cohen Ltd, 1983.

A Holocaust survivor's account. Agnes Sassoon's family fled to Budapest from Czechoslovakia, but Agnes was captured and sent to Dachau at the age of 11, in 1944. She survived, and was reunited with her parents.

Singer, Israel Joshua, trans. Joseph Singer, *Of a World That is No More*, Faber, 1987.
    Evocative memoirs, written in Yiddish, of a childhood in rural Poland, as the son of a rabbi. By the brother of Esther Kreitman, who based her novel *Deborah* on her harsh memories of this time.

Segal, Aranka, *Upon the Head of the Goat: A Childhood in Hungary, 1939–1944*, Signet Vista, 1981.
    Account of growing up in Hungary during the war. Insights into provincial Jewish life, as well as detailing life under fascism. Ends with deportation to Auschwitz.

Yezierska Anzia, *Red Ribbon on a White Horse*, Virago, 1989.
    An account of her life as she saw it and fictionalised it, from the sweatshops of New York to success and fame in Hollywood. The contradictions of becoming rich from writing about the sufferings of the poor silenced her for many years until she wrote this autobiography, which many see as the best of her books.

Zyskind, Sara, *Stolen Years*, Signet, 1983.
    Moving account of years in the Lodz ghetto, and then the concentration camps. Survival in the camps depended partly on the loving support she shared with four 'sisters' from the ghetto.

FICTION

Adler, Ruth, *A Family of Shopkeepers*, Hodder and Stoughton, 1985.
— *Beginning Again*, Hodder and Stoughton, 1985.
    Two vivid fictional accounts of life in the Jewish East End, covering the period from the turn of the century till beyond the Second World War, written by one of the contributors to this volume.

Esther Kreitman, *Deborah*, Virago, 1983.

A powerful autobiographical novel by the sister of Isaac Bashevis and Israel Joshua Singer. Though melodramatic at times, it is full of strong and bitter personal feeling about her own confined life as the daughter of a Chassidic rabbi. Bella Chagall's book offers a strong contrast as a memoir.

Tax, Meredith, *Rivington Street*, Heinemann, 1983.
Racy historical novel by American socialist-feminist telling an American Jewish family saga.

Yezierska, Anzia, *Hungry Hearts and Other Stories*, Virago, 1987.
Classic collection of stories about the lives of immigrant Jewish American women, first published in 1920.
— *Bread Givers*, The Women's Press, 1984.
Novel drawing on the same experiences of Jewish immigrant life on the Lower East Side.

JOURNALS

Jewish Socialist, JSG BM 3725, London WC1N 3XX.
Quarterly journal of politics and culture, produced by the Jewish Socialist Group.

Jewish Quarterly, PO Box 1148, London NW5 2AZ
Long-established political, cultural and literary journal.

POETRY

Klepfisz, Irena, *Different Enclosures*, Onlywomen, 1985.
Klepfisz's vibrant poetry includes what are arguably some of the finest and most moving responses to the experience and the knowledge of the Holocaust. As a child, she was hidden and had to pass herself as a gentile in Nazi-occupied Poland during the war years; she now lives a committed lesbian and Jewish-identified life in the US.

POLITICS

Cohen, Steve, *That's Funny, You Don't Look Anti-Semitic*, Beyond the Pale Collective, 1984.

A discussion of anti-Semitism on the Left in Britain, covering the period from the late nineteenth century to the aftermath of the Israeli invasion of the Lebanon in 1982; also provides a critique of anti-Semitic elements in classic Marxist and Trotskyist writings, including those of Marx, Lenin and Abram Leon.

— *From the Jews to the Tamils*, Manchester Law Centre, 1988.

A brief analysis of the history of the way in which British immigration laws in the twentieth century have enshrined racist practice; includes previously unpublished material on the treatment of Jews interned in the north of England during the First and Second World Wars; attempts to highlight parallels between treatment of Jews and Tamils, drawn from case histories.

Harway, Danielle, Chester, Gail, Schwartz, Ros and Johnson, Val (eds.), *A Word in Edgeways: Jewish Feminists Respond*, JF Publications, 1988.

A contribution by Jewish feminists from a range of political positions to a debate initiated by anti-Zionist Jenny Bourne in *Race and Class* and *Spare Rib*, about Zionism and 'identity politics'.

Seidel, Gill, *The Holocaust Denial*, Beyond the Pale Collective, 1986.

A discussion of the rise of the new international neo-Nazi network, which argues that in denying the existence of the Holocaust the new extreme Right are seeking to rehabilitate National Socialism. Neo-Nazis and some far-right 'revisionists' argue that the 'myth' of the Holocaust is the product of a Jewish conspiracy, and thus use the Holocaust denial to incite further anti-Semitism.

JWIL Resources

Parts of the Jewish Women in London archive have been duplicated for ease of access. The interviews were originally recorded on reel-to-reel tape. Cassette copies, printed summaries of all the interviews and some full transcripts are now housed at both the London Museum of Jewish Life and the Fawcett Library, along with conditions of use and access.

The reel-to-reel tapes and the collection of photographs are now at the London Museum of Jewish Life.

The Fawcett Library, City of London Polytechnic, Calcutta House, Old Castle Street, London E1 7NT. 01 283 1030

The London Museum of Jewish Life, Sternberg Centre, 80 East End Road, London N3. 01 349 1143

The exhibition, 'Daughters of the Pale' and the tape/slide show, 'Three Jewish Women', are available for hire from the Cockpit Gallery. The tape/slide show is distributed on video by Circles Women's Film and Video Distribution.

Cockpit Gallery, 15 Wilkin Street, London NW5. 01 482 2551

Circles, 113 Roman Road, London E2. 01 981 6828